SPONSORS

Society for Information Science, New Delhi-110 012

Jawaharlal Nehru Centre for Advanced Scientific Research,
Bangalore - 560 064

Council of Scientific and Industrial Research,
New Delhi-110 012

National Informatics Centre, New Delhi-110 003

Centre for Scientific and Industrial Consultancy
Indain Institute of Science, Bangalore-560 012

M/s Capital Market Publishers, Bombay-400 071

The Printers (Mysore) Ltd., Bangalore-560 001

M/s Silver Platter Information Ltd., U.K.

M/s Informatics (India) Pvt Ltd., Bangalore-560 003

CONFERENCE ORGANISING COMMITTEE

Chairman

Shri N.V. Satyanarayana, Informatics India Pvt. Ltd. Banglore

Organising Secretary

Shri N.M. Malwad, JRDTML, IISc. Bangalore

Treasurer

Dr. T.B. Rajashekar, NCSI, IISc. Bangalore

National Members

Prof. N. Balakrishnan, SERC, IISc, Bangalore
Shri Chikkamallaiah, IIM, Bangalore
Prof. M.A. Gopinath, DRTC, ISI, Bangalore
Prof. R.G. Gupta, SIS, New Delhi
Shri K.N. Harikumar, Deccan Herald, Bangalore
Dr. H.C. Jain, SIS, New Delhi
Shri N.C. Jain, SIS, New Delhi
Dr. C.R. Karisiddappa, Karnataka University, Dharwad
Dr. S. Mallick, SIS, New Delhi
Dr. S.S. Murthy, DESIDOC, New Delhi
Shri Ramesh Kundra, SIS, New Delhi
Prof. I.K. Ravichandra Rao, DRTC, ISI, Bangalore
Dr. Shalini R. Urs, Mysore University, Mysore
Prof. T. Viswanathan, INSDOC, New Delhi

Local Members

Shri N. Chowdappa, , B.M.S. College,Bangalore
Shri I.H. Jahagirdar, British Council, Bangalore
Shri V.L. Kalyan, BEL, Bangalore
Shri A.D. Kulakarni, INSDOC, Bangalore
Shri T. Malleshappa, Department of Public Libraries, Bangalore
Shri S.G.K. Murthy, NAL, Bangalore
Shri C.K. Pattanasetty, Bangalore University, Bangalore
Shri T.N. Prakash, ADA, Bangalore
Shri Puttabasavaiah, IISc, Bangalore
Shri H.S. Siddamallaiah, NIMHANS, Bangalore
Shri K.T. Somashekar, UAS, Bangalore
Dr. M.S. Sridhar, ISRO, Bangalore

PREFACE

Microcomputers have revolutionized management of information in relation to speed, efficiency and effectiveness which was not possible other wise. In addition, microcomputers together with communication technologies have altered the ways information is collected, stored, processed and transmitted. Consequently, this has resulted in the evolution of digital libraries.

Digital Libraries are heterogeneous in nature. They encompass the work related to information and how to digitize it, store it, find it, link it, visualize it, use it, publish it, manage it, and share it. They aim to provide instant access to digitized information and consist of a variety of information sources — paper to paperless forms, including multimedia.

To study and understand their implications, the Society for Information Science (SIS), New Delhi, has rightly chosen the topic Digital Libraries: The Dynamic Storehouse of Information as the theme for their 15th Annual Convention and Conference, which is being held at IISc, Bangalore, between 18-20 January 1996.

More than 30 papers have been included in this volume. Also, a select bibliography on digital library consisting of about 300 references is given. The papers mainly discuss the following aspects:

Digital libraries: Challenges, issues, architecture, features, fear and aspiration.

Collection, storage, organization, and transmission of digital information,

Sources and tools to handle digital information

Creation and use of Hyper text and Hyper media systems.

Electronic publishing

Networks and their implications

Manpower development

User interfaces

Case studies, etc.

It is hoped that this set of papers will facilitate better understanding of the concept of digital libraries and will be useful as a reference document for information professionals aspiring to go for Digital Libraries in India.

Bangalore
Date : 22nd December 1995

Editors

N.M. Malwad
T.B. Rajashekar
I.K. Ravichandra Rao
N.V. Satyanarayana

ACKNOWLEDGEMENTS

We are indebted to the authors who have contributed papers on various aspects of digital libraries even though it is a new and emerging topic in the Indian context. Grateful thanks are due to Shri Puttabasavaiah for his painstaking efforts in organising the materials. The editors acknowledge with thanks the unstincted help rendered by Shri Sadananda Rao in going through the proofs so meticulously. It is a pleasure to extend our grateful thanks to Shri V.A. Subhan for compiling a select bibliography on digital libraries in a very short period of time. We also extend our thanks to Shri V.N Nagendra for keying in the bibliographic entries.

The editors wish to thank the Campus Xerox Centre, IISc. for preparing camera ready copy in time.

We are personally thankful to the Society for Information Science, the Co-sponsors, the Technical Session Sponsors, the members of the Conference Organising Committee, and the Conference Secretriat including the staff of the J.R.D. Tata Memorial Library, IISc., in organising this conference.

We gratefully thank the New Age International Ltd.. Publishers, New Delhi and in particular, Shri Vinayak for their painstaking efforts in providing a quality publication within a record time. If inspite of their and our best efforts some errors of omission and commission have escaped attention, the editors apologise sincerely to the authors and readers.

CONTENTS

SESSION THREE:

Cataloguing, Indexing, Processing

SESSION FOUR:

Networking Systems and Electronic Access

SESSION FIVE:

Information Professionals for Digital Information Systems

SESSION EIGHT:

Indian Scenario, Problems and Prospects

A SELECT BIBLIOGRAPHY

CONTRIBUTORS

K.T. Anuradha
NationalCenterfor Science Information,
Indian Institute of Science,
Bangalore 560 012.

Dr. A.Y. Asundi
Professor,
Dept. of Library and Information Science,
Bangalore University, Bangalore 560 056.

Prof. N. Balakrishna
Chairman,
National Centre for Science Information,
Indian Institute of Science, Bangalore 560 012.

Bhagavan Das,
Sr. Librarian, KDMIPE, ONGC, Dehradun.

S. Chandrashekar,
Informatics (India) Private Limited,
Bangalore 560 003.

Chikkamallaiah
Librarian,
Indian Institute of Management, Bangalore.

Ms. K.S. Chudamani
J.R.D. Tata Memorial Library,
Indian Institute of Science, Bangalore 560 012.

W.B. Croft
Center for Intelligent Information Retrieval (CIIR),
University of Massachusetts, Amherst, MA 01003, USA.

Mrs. M. Deb
Dy. Suptdg. Librarian,
KDMIPE, ONGC, Dehradun.

S.T. Fazzuludin
Manager, Computer Centre,
Indian Institute of Management, Bangalore.

Ms. D. Gayathri
Library and Documentation,
Indian Institute of Chemical Technology,
Hyderabad.

Prof. M.A. Gopinath
Documentation Research and Training Centre,
Indian Statistical Institute, Bangalore.

Dr. R.K. Goyal
BASIS PLSS Division,
National Informatics Centre, A-Bloc, CGCO Complex,
Lodi Road, New Delhi 110 003.

Jagtar Singh
Department of Library and Information Science,
Punjab University, Patiala 147 002, Punjab.

Mrs. Archana Kakodakar
Centre for Latin American Studies,
Goa University, Goa.

N. Kalidas
Library and Documentation,
Indian Institute of Chemical Technology,
Hyderabad.

H.P.S. Kalra
Department of Library and Information Science,
Punjab University, Patiala 147 002, Punjab.

Dr. C.R. Karisiddappa
Department of Library & Information Science,
Karnatak University, Dharwad 580 003.

Prof. M.M. Kashyap
201, Kadambari Apartments,
Sector IX, Plot XIX, Rohini, Delhi 110 085.

A.K. Katna
Indian Institute of Technology, Kharagpur.

A. Lakshmana Moorthy
DESIDOC, New Delhi.

M.A. Malini
Supercomputer Education and Research Centre,
Indian Institute of Science, Bangalore 560 012.

N.M. Malwad
Librarian,
J.R.D. Tata Memorial Library,
Indian Institute of Science, Bangalore 560 012.

Kamelendu Majumdar
Indian Institute of Technology, Kharagpur.

Naina Pandita
National Information Centre, New Delhi.

Mrs. N. Parvathamma
Reader, Department of Library and Information Science
Gulbarga Univeristy, Gulbarga 585 106, India.

B.P. Prakash
Hindustan Photo Films
Ootacamund 643 005.

C.E. Prakash
Supercomputer Education and Research Centre,
Indian Institute of Science, Bangalore 560 012.

T.N. Prakash
Aeronautical Development Agenzy, Bangalore 500 017.

Dr. T.B. Rajashekar,
National Centre for Science Information (NCSI),
Indian Institute of Science, Bangalore 560 012.

Ms. Ramadevi
Naval Science and Technology Laboratory,
Visakhapatnam 530 027.

D.B. Ramesh
Library and Documentation,
Regional Research Laboratory,
Bhubaneswar 751 013.

Dr. I.K. Ravichandra Rao
Documentation Research and Training Centre,
Indian Statistical Institute,
Bangalore 560 059.

J.R. Sahu
Library and Documentation
Regional Research Laboratory
Bhubaneswar 751 013.

Ms. B.C. Sandhya
J.R.D. Tata Memorial Library,
Indian Institute of Science,
Bangalore 560 012.

Md. Sibili Sirajee
National Information Centre, New Delhi.
H.S. Siddamallaiah
Chief Librarian,
NIMHANS, Bangalore.

A. Sreenivasa Ravi
National Centre for Science Information (NCSI),
Indian Institute of Science,
Bangalore 560 012.

Dr. M.S. Sridhar
Head,
Library and Documentation,
ISRO Satellite Centre, Bangalore 560 017.

A.K. Srivastava
Senior Librarian, KDMIPE Library,
Oil and Natural Gas Corporation.

Dr. Shalini R. Urs
Department of Library and Information Science,
University of Mysore, Mysore 570 006.

P. Subbaramaiah
Naval Science and Technology Laboratory,
Visakhapatnam 530 027.

V.A. Subhan
JRD Tata Memorial Library,
Indian Institute of Science,
Bangalore 560 012.

Ms. P. Suma
Documentation Research and Training Centre,
Indian Statistical Institute,
Bangalore 560 059.

B. Venugopal
Bharathidasan University Library,
Tiruchirapalli 620 024, Tamil Nadu.

DIGITAL LIBRARY FACILITY -
A boon to the learning community

With fantastic developments in Electronics ***fields,***
Computers having acquired enormous power to ***wield,***
*And touching our daily lives in one-way-or-the-****other,***
Changing they are, our work life ***altogether****.*

With Computers storing data in digital ***code,***
With their ability to communicate in network ***mode,***
Holding volumes of information in a manner ***compact****.*
Made they have, on library management a great ***impact****.*

A treasure house of knowledge from Alexandrian ***days,***
Libraries have promoted the progress of mankind in many ***ways****.*
Being a repository of peoples intellectual ***attainment,***
Delightful resources they are for people self ***development****.*

Keeping in tune with the technological ***pace,***
Overcoming the barriers of time and ***space***
And supporting the cause of informal ***education,***
A helpful aid it is, to the evergrowing student ***population****.*

"Mountain coming to Mohammed " is a part of an age old ***adage,***
Digital libraries, how truly bring this concept to actual ***usage****?*
With the abilities to display instantly information ***sought,***
No doubt they will be a boon to the teacher and the ***taught****.*

B.N. JAGADEESH PRASAD
Bharat Electronic, Bangalore-560 013

One

Electronic Publishers, Developers and Users

SIS–96, 18–20, Jan. '96, Bangalore

Electronic publishing with SGML

S. CHANDRASHEKAR
Informatics (India) Private Limited, Bangalore-560 003

Abstract

Distribution of information has played and is playing a key role for mankind. Limitations in accessing this information has been one of the major factors costing time, effort and resources. Information has to be accessible to people in various media with the least effort in conversion.

This paper presents a brief introduction to the world of structuring information/data/documents using the international standard ISO 8879 (SGML). It also presents the advantages, features, and functionalities of presenting the structured information for distribution on both paper as well as electronic medium without duplicating efforts.

Information and its Classification

Information is knowledge concerning facts, concepts, objects, events, ideas, and processes, which within a specific context has a particular meaning. Information presented in a structured format is referred to as a database. Depending on the major content a database can be broadly classified depending on the content, under:

- Full text databases — Books and journals in electronic format structured for storage and presentation enabling search the complete content of the book for retrieval of the required information.
- Bibliographic and directory databases — Structured databases in the form of a directory or references to information are some of the typical examples of this database.
- Multimedia — Representation of synchronized digital information (audio and video) on the electronic medium is referred to as multimedia.
- Image database — Storage of images as a component of the database referenced by information about the stored image is the main content of the database.

Electronic publishing

Electronic publishing is defined as a process for production of typeset-quality documents containing text, graphics, pictures, tables, equations, etc. with the assistance of a data processing system. The synonym for Electronic Publishing is: Computer aided/assisted publishing. The published information is distributed on state-of-the-art medium — CD-ROM, Networks (on-line, Internet, ISDN, etc.).

Advantages of Electronic (Books) Publishing

- Minimizes time and cost-effective than publishing on paper
- Streamlines update process and promotes availability of accurate documents instantaneously
- Reduces distribution and storage overhead
- Allows media enhancement of existing reference materials with sound, animation, and video
- Increases user effectiveness and productivity
- Error reduction in production process

Standards

Standards are necessary for the exchange/interchange of information across the hardware-software borders. Non-standard documents are not accessible across hardware and software platforms. The International Organization for Standardization (ISO), has introduced two sets of standards for exchange of information:

- Office Document Architecture — ISO 8613
- SGML — Standard Generalized Markup Language — ISO 8879

The aim of ISO 8613 was to define the structure, presentation style and the layout of the various classes of documents. Documents are classified based on their structure and area of utilization. The aim of ISO 8879 was to enable users to access the documents across platforms.

What is SGML?

- Standard Generalized Mark-up Language is an ISO (International Standards Organization) standard. ISO 8879.
- SGML permits exchange of information across hardware platforms and software applications.

SGML was designed keeping the author and publisher relationship in mind. The author was responsible in defining the structure of the content and the publisher was for the presentation. As the author and the publisher rarely had the same hardware platform and application tools. converters and filters were necessary to access the information. As publisher cannot foresee the input format of the documents, filters were necessary for conversion from all formats to the required format. This cost factor was unacceptable to publishers.

Example: Imagine an author uses MS Word to produce an article. The publisher uses TEX system for printing articles. To print the article he/she will have to convert the MS Word format into a TEX format. This is obviously an inefficient way of interchanging information.

The idea behind SGML is to allow interchange of information without the overheads inherent in conversion of proprietary formats.

Characteristics of SGML

- SGML is a tagging language
- It handles logical structures
- It is a database language for text
- SGML supports multimedia and hypertext
- SGML with the present day tools enable users to view the documents using the WYSIWYG (What You See Is What You Get) concept.
- SGML is a syntax for text processing style-sheets
- SGML allows coded text to be reused in ways not anticipated by the user
- SGML is a document representation language for any architecture
- SGML is a annotation for any kind of structure
- SGML is a meta-language for defining document types
- SGML represents hierarchies
- SGML is an extensible document description language
- SGML is a standard for communication among different hardware platforms & software applications

SGML and Presentation Styles

SGML separates formatting instructions from content. In a word processor format the formatting instructions are imbedded within the content. This means if you want to re-use the information but in a different style or software package you have to go through a conversion process.

Advantages of SGML

- Cost control in Data Preparation — Documents from a publishing system producing SGML can extensively reduce the cost of on-line publishing a dynamic electronic book.
- Hypermedia Link Behavior — SGML markup is used to automatically generate links for figures, tables and footnotes associated with the content in the document. This enables the user to navigate to the required location with ease.
- Ease in Handling Large Document Collections — The convenience in delivering entire collections of reference manuals (thousands of pages) on an electronic media such as CD-ROM is faster and less expensive than paper.
- Document Control — Stylesheets are also used to specify the dynamic behavior of an electronic book. Stylesheets work consistently across all documents of a particular type. This enables publishers to design the behavior of the book and its appearance with ease.
- Multiple Dynamic Views — One key feature of SGML is the ability to add attributes/values to document elements. These can be used to label elements with security clearance ratings, product configuration ID's, revision levels, language, etc.
- Dynamic filtering enhances the clarity of the document. Example: display information relevant to a specific task, system configuration, security clearance, language, etc. only.
- Hardware independence, meaning easy interchange of texts
- Separation of structure and layout
- Software independence, giving an open-endedness to data
- Unambiguous format, enabling database storage and retrieval.

SGML - Areas of Application

- The areas in which the utilization of SGML is advantageous to the user/publisher are:
- Multiple purposes document presentation
- Interchange a document across hardware platforms and software applications
- Add a document to a database or document filing system
- Revise a document later in its lifetime
- Exploit the full lifetime of a document
- Retrieve information in a structured document

Contents of a SGML Document

- The SGML Declaration — It is a formal part of each SGML document, specifying which characters and delimiters are used.
  - — it is usually common to all documents in an SGML installation
  - — may or may not be part of the document (a default will be used in its absence)
  - — gives the precise details on how SGML was applied to this document
  - — defines which characters should be used as delimiters (e.g. , , /)
  - — defines which character set (ASCII or other) is used
  - — defines which features of SGML are being used
- Document Type Definition(DTD) — defines the rules for marking up a class of documents.
  - — defines the structure of a document
  - — is written for SGML documents
  - — may be stored externally to the document
  - — is different for each set of documents, specific to a structure (memo's, articles, books)
- Document instance: It is the document itself which:
  - — contains data (contents)
  - — contains markup
  - — includes a reference to the DTD (if it is not present in the document).

SGML Software Tools

- DTD Designer: Enables the user to design and develop the DTD. Examples: RulesBuilder, Near&Far, etc.
- DTD Validator: Enables the user to validate the DTD created. Example — Near & Far Lite.
- SGML Parser, a software tool, ensures that the markup of an SGML document is consistent, error free, and correctly interpreted. The parser checks for the SGML standard conformance of the document's DTD. An SGML parser is essential in the validating of data, it does not check

the content of the data but checks that the structure is correct. Examples of the SGML parser are: SP, AuthorEditor, DynaTag, etc.

- SGML Viewer — Enables the user to view SGML documents on the screen.
- SGML Database: Stores the documents in a database especially designed to handle SGML documents. DynaBase, etc.
- SGML Indexer — Enables indexing of SGML documents
- SGML Style Sheet Editor — Representation of information and its modification.

SGML Representation

There are three main markup items defined in a DTD

- Elements
- Attributes
- Entities

Element is a tag delimiter. It is the building block that marks the content and structure of the data.

e.g. <title>Document analysis and SGML</title>

The operating tag has < > with the name given to the tag and the end tag has / to denote it as the closing tag. It is possible to close an element by using the < /> construct thus saving time and space. It is also possible to define in the DTD that a start or end tag is optional. This should be done with care otherwise ambiguities can occur.

Attributes — Elements can have one or more optional or mandatory attributes that provide further information about the element. An example of this could be that you have an <article> element and you want to specify the article is a review article.

e.g. <article arttype = "RA">

Attributes must be given in the start tag. Attributes values can be letters, digits or other characters provided they are delimited by quotes or apostrophes.

Entities - Documents may contain characters (Greek letters and mathematical symbols), illustrations or text from another file. In all these cases SGML uses an entity reference.

This reference is represented by a character string. Entities are used:

— as a shorthand notation for text strings

— as a common way of coding special characters, accents, symbols

— for including external files

— as variable in a DTD.

Document Type Definition (DTD)

DTD is a set of rules defining the hierarchical structure of a class/set of document defined in the SGML standard. A document class consists of a group of documents with similar properties. Existing DTD's, written for a specific application, can be modified to suit the requirements or new DTD's can be defined for a set of documents.

Note: A DTD for converting existing data into SGML will differ from a DTD for new documents.

SGML Conversion Process

SGML conversion is a process of inferring information from existing documents and converting that information into formally-defined SGML structures. It is a process which attempts to infer, from lexical patterns within text and from visual layout clues, the implicit structure within the input documents, and convert that implicit structure into a formally-defined explicit structure (describes an SGML DTD). The process of converting existing documents to SGML involves the following steps:

Document analysis

Document analysis consists of the following points:

- delimit the area of applicability
- define a strategy for the creating the DTD
- determine the type of end-users
- recognize the logical elements in the document class
- determine structure of a document class and structure diagrams for the contents of the elements.

Designing the DTD

The design of DTD involves the structuring of the document that includes identification of:

- The generic identifier (GIs, that is the mnemonic name that the user feels best characterizes the element) that are permissible in a document of this type.
- For each GI, the possible attributes, their range of values, and defaults.
- For each GI, the structure of its content, including
  - — which sub-element GIs can occur and in what order
  - — whether text characters can occur
  - — whether noncharacter data can occur.

Conversion of Existing Document Format

The user can either use tools and utilities available in the market for converting existing document formats to SGML format or can tag the contents of the document. In the former case, the SGML formatter confines the document structure to the vendor specific DTD. The user will then have to structure the document to suit the specific DTD designed for the document class.

In the latter case user locates each significant element of the document and marks it with the generic identifier. The process of marking start and end of the element in the document is known as tagging. The tagged document is then validated using tools and utilities designed for the task. The tagged content of this paper has been presented in annexure 1.

Presentation of the Document

The document can be presented in a form desired by the user by using Style Sheets. Style Sheets associate an extensive set of display characteristics (font, size, weight, color and so on) with the elements of a DTD. All documents based on a particular DTD, can, therefore, share stylesheets. The user can create more than one stylesheet for a DTD and thus have different presentation formats for the same document.

Utilization of SGML

SGML entered the domain of publishing with the main objective of standardizing presentation of structured information, independent of hardware platforms and software applications. Documents coded with SGML can be accessed irrespective of the text processing system. Updation of documents can be carried out with ease without changing the actual structure of the content. Due to these reason SGML has found a strong base in the following industries: IT, airline, oil, automobile, space, defense, telecom, publishing, etc.

The US Government has passed a rule stating that all documents must also be published in Braille enabling the blind community to read the papers/ documents available to the normal man also. For this purpose i.e., converting and presenting documents in Braille, SGML uses the ICADD (International Committee on Accessible Document Design).

SGML documents can be printed using either the SGML native tools and utilities or using the Microsoft Rich Text Format (RTF).

The WWW, a new wave in the IT industry, uses HTML documents. The process of conversion of SGML to HTML is a lot easier than writing new HTML documents.

Conclusion

Normally in the IT industry no person has been successful in predicting the future of a standard or product. However in case of representation (internal/ external) of information, here SGML, the IT community is confident that this standard will be modified to suit the requirements but will outlast the conventional and the regular text processing systems.

References

1. Eric van Herwijnen, NICE Technologies, Veraz France. Practical SGML, 2nd Edition Kluwer Academic Publishers, Dordrecht, Netherlands 1994.

2. Charles S Goldfarb. The SGML Handbook, Oxford University Press Inc, New York, US 1993, ISBN 0-19-853737-9.

3. Anders Berglund (Editor). Information processing — SGML support facilities — Techniques for using SGML, ISO/IEC/TR 9573, 1988.

4 Martin Bryan. SGML: An author's guide to the Standard Generalized Markup Language, Addison-Wesley 1988, ISBN 0-201-17535-5.

5. Joan M Smith, and Robert Stutely. SGML: The User's Guide to ISO 8879, Ellis Horwood 1988, ISBN 0-7458-0221-4.

Annexure 1.

<DOC> <DTITLE> Electronic Publishing with SGML </DTITLE>
<ABS> <PARA> Distribution of Information has played and is playing a key role for mankind.
Limitations in accessing this information has been one of the major factors costing
time, effort and resources. Information has to accessible to people in various
media with the least effort in conversion. </PARA>
<PARA> This paper presents a brief introduction to the world of structuring information /
data / documents using the international standard ISO 8879 (SGML). It also
presents the advantages, features, and functionalities of presenting the
structured information for distribution on both paper an well as electronic medium
without duplicating efforts. </PARA> </ABS>
<CHP> <CTITLE> </CTITLE>
<SEC> <STITLE> Information and its Classification </STITLE>
<PARA> Information is knowledge concerning facts, concepts, objects, events, ideas, and
processes, which within a specific context has a particular meaning. Large
volume of information presented in a structured format is referred to as a
database. Depending on the major content a database can be broadly classified
depending on the content, under: </PARA>
<LIST> <ITEM> <PARA> Full text databases - Books and journals in electronic format structured for store
and presentation enabling search the complete content of the book for retrieval of
the required information. </PARA> </ITEM>
<ITEM> <PARA> Bibliographic and directory databases - Structured databases in the form of a
directory or references to information are some of the typical examples of this
database. </PARA> </ITEM>
<ITEM> <PARA> Multimedia - Representation of synchronized digital information (audio and video)
on the electronic medium is referred to as multimedia. </PARA> </ITEM>
<ITEM> <PARA> Image database - Storage of images as a component of the database referenced
by information about the stored image is the main content of the database. </PARA> </ITEM> </LIST> <
<SEC> <STITLE> Electronic Publishing </STITLE>
<PARA> Electronic publishing is defined as a process for production of typeset-quality
documents containing text, graphics, pictures, tables, equations, etc. with the
assistance of a data processing system. The synonym for Electronic Publishing is
: Computer aided / assisted publishing.
The published information is distributed on state-of-the-art medium - CD-ROM, </PARA> </SEC>
<SEC> <STITLE> Advantages of Electronic Books Publishing </STITLE>
<LIST> <ITEM> <PARA> More time and cost-effective than publishing on paper
</PARA> </ITEM>
<ITEM> <PARA> Streamlines update process and promotes availability of accurate documents
instantaneously </PARA> </ITEM>
<ITEM> <PARA> Reduces distribution and storage overhead </PARA> </ITEM>
<ITEM> <PARA> Allows media enhancement of existing reference materials with sound, animation,
and video </PARA> </ITEM>
<ITEM> <PARA> Increases user effectiveness and productivity </PARA> </ITEM>
<ITEM> <PARA> Error reduction in production process </PARA> </ITEM> </LIST> </SEC> </CHP> <

SIS–96, 18–20, Jan. '96, Bangalore

Electronic publishing: Impact and implications on library and information centres

A. LAKSHMANA MOORTHY AND C.R. KARISIDDAPPA*
Defence Scientific Information & Documentation Centre, Delhi-110 054
*Department of Library & Information Science, Karnataka University, Dharwad-580 003.

Abstract

This paper overviews electronic publishing, electronic journal, and electronic publishing programmes of ADONIS, OCLC, IEL, ACM, and Elsevier publishers. The advantages and disadvantages of electronic publishing are briefly discussed. The paper attempts to assess the impact and the implications of electronic publishing on the libraries and information centres (L&ICs) and their services. Issues and concerns arising out of the use of electronic publications in L&ICs have been discussed. The paper also deals with digital libraries and their impact on the L&ICs.

Introduction

The next chapter in the history of publishing is being written and published electronically[1].

The ever increasing number of users of information and the difficulty in having informal, personal communication; the large geographic distances involved in certain routines of information acquisition; the urge to use modern developments in the related fields of electronics, computers; and telecommunications; the increasing role of information in shaping the economy of a society (the countries which produce more information have an edge over others because of the use of that information results in technological developments and the dissemination brings in financial resources in foreign exchange); and the changing notion of the information from something to know to something to have as any other commodity[2] have resulted in the need for improving the information services.

In recent times, developments in information technology (IT) have made it possible to overcome many of the above mentioned problems. Application of IT in libraries and information centres (L&ICs) raises the efficiency of information acquisition, processing, storage, and retrieval. The use of IT and the electronic document delivery systems on the library and information services are discussed in detail elsewhere[3,4]. The present paper briefly discusses the impact and implications of electronic publishing [EP] on L&ICs.

Electronic publishing

The exponential growth in the volume of published information, difficulty in retrieving information from libraries due to the literature seepage and scattering, the need to control and provide access to ever increasing volume of information, the faster rate of increase in the costs of raw materials used in publishing leading to the escalation of manufacturing costs of books and journals, the need to reduce the time required in conventional publishing, and the realization of the potential and unique features of electronic media are some of the reasons which resulted in the shift of emphasis from conventional publishing to EP.

Electronic publishing can be defined as the publication process where the manuscripts are submitted in electronic format, edited, printed, and even distributed to readers (users) by employing computers and telecommunications. In the most pedestrian interpretation, computers and related devices are used for economy and convenience in producing a conventional print-on paper publication. In the most sophisticated interpretation, the full capabilities of the electronic media — including motion, sound, and interactive features — are exploited in the creation of completely new publication forms[5]. In general, the fusion of electronic, computer and communication technologies with publishing can be termed as EP to mean any information source published in electronic (machine-readable) form. This would include sources distributed on magnetic tape and such media as videodisc as well as sources not really distributed at all but only accessible (like databases)[6].

Lancaster reported[7] that 25 per cent of reference books will be in electronic form by 1990, 50 per cent of the existing abstracting services will be available only in electronic form by the year 2000, and 25 per cent of the periodicals in science and technology, social sciences and humanities will not reach this conversion level until after the year 2000. It is an established fact that many journals and reference books including abstracting and indexing periodicals are available in electronic form now. If the current trend in the publication and marketing of CD-ROM products is any indication, there is no doubt that the above statement will become a reality soon.

Ever since the first electronic book was published in 1985 in Germany[8] there has been a steady growth in the number of electronic publication. More and more publishers of scholarly, academic and reference works from almost all fields of human knowledge are entering into the EP field. Though many publications exist in 'dual' (both on paper and electronic) versions, some 'electronic only' publications have also emerged. The first EP products were mostly reference works, secondary publications, and machine-readable databases of indexing/abstracting services.

American Chemical Society (ACS) was the first professional association bringing out scholarly periodicals to offer its publications in electronic from when it made available full text of 18 primary journals over Bibliographic Retrieval Services (BRS) in June 1983[9]. Earlier ACS has offered full-text papers of its Journal of Medical Chemistry published between 1976-78. However, this service did not include tables and instructions. Harvard Business Review was made available online providing full text articles via BRS since 1982. For a long time now, most of the major abstracting and indexing periodicals are available in electronic medium. According to online databases directory, in 1993 there were 6,998 online and CD-ROM databases[10]. Out of these, abstracting and indexing databases issued on CD-ROMs accounted for 16 per cent of the total titles produced in 1993. It is well established that online or CD-ROM databases of the secondary periodicals are more frequently consulted by the users than the printed versions.

Optical discs and electronic publishing

Optical information storage systems have become synonymous with EP. This is because of the success of the CD-ROM as the optical medium of choice for the publishing industry and also due to its adoption by major L&ICs around the world. Durability, capability to hold large volumes of data, and, of late, affordability are the important factors for the success of CD-ROMs. Many publishers including McGraw-Hill, Wiley, Elsevier-North Holland, Meckler, Grolier, Prentice-Hall, Oxford University, etc. have all ventured in this area. In due course, CD-ROMs may replace microform publications such as microfiche and microfilm primarily due to the ease of use. The usability of CD-ROMs in networking environment made this technology more attractive and acceptable to the library community. CD-ROMs, videodiscs and online bibliographic databases form a major part of the EP field.

There were only 53 CD-ROM titles in 1986 which rose to 230 titles in 1988, to over 5,000 titles in 1993 and was expected to reach about 8,500 titles by 1994. In 1993, CD-ROM titles have shown a growth of 38 per cent over the titles produced in 1992. Out of the 4,422 unique commercially available titles in 1993, science & technology accounted for 1,070 titles (24 per cent) followed by general works (931 titles — 21 per cent) and medicine (298 titles — 7 per cent). Social sciences and humanities & arts together accounted for 2,119 titles (48 per cent), indicating that these fields too are embracing CD-ROM as a publishing medium along with science and technology. In 1993, there were over 2,500 CD-ROM producers. The industry had a base of 11.4 million CD-ROM drives which was expected to reach 15 million by 1994[11]. Now, many publishers (for example, Elsevier, OCLS, IEEE, etc.) are distributing primary peer-reviewed periodicals in CD-ROM format. This shows that CD-ROMs have penetrated all branches of professional and scholarly publishing. Electronic publishing started with reference books and replaced the print-on-paper reference sources to a large extent; the remaining being converted to electronic medium in the next few years.

Further CD-interactive (CD-I), digital video interactive (DVI), and CD-recordable (CD-R) are expected to provide audio and graphic capabilities in addition to the text and data. DVI has additional capability of full motion video. Other variant forms such as erasable optical discs, WORM (write once read many times), EPROM (erasable programmable ROM), holograms, have been developed as solutions to problems or as spin-offs from research by the information industry.

Electronic journal

There is considerable difference of opinion on the definition of electronic journal (EJ). McMillan defined[12] it as any serial produced, published and distributed nationally or internationally via electronic networks such as Bitnet and the Internet. According to Langschied[13], the EJs are different from online journals. The latter are the electronic counterparts of journals in print.

Electronic journal can be defined as a periodically available online or in CD-ROM format. Generally, EJ is a full-text delivery system and differs from conventional bibliographic databases available online. The full-text databases produced on CD-ROM during 1993 accounted for 47 per cent of the total CD-ROM titles.

Many factors spurred the interest in the concept of EJ. The ever increasing overhead costs such as printing, binding, packaging and mailing charges and the decreased buying power of L&ICs due to the insufficient budgets are the major factors. Other factors include the delays experienced in communicating the research results, the slowness in the flow of manuscripts, the peer evaluation process, the time required for editing, typesetting, page layout, and page proofs.

In an EJ, there is less involvement of paper. All the routines of publishing, from the initial stages of paper submission to publishing and distribution including accessing can be performed using electronic media. The author writes an article using a computer at his end. Alternatively, a paper can also be authored by more than one author separated/scattered over a large geographical area but connected through a network through e-mail or by teleconferencing. The completed paper is then sent through e-mail to colleagues and peers for comments and incorporate suggestions made, if any. Now the paper is ready to be transferred from the authors domain to the publisher's or editor's domain by way of e-mail[5]. The paper, then will be under editorial processing. Referees upon hearing a message or transfer of paper to their domain, evaluate and transmit back to the editor with comments. These reviewed papers are then processed further based on the final status, viz. accepted for publication or modifications needed or rejected. Once accepted for publication, the paper will be transferred into the users' domain when it is available online. This could be either issue-wise (as is the case of many EJs) or by sending periodical updates of papers automatically by matching the subject interest profiles (or upon request). When a subscriber or user accesses the EJ, the latest additions after his prior access will be tagged. Upon scanning the tagged entries, the subscriber can decide whether the paper is useful or not. Others may browse by means of search queries the titles added after their previous access.

For quite some time now, many journals are accepting papers in electronic form. The author is expected to submit the final paper in floppies or send by e-mail using the word processing software adopted by the journal. In case the author uses a different software, it is possible to export them into the target software through conversion software. The electronic submission helps in reducing the time consuming, painstaking work of inputting and proof-reading, the time involved in editorial processing, and enhances the accuracy of the typeset material. The figures/illustrations, scanned or drawn using software like Harvard Graphics, Corel Draw, Exel, Lotus 1-2-3, etc, can also be sent on separate floppies. But, these files take a large memory and sometimes it is impossible to transfer them to floppies even after using compression techniques.

Some of the ongoing EP and EJ programmes are dealt in the following sections.

ADONIS

Advanced Document Over Network Information Services (ADONIS) initially covered, in its trial version, only 224 biomedical journals published in

1987 and 1988. However, by 1994 the number of journals included in the service rose to 505 from 40 participating publishers and about 160 new titles were added to the service in 1995. The journals are primarily from the biomedical field; they also cover related disciplines such as chemistry, biochemistry, bioengineering and biotechnology. Each week, a new CD-ROM is sent to the subscribers which contains all articles (about 10,000 pages) including figures as bit-mapped graphic images.

ADONIS has benefited both the publishers who like to have a control over photocopying and the librarians looking for a change from conventional stock-room and photocopying to a space and time saving mechanism. Each time a print out is taken, the system automatically stores the information in the respective statistics file for calculating the royalties payable to ADONIS.

IEEE/IEE Electronic library

Institution of Electrical and Electronics Engineers (USA) and Institution of Electrical Engineers (UK) are offering IEEE/IEE Publications Ondisc (IPO). The service combines records from the INSPEC database with full images of the original documents. These include over 100 IEEE and IEE journals, standards of the IEEE, conference proceedings and colloquia. The index disc contains records with abstracts and index from INSPEC database corresponding to the documents available on the image disc. Approximately 25,000 records are added each year.

Starting from January 1996, IEEE/IEE Electronic Library (IEL) is being introduced. The IEL is an extension of IPO with full-text information resource in the fields of electrical engineering, electronics, computer science, information technology, applied physics and related disciplines. IEL comprise more than 200 CD-ROMs of over 2000 publications of IEEE and IEE published since 1988. These publications include over 100 scientific journals published by IEEE and IEE, about 600 IEEE standards, and 700 conference proceedings.

IEL is expected to be a premier source for the state-of-the-art information which combines a subset of INSPEC database with abstracts and index to the IEEE and IEE publications, full images of matching documents and a powerful search and retrieval software. Subscribers will receive monthly updates of 3-5 discs with over 15,000 pages of scanned images and text covering current journal titles, newly published conference proceedings and latest versions of IEEE standards. There is no limit to the number of laser prints taken from the IEL database.

OCLC online library computer centre

Through its Electronic Journals Online (EJO) service, OCLC offers peer-reviewed journals online. The EP programme of OCLC started in July 1992 with the introduction of the Online Journal of Current Clinical Trials in association with the American Association for the Advancement in Science. This is the first scholarly peer-reviewed journal made available in the online environment[14]. This was followed by the Online Journal of Knowledge Synthesis in Nursing and Electronics Letters Online (September 1993).

American Institute of Physics is offering online version of its Applied Physics Letters (APL) via OCLC's EJO. APL Online is also available on CD-ROM form on an yearly subscription. OCLC has designed a World Wide Web (WWW) interface for the EJO service which makes subscribers to access journals using NCSA's Mosaic software. APL Online and the Online Journal of Knowledge Synthesis in Nursing are now available on the WWW and can be accessed through the Internet.

In 1995, six Current Opinions journals in the biological sciences and 24 Current Opinions journals in the clinical medicine were added to the EJO service. The Current Opinion journals are available to the readers prior to their print version and offer unlimited SDIs and links to MEDLINE database. Further, Immunology Today Online and Vaccine Online from Elsevier were also added to EJO service. From 1996, all the eleven IEE proceedings journals will be available through EJO service. Many of these online journals are covered by the abstracting/indexing databases like MEDLINE, INSPEC, SPIN, etc. and are linked to the databases to enable the user to browse the abstract to decide if the paper is suitable.

Subscribers can browse the contents of the online journals or search the entire collection by a variety of indexes, Boolean operators and proximity indicators. The Windows-based software Guidon of OCLC provides both colour and graphical images and equations along with the text[15].

The CORE project

The Chemistry Online Retrieval Experiment (CORE) is an electronic library of the future available at the Cornell University's Mann Library. American Chemical Society (ACS) and Chemical Abstracts Service (CAS) are pursuing this project with OCLC to provide electronic access to all the journals of ACS with associated CAS indexing dating back to 1980. In the testing phase, a sample of 31,000 papers (approximately 165,000 pages of information) from 20 chemistry journals of 1991 and 1992 and associating abstracting information from CAS were used. Eventually the project will mount all the 20 journals from 1980 on OCLC. The CORE database, the full-text component of which is encoded in Standard General Markup Language (SGML) is translated from original typesetting files. When completed, it will have more than 250 journal-years of data. The database can be searched using XSCEPTER (X-Windows Scientific Electronic Publishing and Retrieval) graphic user interface with a variety of search options such as find, browse, table of contents, and display options[16].

The ACM electronic publication plan

The Association of Computing Machinery (ACM) is exploring ACM Electronic Publishing programme with a vision to meet the future challenges of 'digital libraries', and plans to move aggressively into EP and preserve openness of ACM publications in the new media[17]. OCLC and its subsidiary Information Dimensions, Inc. have jointly developed OCLC/IDI System of Total Electronic Publishing Services (STEPS) which is implemented at the ACM. The STEPS, an end-to-end EP system for scientific journals, is designed to encompass data capture, conversion of the paper, SGML editing, composition of the finished document, electronic distribution and work flow tracking, i.e., from author's draft to the reader's computer. STEPS automatically translates the papers written by the authors in any of the four word processing software — LaTex, Word Perfect, MS Word, and Framemaker — under DOS/Windows, Macintosh, OS/2, and Unix environments into SGML[18].

Elsevier's TULIP project

Elsevier Science Publishers in association with OCLC and a few American universities, under its TULIP (The University License Project) programme, is exploring electronic access to journals without SGML tags. The information will be supplied by Elsevier in non-SGML coded TIF files (created as page images scanned at 300 dpi) and ASCII files (created using OCR software). Under this project, Elsevier would supply bitmapped images of about 45 journals in materials science to eight implementing American universities for mounting on experimental basis during 1993-1995 for usage data collection. The project has three primary objectives: to gain insights into the technical issues involved in providing access to bit-mapped images of journals, new economic models for the transition of commercial journal publishing into the networked environment, and how readers used journals in the networked environment. The project has been an overwhelming success with technology issues. The OCLC provides its database retrieval engine Newton and the user interface Guidon software for the TULIP programme[19].

Benefits and drawbacks

Advantages

In electronic publishing, the data can be maintained uptodate so that the buyer will be able to purchase the latest version of publications (for example, encyclopedias, directories). This enables 'on demand publishing', and allows retrospective searching and SDI. The individual subscribers can be provided with only those documents which match their profiles, and can be charged accordingly. An important factor is that the L&ICs need not 'buy publication' to access the information in it; they can have online access to the EP and download or print the required material. The EPs provide aids for connectivity, audiovisulisation, customizability, creation and revision of documents, interactivity, and rapid information retrieval.

The most important advantage of EJs over the conventional journal is the saving in the turn-around time, i.e., the time lag in submission, refereeing, revision, editing, composing, printing, binding, and forwarding eliminated by using computer and communication networks. This enhances timely publication and is suitable to the letters-type journals where rapid communication is of utmost importance. The electronic version also offers Boolean search of the full text to browse and read only the selected items. Further, when computer and communication facilities are available, the reader need not go to the L&IC and need not have to sift through unwanted material as in conventional journals to retrieve the relevant papers. Electronic publications may help in overcoming the restrictions on the length of the paper imposed by many scholarly journals.

Disadvantages

Some of the problems of EP include high initial costs to the publishers as well as L&ICs have to invest before benefits are expected, the non-compatibility of hardware (and hence the market potential) due to the absence of common standards, and the usage of different retrieval software by different publishers. The acceptance of EJs depends upon the user-friendly retrieval software. As a prerequisite, EPs necessitate the availability of a computer and communication network to the subscriber. The gap between developed and developing countries (those who can access and those who cannot) makes the EPs an elitist technology.

Electronic journal may take some time to percolate down to the reader level mainly due to the problem of displaying page images conveniently on a computer screen. For an entire page to be accommodated, the size of the image has to be reduced and the low resolution makes it difficult to read.

Ease of use, i.e. reading at a convenient time and place, is not possible with EPs. As there are no restrictions on the length of the papers and of course no page charges, the quality of papers may be poor if lengthy papers are accepted. Other disadvantages include the psychological feeling that researchers generally read more outside their work place, thus requiring portable reading material, though this problem can be solved by taking a printout of the required literature.

One major drawback of the Ejs at present is their delayed release. Though there are many publications which are available only in electronic medium, in many instances, when the publication is issued in both printed and electronic forms, the electronic version is released after a gap of three to four weeks. Other problems include the necessity of training for the subscribers and readers, and multiple copying license/charges (for example, ADONIS). Due to these factors, unlike their printed counterparts, EJs are not open to all but somewhat restricted.

Not withstanding these drawbacks, EJs will become all pervasive as their printed counterparts, at least in some subject fields. The day may not be too far when a researcher is able to read an EJ at a convenient place and time using laptops (to read in journeys, leisure, etc) and computers at home.

Impact on L&ICs and avenues for exploitation

The impact of EP in general and EJs in particular are four-fold. These are more useful due to inherent capabilities for manipulation and searching, providing information access is cheaper to acquiring information resources, savings in storage, maintenance, etc. and sometimes electronic form is the only alternative available. These offer a variety of capabilities to enhance the quality of services offered by L&ICs. A few avenues where the potential of EPs can be exploited are discussed in the following sections.

Accessing information

Electronic publishing has changed accessing of information by end-users to some extent. Unlike printed publications which offer unlimited and personal access, EPs provide access mostly through intermediaries, though direct access by individuals is possible to a limited extent. This is mainly because of technical reasons which include availability of suitable technology training end-users in handling a variety of retrieval software, search strategy formulation, and security and cost considerations in the case of online resources.

Quality of services

The major impact of electronic information on an L&IC would be directly on the quality of information services. In future the L&ICs would continue to provide access to information after locating in databases rather than having comprehensive acquisitions. Personalised/mission or project-oriented databases will be developed by downloading information from electronic publications. The downloaded information would be edited, revised or repackaged as per the requirements.

Electronic publishing facilitates faster and better quality of services including value-added products, enhancement in the number of clientele served with little or no extra inputs, marketability of information services, and networking and remote log-in for geographically, distributed users. These factors certainly will enhance the reputation of the L&IC. The impact of EP on research scholars and other users, publishers, and L&ICs have been dealt in detail by Aluri[20] including the role of L&ICs in the changing environment, the distinction between local and external collection, the role of inter-library loan and reference services in the new environment.

Electronic clipping services

On the lines of selective dissemination of information, many database services have developed new ways to provide professional news, both in real-time and with periodic updates. These are called 'Electronic Clipping Services'. Users can set up profiles on most major databases to monitor customised news including current events, company and industry news, evolving issues and other topics of interest[21]. These include P.A.S.S.PORT of Data Times, Alert Service of Dialog, CLIP of Dow Jones/Retrieval, News Flash of NewsNet, Eclipse of Nexis, etc. Some are same day services covering about 100 newspapers, a few search all databases held by the vendor. These will have an effect on the information services offered by the L&ICs.

Electronic reference services

Since 1993, the Atlanta-Fulton Public Library is offering an electronic reference service called PASSPORT which provides access to the library's online catalogue, commercial databases and electronic reference sources such as *Master File* (a collection of 350 full-text magazines), *Facts On File, Company Profile,* and *Academic American Encyclopedia.* From 1995, dial-up access was provided to all the patrons who can access all the library's databases from their homes, offices and work places. The library also provides connectivity to Internet[22]. Many L&ICs are already involved in such activities (both online and off-line). This phenomenon is going to increase in future.

Issues and concerns

Though many talk about global information revolution, it is mostly experienced in developed and wealthy countries where interactive CD-ROM products are released more and more and high-bandwidth computer networks are available. This is evident from the following figures. Out of the 6,998 online and CD-ROM databases listed for 1993, only 41 (i.e., a mere 0.6 per cent) are from the developing countries; of the 1,433 CD-ROM titles published through out the world during 1993, only 31 (i.e., about 2 per cent) came from the Third World. The country-wise number of Internet hosts/nodes in the developing countries is too few to feel happy. About 97 per cent of the nodes of Internet in the year 1992 were located in developed countries (about 62 per cent in USA alone)[23].

The problems and concerns of publishers, L&ICs as well as subscribers include issue of single articles versus full issues of EJ, copyright, user-friendliness, pricing, networks, incompatible hardware and software, formatting, graphics, scholary recognition, and obsolescence. The problems of an EJ like credibility, accessibility, permanence and the associated technical issues concerning the dissemination over networks (Internet), scholarship, etc. were dealt by Collins and Berge[25]. A few are dealt here.

Accessibility

The EJs will be easier to access only when the necessary telecommunication link and computer system are available to the user. Incompatible hardware and software, the gap between developed and less developed countries, geopolitical compulsions are also some of the related issues which influence the accessibility of an EJ. Further, unless the users/subscribers are trained in the mechanics of search and retrieval techniques, the EJ though 'available' will be inaccessible. This calls for establishing training facilities for the subscribers/users to access EJs through networks.

In an evaluative study of the electronic issue of the New Zealand Journal of Marine and Fresh Water Research, doubts about universal access to information, preference to hard copy over screen displays, and disappointment with the quality of graphics were expressed. The respondents described that electronic publication must supplement and not replace the printed journals[26].

Acceptability

The readers as well as authors prefer conventional prestigious journals to consult or publish. This may be linked to their promotions, appointments etc. More over, the technology has not percolated to the required level to make the electronic publications acceptable on par with their printed counterparts. However, in future, the research community is expected to heavily use networks, e-mail, bulletin boards, etc. for scientific communication. This will necessitate speedy publication and distribution of scholarly publications, thus enhancing the acceptability as well as the number of EJs.

Accountability

The question of cataloguing electronic (online) journal issues, volumes and back volumes needs to be answered. Some issues like the agency to oversee stability and authenticity of material, maintain the collection including archival, long-term storage and access, and granting equal access to the information are to be addressed in depth[27].

Awareness and coverage in secondary periodicals

An important point which influences the accessibility of an EJ is the awareness. The reader should know about the existence of the EJ, its mode of access, and charges/tariff, if any. This calls for reference tools such as directories and also bulletins/newsletters to announce such information.

Another point which greatly enhances the access of EJ is their coverage in abstracting and indexing periodicals and databases. As of now, very few are covered by these services. Perhaps this may be one of the reasons which made many publishers to opt for both print and electronic versions. Further, it is difficult to cite material from EJs due to their non-coverage in secondary publications. The reluctance of authors in submitting their papers stems from the lack of audience and uncitedness due to the non-coverage in secondary services. In due course as the EJs gain wide acceptance from researchers and professionals, we may see increased coverage in the secondary periodicals.

Preservation and archiving

Selection, acquisition, organisation, provision and preservation of back volumes are the functions of L&ICs and not the computer centres or networks which are at present providing access to the electronic publications. When the 'copy' is available through networks, who will ensure it archiving and in what form? CD-ROMs, video discs, magnetic tapes, and online databases are some of the forms which can be used for archiving the EJs. Agencies like the

National Academy of Public Administration of USA are taking steps to develop standards for preservation of EJs. This may influence the nature of availability and preservation of EJs[28]

Readability

Even computers with the best resolution cannot match the print equivalent for reading. This in addition to the lack of pagination (for example, IPCT), ease of usage, and the transportability of publication for a leisurely reading at a convenient place and time still make the printed journal preferable over the EJ.

Ethical and sociological factors

One important concern of electronic information is its vulnerability to manipulations, additions, deletions, etc. This may raise problems such as integrity, authenticity and stability of published data. This may be one of the important reasons for the author's unwillingness to publish in the online journals. Further, these cannot be closely monitored or their use cannot be restricted as in the case of printed journals. These may result in plagiarism, authorship conflicts and impersonation. Some of these problems have been addressed by Lynch[29] who suggested dedicated server, document digest algorithms, and cryptographic signatures to overcome some of these problems.

The issue of sociological and psychological impact on the profession and the traditional role of the L&ICs in the event of the researchers accessing information resources from all over the world through networks without actually entering into a L&IC is difficult to understand and address at present. Perryman provided some guidelines to avoid the latter situation[30]

Copyright and pricing

Legal issues relate to the copyright and ownership and also with respect to rules and regulations governing multiple usage. Publishers may not get returns when copyright violations (illegal photocopying) are taking place resulting in revenue losses and to avoid this situation, they are bound to impose stringent copyright rules and mechanisms to collect photocopying charges. To overcome this problem, many projects are underway. The ISI Electronic Library Project is developing[31] a security and rights management system which will take care at the client, and local and central server levels. The system provides secure viewing through password, secure printing through session encryption and water-marks, guaranteed document authenticity by means of a 'digitally signed finger print', and use privacy. A hidden watermark in the image file of each page of an article will discourage unauthorised copying.

These attempts may be seen as non-user-friendly by the end-users. Copyright is a social construct that has been and should be tailored to achieve the purposes meant for it. It is not a predestined, static law of humankind; some leakage (unauthorised copying) has always been there. Tolerating some leakage, as long as it does not hemorrhage, may be of interest to publishers in the long run[32].

Determining how to charge an L&IC for the use of online reference works is a challenge for publishers. When cooperative acquisition and inter-library loan are being followed by a group of L&ICs, this issue becomes even more problematic. A few such scenarios are dealt in detail by Gold [33]. However, the Usage Statistics Collection and Management System being developed[34] by ELINOR Electronic Library Project at Milton Keynes (UK), to analyse the usage of electronic or digital libraries may be able to help solve such problems. This project aims to analyse two types of statistics. The first type is for the publisher concerning the number of pages browsed, time spent and the number of pages viewed and printed by the users. This will also enable the system to calculate charges, if any, towards photocopying. The second type of statistics relate to maintain users' accounts, monitor and find out the heavily used documents, and to know the user reading patterns.

Standardisation

At present the EJs are available in various forms, formats and through different access points. This is a problem for the reader for accessing. Some of the EJs do not include page numbers as the size of the page in different computers (VDUs) is different. This raises citation problem when the same material to be cited can appear in different pages. The hardware and software are also to be standardised to enable the end-user to retrieve information irrespective of the make of the machine. A common command information retrieval language which can work with any sort of computer and retrieval software may be useful in such situations.

Digital library

Libraries and information centres have been described to be in transition; their change to 'electronic libraries' has been felt in the nature of functions and services offered by them and also in the behaviour of users in terms of enhanced information access and increased demands. However, the transformation of 'electronic libraries' to 'digital libraries' is perceived as a matter of term preference and not due to any change related to duties, functions or objectives of L&ICs, much the same way as bibliometrics (a preferred term to librametry) given way to informetrics, a term widely in use now. A digital library, though popularly taken as an electronic version of the L&IC (digital storage of information), may mean differently to different users.

Libraries and information centres may have to face many challenges while transforming to digital libraries; addition of more and more electronic, and digitized information, providing access to the digitised information, sorting out issues like access to information versus ownership and reappropriation of budgets towards maintaining computer systems, databases etc. versus maintaining stock.

Yerkey defined[35] digital libraries as electronic libraries in which large number of geographically distributed users can access the contents of large and diverse repositories of electronic objects. Electronic objects include networked text, images, maps, sounds, videos, catalogues of merchandise, and scientific, business and government datasets. They also include hypertext, hypermedia, and multimedia compositions. Many variant definitions can be found in the literature.

The three main characteristics of digital libraries are the storage of information in digital form, usage of communication networks to access and obtain information, and 'copying' by either downloading or on-line/off-line printing from a master file. Preservation, search and access, content creation, and delivery are its essential components. Digital libraries use and provide information in digital format[36].

Recognising the way digital libraries will forever change the existing cultural, social, organisational, economic, intellectual and technical infrastructures for information delivery, the School of Information and Library Studies at the State University of New York at Buffalo is offering a course in digital libraries from 1995[35]. The Department of Library and Information Studies at Loughborough University of Technology, with the support of British Library, is planning to establish and evaluate a training electronic journal. The aim of the journal is to provide a test bed to train L&IS students in editing, running and using EJs. There will be five sites, three in UK, and one each in Australia and Sweden which will mount information for use by their students. All five sites will be inter linked with each other for accessing of information in the EJ[37].

Many objects and initiatives are underway to solve problems, discuss the issues and concerns involving digital libraries[38]. ARPA, NASA and NSF of the USA have jointly announced several digital library projects over four years to advance the means to collect, store and organise in digital forms and to make it available for searching, retrieval, and processing via communication networks (see Yerkey[35] for more information).

The topmost priority of an L&IC, digital or otherwise, is to serve the information needs of its clientele. While traditional libraries, a meeting place of researchers, support formal, interdependent, collaborative learning and research, digital libraries however, may facilitate individual, independent and informal learning. Digital libraries are expected to play a major role in formal learning as well by providing the teachers and learners with more information in a variety of media. The potential role of digital libraries in teaching has been discussed elsewhere[39].

Conclusion

The number of journals available 'on line only' are increasing by day. For example, some of the journals offered by OCLC like Current Clinical Trials and the Online Journal of Knowledge Synthesis in Nursing have no print equivalent. These are published fast, the peer-reviewed papers are edited and marked up in SGML and sent to OCLC which are made available online within 24 hours. Even software companies are entering into this area. Microsoft is planning an online EJ (no print version) which will be available on Internet and Microsoft Network[40].

Business India magazine is internationally available now on CD-ROM. Launched in December 1995, the new version is a quarterly periodical and cumulative in nature, i.e., each issue of the volume will contain the previous issues. The publication is already accessible over Internet[41]. McGraw-Hill is offering electronic version of its Business Week on America Online which has resulted in attracting new readers. It receives over half a million clicks on its pages every week and each 'click' generates revenue. This 'feedback' enabled editors to analyse and feel the pulse of the readers' interest to revise content. If desired, readers of the online version can also have a chat session through e-mail with the authors of the lead articles. It was reported that the electronic products account for 35 per cent of the McGraw-Hill's total revenues[42]. Magazines like Time, Newsweek, PC Magazines and PC/Computing are already issuing CD-based versions. Electronic interactive magazines distributed online or on CD-ROM have tremendous potential as complementaries and companions to their printed counterparts.

The Internet is changing the notion of library as a place into a library without walls. Internet, the global network of networks, has over 1.77 million host computers with a new host added every ten minutes[43]. And in North America alone, the Internet has over 30 million users. About 200 daily newspapers, 600 magazines, over 1000 newsletters and other products are available, online via communication networks and Internet[40].

However, the rate of progress depends upon several factors such as user acceptance, economics, commitment to established products and services and also the pace of technological advances. The usage of electronic information networks such as Internet, Gopher, WWW, Easynet, etc. are on the increase. This has a positive impact on the way the information is generated, communicated, processed, acquired, retrieved and disseminated. The availability of bulletin board services, e-mail, file transfer capabilities, etc. have made it possible to disseminate the information faster across continents.

The day is not too far when one may be reading a favourite magazines interactively.

Acknowledgements

The authors are thankful to Dr. S.S. Murthy, Director, DESIDOC for his kind permission for providing the facilities and for the permission to present this paper. They are also thankful to Dr. C.K. Ramaiah for his valuable suggestions in preparing the paper. Thanks are also due to Shri D.V. Rao and Smt. P.K. Annapurna for their help in various stages of preparing this paper.

References

1. Pedek, Robin P. Introduction and overview. *Journal of the American Society for Information Science*, 1994, 45(10), 727-729.

2. Jones, Barry O. Social implications of information-based society: The role of libraries and librarians. In Meeting the challenge of technology, Proceedings of the VALA National Conference on Library Automation, Vol.1. Victoria Association for Library Automation, Melbourne, 1982, 3-4.

3. Lakshmana Moorthy, A. and Rajendran, V. Information technologies for libraries and information centres. *Aglis Journal*, 1990, 81(1-4), 6-16.

4. Lakshmana Moorthy, A., Pant, Manoj Kumar and Rajendran, V. Electronic document delivery systems. In New Vistas in Library and Information Science: Papers in honour of Prof GVSL Narasimha Raju edited by L.S. Ramaiah, et al. Vikas Publishing House, New Delhi, 1995.

5. Lancaster, F.W. Electronic publishing. *Library Trends,* 1989, 37(3), 316-25.

6. Lancaster, F.W. Electronic publishing and their implications for libraries: In Beyond 1984, edited by Peter Gellaty. Howarth Press, New York, 1983. p. 245.

7. Lancaster, F.W. The future of the library in the age of telecommunications. In Telecommunications and libraries: a primary for librarians and information managers, edited by D.W. King and others. Knowledge Industry, White Plains, 1981.

8. Gurnsey, John. Electronic publishing: A state-of-the-art review. *Information Media & Technology*, 1992, 18(3), 101-104.

9. Garson, Lorrin R. and Howard, Jeanne H. Electronic publishing: Potential benefits and problems for authors, publishers and libraries. *Journal of Chemical Information & Computer Science,* 1984, 24(3), 119-123.

10. Marcaccio, K.Y., Nolan, K.L. and Turecki, G. Gale directory of databases, 2 V. Gale Research, Detroit, 1993.

11. Chakravarti, A.K., Vasanta, B., Shroff, N. and Krishnan, A.S.A. CD-ROM. *Electronics Information & Planning*, 1994, 22(2), 106-112.

12. McMillan, G. Embracing the electronic journal: One library's plan. *The Serials Librarian*, 1991, 21(1), 97-108.

13. Langschied, L. Electronic journal forum: Column 1. *Electronic Journal Forum*, 1992 (Spring/Summer), 131-136.

14. Dykhuis, Randy. The promising of electronic publishing: OCLC's program. *Computers in Libraries*, 1994, 14(10), 20-22.

15. OCLC *Newsletter*, 1995 (July/August), 22.

16. Weibel, Stuart L. The design and implementation of XSCEPTER, an X-Windows graphic user interface to the CORE Project. In Annual Review of OCLC Research, 1994. OCLC Online Computer Library Centre, Dublin, 1995, 40-45.

17. Denning, Peter J. & Rous, Bernard. The ACM electronic publishing plan. *Communications of the ACM*, 1995, 38(4), 97-103.

18. Promenschenkel, George. STEPS: Towards a new era in electronic publishing. *OCLC Newsletter*, 1995 (July/August), 20-21.

19. Lynch, Clifford A. The TULIP project: Context, history and perspective. *Library Hi Tech*, 1995, 13(4), 8-22.

20. Aluri, Rao. Electronic Publishing: Unfolding of an information revolution. DESIDOC *Bulletin of Information Technology,* 1996, 16(1), in press.

21. Bates, Mary Ellen. Electronic Clipping services: A new life for SDIs. Online, 1994, 18(3), 43-51.

22. Agnew, Grace B. The Internet initiative at the Atlanta-Fulton Public Library. DESIDOC *Bulletin of Information Technology*, 1996, 16(1), in press.

23. Jacobson, Thomas L. The electronic publishing revolution is not 'global'. *Journal of the American Society for Information Science*, 1994, 45(10), 745-752.

24. Catenazzi, Nadia & Gibb, Forbes. The publishing process: The hyper-book approach. *Journal of Information Science*, 1995, 21(3), 161-172.

25. Collins, Mauri P. & Berge, Zane L. IPCT Journal: A case study of an electronic journal on the Internet. *Journal of the American Society of Information Science*, 1994, 45(10), 771-776.

26. Jasperse, Jaap A. Primary science on CD-ROM: The New Zealand experiment. *Journal of the American Society for Information Science*, 1994, 45(10), 777-784.

27. Von Ungern-Sternberg, Sara & Lindquist, Mats G. The impact of electronic journals on library functions. *Journal of Information Science,* 1995, 21(5), 396-401.

28. Sasse, Margo Q. Winkler, B. Jean. Electronic journals: A formidable challenge to libraries. In Advances in Librarianship, Vol.17, edited by Irene P. Godden. Academic Publishers, New York, 1993, 149-173.

29. Lynch, Clifford A. The integrity of digital information, mechanics and definitional issues. *Journal of the American Society of Information Science*, 1994, 45(10), 737-744.

30. Perryman, W.R. The changing landscape of information access: The impact of technological advances upon the acquisition, and dissemination of information resources within the research library community. *Journal of Library Administration*, 1991, 15(1/2), 73-93.

31. Anderson, Laura Challman & Lotspiech, Jeffrey B. Rights management and security in the electronic library. *Bulletin of the American Society for Information Science*, 1995, 22(1), 21-23.

32. Samuleson, Pamela. Copyright and digital libraries. *Communications of the ACM*, 1995, 38(4), 15-21, 110.

33. Gold, Jon D. An electronic publishing model for academic publishers. *Journal of the American Society for Information Science*, 1994, 45(10), 760-764.

34. Zhao, Dian G. Usage statistics collection and management in the ELINOR electronic library. *Journal of Information Science*, 1952, 21(1), 1-9.

35. Yerkey, A. Neil. A course in digital libraries. DESIDOC *Bulletin of Information Technology*, 1996, 16(1), in press.

36. Riggs, Donald E. Digital libraries: Assumptions and characteristics (editorial). *Library Hi Tech*, 1995, 13(4), 5, 60.

37. CTI *Newsletter,* 1994, 5(5), 5.

38. See *Communications of the ACM*, 1995, 38(4), 22-110; and *SIGLINK Newsletter,* 1995, 4(2), 2-28.

39. Marchionini, Gary & Maurer, Nermann. The roles of digital libraries in teaching and learning. *Communications of the ACM,* 1995, 38(4), 67-75.

40. *The Economist*, 11-17 November 1995, p.84.

41. Pande, Manisha. *Asian Age*, 12 December 1995, p.13.

42. *Economic Times,* 29 November 1995, p.37.

43. Treese, Winn. The Internet index. treese@orl.dec.com. 1994 (quoted in Shaw, Debora. Libraries of the future: Glimpses of a networked, distributed, collaborative, hyper, visual world. *Libri,* 1994, 44(3), 206-223.)

SIS–96, 18–20, Jan. '96, Bangalore

BASISplus: A tool for developing digital library

R.K. GOYAL
BASIS PLUS Division, National Informatics Centre, New Delhi-110 003
(E-Mail-goyal@basis.nic.in)

Abstract

BASIS WEB server based on BASISplus is a tool for publishing large scale document databases on the WWW. The various features of the software and its applications are discussed. The information available in libraries has to be converted into digital format and has to be put on WEB server for world wide use. The BASISplus along with the related software is used to achieve the goal.

Introduction

A digital library is visualised as a server which is having linkages to various other sources of information in digitized format. These linkages can lead to a number of sources such as FTPservers, LISTservers, NEWSservers, EBservers, Wired Service articles, etc. Digital library has mainly three characteristics, first, storage in digital form, that is, works such as books, magazines, newspapers, records, videos, etc. are to be stored in digital form. Second, readers no longer need to come to a library, they use electronic methods to have material delivered to them. Third, material is always copied from the master version of the work in the electronic library. To create/develop such digital libraries, various tools are available. BASIS WEBserver, based on BASISplus, is one such tool for publishing large scale document databases on the World Wide Web (WWW). National Informatics Centre (NIC) has procured BASISplus, BASISDesktop, TECHLIPplus and BASIS WEBserver software from Information Dimensions Inc., (IDI) USA. A brief description of these software products is provided in this paper.

BASISplus

BASISplus is a Client-Server relational database system (RDEMS) for text and mixed object documents that adheres to fundamental principles of open system including interoperability, portability and scalability. It has multiprocess server architecture which allows BASISplus to perform, not only on single processor system, but also on state-of-the-art symmetric multiprocessors. The database engine provides user authentication, document access control, concurrency control, deadlock protection, rollback and recovery.

It combines the most comprehensive concept retrieval (thesaurus) capabilities available with the full power of an extended relational database management engine. It supports document management needs such as large object storage, text manipulation, document navigation and full journalling, backup and recovery for documents. It also allows users to search the text of all documents to locate relevant information. It provides electronic delivery of full text documents. BASIS Desktop is a windows application of BASISplus and a toolkit for building customized document database applications in a Client-Server environment. The main features of BASIS Desktop are as follows:

- Document Routing — BASIS Desktop integrates with Windows e-mail applications so that users can route documents throughout their workgroup, adding notes and conducting online editing sessions.
- Flexible Display — BASIS Desktop displays and prints each document in its original format regardless of whether the authoring application is resident on the user's machine.
- Protected editing — The review documents, users can check them out of the database and edit them in their preferred word processors.
- Automatic Versioning — During the editing life-cycles, users can track the evolution of the their documents.
- Mixed Object Management — It manages images and mixed object data as well as text, and can launch other desktop applications to edit word processing documents, images, graphics and spreadsheets.

TECHLIBplus

TECHLIBplus is a comprehensive library automation package over BASISplus RDBMS and Text Retrieval system. Designed to streamline and facilitate all the day-to-day operations of a fully electronic library. It provides Online Patron Access Catalog (OPAC), catalog maintenance, circulation, serial management, acquisition processing and MARC cataloguing, image references can be stored directly in TECHLIBplus databases, or users can access images and information stored in BASISplus databases. TECHNLIBplus also provides direct access to information in Current Contents. It supports Z39.50 connectivity to facilitate access of other databases.

Application development

As discussed earlier, BASIS WEBserver can be a ideal tool for development of digital libraries in a networking environment. NIC has setup a satellite based nation wide computer-communication network called NICNET, with over 750 nodes connecting the national capital, the state capitals and district headquarters to one another. NIC has also setup Information Super Highway nodes in major cities of India. These high speed nodes can transmit images, video, long text, etc. stored in BASIS WEBserver at C-WEB at NIC HQ, New Delhi. Similarly, about 70 high speed nodes in major cities will also provide the above facilities to serve the whole country. Main features of BASIS WEBserver which help in conversion of applications to digital are described below.

BASIS WEBserver employs powerful text and attribute-retrieval functionality, enabling users to easily access information that meets their needs. Its key functionality includes automatic export of information as valid HTML (Hyper Text Markup Language) documents, Full Text databases, HTML databases, concurrent information updating, and intelligent navigation. It is capable of managing hundreds of gigabytes of information. The WWW offers greater opportunities to take your documents into the next century. It accommodates the electronic publishing requirements of any kind of document format. One can publish multiple document types today while planning electronic publishing projects of tomorrow. It also ensure quality and security aspects of WEB management. It also supports Forms, Common Gateway Interface (CGI), Inline images, etc.

Application developed on BASIS WEBserver

- C-WEB (http://www.nic.in/): NIC has started WWW on Internet in Jan. 1995. Various application databases using BASISplus are being developed and made available for browsing. Legal information, NBWSNIC, GISTNIC, S&T databases, Patent database, etc will be shortly available on C-WEB.

- BOLD (http://www.idi.oclc.org/): BOLD (BASISplus Online Documentation), BASISplus Documentation is available Online on IDIs WEBserver.

- VOLNET (http://orca.unl.ac.uk:8001/): University of North London (UNL) publishes the VOLNET database which is bibliographic database of documentary sources in the "voluntary sector" (i.e., charities and social science).

- CHIN (http://www.chin.gc.ca/): Canadian Heritage Information network has published the Humanities National database as part of its reference databases.
- Global Directory (http://www.one-global.com/): Global directory has databases and information on international business, travel and economic facts.

Conclusion

Information can be exchanged with one WEBserver to another WEBserver with hyperlinks/weblinks. Now it is important that the information in libraries has to be converted to digital format. This has to be done subject/sector wise, each library focusing on one specialized subject to put on the WEBserver. One library cannot produce the entire digital library, since it will be time consuming and costly affair. Giving everyone fair access to digital libraries must be a concern, and linkages must be rapid and economical communication and access options from NICNET provide easy and cost effective way for libraries to participate in emerging global digital community. Enhanced connectivity and flexibility of the NICNET network offer libraries ways to reduce telecommunications costs.

Scholars and research scientists will use the medium to transform ways in which information is acquired, used and shared in the conducting of research. One can communicate with peers, consult databases, transmit or analyze large quantities of data and manage personal libraries.

Teachers and students will use the medium to augment the classroom and textbook with a shift from passive printed page to interactive digital screen that could pose or entertain questions, provide or analyze answers. Writers, editors and publishers will create and produce books and journals, but the pattern of use and productions will gradually shift to favor the faster and more powerful methods afforded by digital means. People will be looking for smaller and smaller needles of information in bigger and bigger information haystacks. They will send more and more documents by fax or by online systems.

Digital medium will create demand for new services such as bulletin board, online data, video and sound data publications. The gradual shift from paper to digital medium that incorporates data, moving images and on demand delivery will pose major challenges to publishers, information users and libraries. Digital libraries will require a new breed of electronic information specialists who will have to reinvent for new electronic environment, the traditional library functions of cataloguing, archiving and providing archives of information.

As we approach the 21st century, the digital medium will increasingly become the medium of choice for the increasing number of people who will create, organise, store, access, retrieve and distribute information in the digital form.

References

1. David M. Levy and Catherine C. Marshall. 'Going Digital': A look at assumptions underlying digital libraries. *Commun. ACM,* 38, 4 (April '95), 77-84.
2. Wiederhold G. Digital libraries value and productivity. *Commun. ACM,* 38, 4 (April '95), 85-95.

SIS–96, 18–20, Jan. '96, Bangalore

Digital libraries : New mechanism for horizontal and vertical integration of information

JAGTAR SINGH AND H.P.S. KALRA
Dept. of Library & Information Science, Punjab University, Patiala 147 002

Abstract

The paper underlines that 'Electronic-skywriting' is the fourth revolution in the history of communication. The first three being, speech, script, and printing. The convergence of computer and communication technologies has linked the human minds worldwide, and a continuous dialogue is now possible cutting across the physical barriers. The digital libraries have appeared along with many uncertainties and possibilities. The biggest uncertainity being the future of 'have nots', within, between and among the advanced and less developed countries, regarding providing access to digitized/networked information. Touches upon a few problems relating to handling of multilingual aspects, and the fluid nature of digitized information. Copyright, security and privacy are the issues which need immediate attention.

Underlines the need for developing user-friendly interfaces, standardising the protocols, and creating general awareness regarding digitized libraries. Mentions the importance of developing national information policies and infrastructure, digitization of the existing records, training of the L&I professionals and end-users in handling the new media. Pleads for collaboration between public and private sectors for digitizing and disseminating knowledge and information. Discusses archives of digitized information, available via Internet.

The mission

Digital libraries as a manifestation of changes in the information media, will not be a thing of the distant future, but will start gaining ground in India in the present century. Therefore, it is not hyperbolic to say that we are heading towards a digital environment in which digital information may substitute to a large extent the print-based information. Even then, this paper is developed on the premise that a library is an organization with a mission, which transcends the barriers of space and time, and its existence is not dependent on the physical form of documents. Its mission is to provide a link between the past and the present and shape the future of society by preserving the records of human culture, as well as, enhance access to global information by integrating the emerging information technologies. This mission of libraries is unlikely to change in the near future. The focus of libraries, therefore, should be the acquisition, organisation and dissemination of knowledge and information, rather than the medium. With digitization of knowledge and information, both have become fluid and separated from the container. As such, there is every likelihood of change in the role and status of traditional library. With the advent of digital technology, the possibility of horizontal and vertical integration of knowledge and information has increased significantly. Historically, communication of knowledge and information has passed through three phases, i.e., speech, script, and printing. 'Information Superhighway' as an outcome of 'electronic-skywriting' is the fourth revolution which has provided us the missing link for instant transfer of knowledge and information. Now it is possible to transmit large quantities of voice, video and data across the globe instantly.

Knowledge and information

In Alvin Toffler's idiom, the computer and communication technologies are leading us to the third wave. The first two being the agricultural and industrial waves, which have made a significant impact on socio-economic development of the people everywhere. He believes that these technologies will also transform the global economy in a profound manner. As such, the library and information professionals must know that today it is not the labour or capital which is major input, rather it is the information which has become strategic resource for socioeconomic development of nations. In this context, knowledge of the information needs is very essential to lead, direct and support the emerging information society in India. Here, it becomes imperative to distinguish between knowledge and information. We know that knowledge is the sum total of what is known to the society and has a greater social value, whereas information is user specific and an essential input for generating and developing more knowledge and knowledge-based products. Hence, library and information professionals must possess knowledge of global information resources; information services in problem-solving; and the system of generating, managing and information skills; value-addition to information, and finally the use of information to analyse and resolve both the personal and work-related decisions.

Digital library

Libraries have always adopted newer technologies for fulfilling their basic commitments, and the adoption of digital technology in libraries is a part of this historical process. The terms digital library, electronic library, and virtual library are being used near synonymously, which is not the exact case. Digital library or electronic library may roughly mean one and the same thing. Digital library or electronic library may not necessarily be networked, but would largely contain digitized information along with print-based publications, but the virtual library is a library without walls, spread across the globe, from where one is able to retrieve the whole world of information through a properly networked workstation. Here, the user gets the impression as if he is moving through a large library. However, digital library, electronic library, and virtual library should only be taken as the means for obtaining the mission of libraries, as well as, their changing complexions in the course of history. Therefore, we the professionals have to adapt to the newer technologies to exploit the opportunities provided by the new media, but not to lose sight of our primary concern, i.e., the massage, which is more important than the medium through which it is communicated. It may be noted that whereas the technologies are becoming smart, knowledge and information are also becoming highly complex simultaneously. This is resulting in a wide variety of media, which were not earlier available. The new media have posed many challenges before us.

The biggest challenge being to ensure equitable access to information to one and all. This requires an effort to change the general attitude of higher authorities, library and information professionals and end-users to transform their way of thinking. To do so would require looking, beyond our mission, towards the professional ethics and philosophy. With the digitization of information the possibility of widening of the existing gap between 'haves' and 'have nots' has increased.

Digital information users

As a matter of fact, users of digitized information in India can be broadly divided into following four groups:

a) Those who have started using the latest technology and digitized information.

b) Those who have been using these technologies and digitized information and are expanding it rapidly.

c) Those who have the fear of using new technologies for information retrieval.

d) Those who are intermixed between the above three groups, but have no training to use the technology for accessing global information.

The last one is the largest of these groups. Therefore, general information literacy is required, to reduce the gap between the 'haves' and 'have nots', and enable us to move towards the goal of providing equitable access of information to one and all. This further raises the issue of providing no-fee or low-fee based services. To ensure equitable access, free information services must form an integral part of our national policy on library and information services. As determined by the market forces, the scope of fee-based value added information services is not ruled out altogether, rather it increases in the face of declining library budgets and growing user expectations.

Challenges and opportunities

Integration and updation of IT; maintaining a fair balance between print-based and digital information (this will depend entirely upon the local needs); education and training of the professionals and end-users, issues related to copyright, security, privacy and multilingual aspects of information, and providing connectivity to Internet/ISDNs, are a few more challenges facing the profession. Digital technology has manifold increased the possibility of breaking the monopoly of commercial publishers, through electronic publishing. This is still a nascent field in which if adequate steps are not taken immediately, we might miss the opportunity. It would require active collaboration between various institutes/organisations in the public sector, i.e., between libraries, publication bureaus and computer centres in universities; as well as, between public and private sectors across the globe. Proper steps in this direction would ensure, decrease in the cost of production and provision of digital information. The opportunity could also be used for enhancing our professional image. Earlier, library and information professionals were at the receiving end, accepting the documents, pushed in by the commercial publishers by manipulating the demand and supply gap. With the possibility of electronic publishing, our role can be enlarged, and we can reverse the situation, by publishing at local levels, with the help of new technologies. University presses, computer centres, library and information professionals, and academics can play an active role in electronic publishing.

The notion that with the digitization of information, the existence of libraries is threatened, is unfounded. As indicated earlier, the mission of libraries is unlikely to change, rather the role of libraries may widen in the wake of digitization of information. No doubt, the present structure and organisation of traditional library may undergo an unprecedented change, but library as an organisation, catering to the needs of the respective community would remain an integral part of society. In spite of all the visions and predictions, print-on-paper publications and libraries will survive the shock of the new media. The digital libraries may change the character of the traditional library but cannot eliminate it altogether.

Networking and digital libraries

The digital library at every level should form an integral part of global networks. The value of library and information networks cannot be underestimated. E-mail, ftp, telnet, http, gophers, WWS, online catalogs, directories, guides, databases, e-journals, e-newsletters, discussion lists, bulletin boards, Usenet news-groups, Archie, Veronica, Wais, Mosaic, Netscape, etc., are a few valuable services available via Internet, which enable us to provide massive access to global information. The value of information for economic, social, and intellectual development has almost become a cliche. But network would ensure a number of value-added services for enhancing access to the world of information. 'Information Superhighway' would facilitate instant transfer of voice, video and data in larger quantities. As such, it will become increasingly difficult for academic institutions to materialize their mission without network connectivity. After all, the Internet is creating a global community which is growing and developing day by day.

Implications

This implies, that there is an immediate need to adopt a National Information Policy and develop National Information Infrastructure. For this purpose, a standing commission at national level should be established. The Chattopadhyaya Committee appointed by the Department of Culture, Government of India, had submitted the draft of National Policy on Library and Information Systems in 1989. Its recommendations have been accepted by the Empowered Committee also, but no follow-up action has been taken so far. In fact, the matter of library and information services should not be put under the Departments of Education and Culture, rather a separate Department of Library and Information Systems, under the Ministry of Human Resource Development (MHRD) should be created, keeping in view the massive growth and development of library and information centres in India. Professional bodies, such as, SIS, ILA, IASLIC, must take up the case and get the needful done. We are also required to generate fierce competition in the telecommunication sector. The DOT is behaving like a big brother and is not providing the routes to Internet in a cost-effective manner. If private companies, like in the UK and the USA are allowed to enter this sector, then many of the problems related to tariff of telecommunication will be solved a good idea for digitizing the existing records. The private sector can provide the necessary infrastructure which the public sector can use for digitization of knowledge and information available with it.

Development of user-friendly interfaces and standardisation of the protocols will be two other activities, which will require continuous attention of L&I professionals and others in the information industry. Information literacy will be a *sine qua non* for drinking from the fire-hoses. For this purpose, education and training of L&I professionals and end users becomes a major issue to be resolved. Information literacy encompasses, traditional literacy, computer literacy, media literacy, and network literacy in the context of information problem-solving skills. In fact, real need and the overall problem-solving process are the basic forces pressing the need for education and training. Access to a number of scholarly electronic archives is now available via Internet. Bulletin Board for Libraries (BUBL) in the UK, North Carolina State University gopher, Infoslug (California), CICNet (Michigan), and the LIbrary of Congress gopher in the USA are valuable sources of quality information of interest to L&I professionals. Similarly, many subject gophers, and archives of electronic information are accessible via WWW on the Internet. Archie, Veronica, Wais, Mosaic and Netscape are very useful tools to locate pertinent networked information across the globe. Now the commercial publishers are also providing access to their resources and services via Internet. OCLC and BLDSC are other sources for enhancing our access to networked information.

Conclusion

The semantics of the synergy between information and the technology associated with it lie in the real needs of the society. This synergy will continue *sine die*. It is for us to decide, how we are to take advantage of this synergy. An opportunity is available to us for enhancing our access to global information by integrating it horizontally and vertically via various networks. If we are able to do this worldwide, then we achieve the real mission of the libraries, i.e., making available the records of human culture to all, at any time, from anywhere and in any form. Digitizing and networking of information resources and services means creating a global community with a vast storehouse of knowledge and a continuous dialogue among its members to solve various problems related to the lives and work of people across the globe. Let us stop for a minute and imagine an enormous volume of multimedia running instantly on the 'Information Superhighway'! What more do we need to enhance our access to global information cutting across the barriers of space and time?

References

1. Britton, W.A. BITNET and the Internet: Scholarly network for libraries. *College and Research Libraries*, Feb. 1990, pp.103-07.

2. Brown, J.A. The global computer network: Indications of its use worldwide. *International Information & Library Review*, 1994, pp.51-65.

3. Dichristina, M. The virtual library. *Popular Science*, Apr. 1995, p.51.

4. Fox, E.A. et. al. Digital libraries. *Communications of the ACM*, Apr. 1995, pp.76-75.

5. Gore, A. The information superhighway: What it will mean. *The World Almanac and Book of Facts*, 1995, pp.35-36.

6. Jagtar Singh and Kalra, H.P.S. Automated libraries and information networks: Their role in furthering access to the world of information. Presented in the Seminar on Services in Automated Libraries: Challenges an Opportunities. Dec. 4-5, 1995, Hyderabad.

7. Karol, E. The whole Internet: The user's guide and catalog. San Sebastapol. CA: O'Reilly, 1992.

8. Larson, S. The idea of an electronic library: A critical essay. *Libri*, 1988, pp.159-77.

9. Lipkin, R. The library that is not there. *Science News*, June 3, 1995, pp.344-51.

10. Lynch, C.A. The integrity of digital information: Mechanism and definitional issues. *JASIS*, 1994, pp.737-44.

11. Marchionini, G. and Maurer, H. The role of digital libraries in teaching and learning. *Communications of the ACM*, Apr.1995, pp.67-75.

12. Martin, S.K. Information technology and libraries: Towards the year 2000. *College and Research Libraries*, July 1989, pp.397-405.

13. Purday, J. The British Library's initiatives for access projects. *Communications of the ACM*, Apr. 1995, pp.65-66.

14. Rajashekar, T.B. Digital libraries. *Information Studies*, Oct. 1995, pp.223-38.

15. Rao, R. et. al. Rich information in the digital library. *Communications of the ACM*, Apr. 1995, pp.29-39.

16. Rogers, M. IBM reenters library market with digital system. *Library Journal*, May 1995, p.25.

17. Salvador, R. IBM helps libraries to go digital. *Electronic Learning*, May 1995, p.6.

18. Samuelson, P. Copyright and the digital libraries. *Communications of the ACM*, Apr. 1995, pp.15-21.

19. Verity, J.W. Welcome to the cy-brary. *Business Week*, May 29, 1995, pp.90-91.

20. Wijasuriya, D.E.K. Access to information: Considerations towards national policy on libraries. *Libri*, 1983, pp.22-36.

Two

Collecting, Capturing, Filtering Digitized Information

SIS–96, 18–20, Jan. '96, Bangalore

Digital imaging: Technology, trends and impact on libraries

B.P. PRAKASH
Hindustan Photo Films, Ootacamund-643 005

Abstract

With the advent of the multimedia era, the needs of electronic imaging are growing rapidly. In addition to traditional text- based information, digital libraries are adding up visual data such as photographs, videos, motion pictures, maps, manuscripts, satellite pictures and other special forms of data. Images of these materials are a significant component of digital libraries and by far the most demanding in terms of conversion, storage and retrieval. This paper examines history, trends and current issues of "Digital Imaging", textual information. The organisation and representation of visual data is discussed and a model of the "Image Database" is presented. The process of image capturing and trends in compression of image data and the standardization efforts (MPEG) are discussed.

Introduction

The dawn of information revolution is considered to be one of the marvels of twentieth century. The new technology has not only transformed the shape of modern libraries but also created very many exciting possibilities and opportunities. With radio, television, computers, communication satellites, cable TV, multimedia, local and wide area networks we are often referred to be living in an "Information Society".

Digital Libraries 'does not mean Libraries' in the classical sense, but a network of multimedia systems. A typical digital library is a media server (group of interlinked workstations) connected to high speed networks. Unlike traditional libraries, digital libraries don't reside in a building. Correctly designed, the information arrives as needed at the users screen, like the ever attendant waiter filling your water glass before you know it is empty.

In addition to traditional text based information data accessible through the digital library system includes non text information (photographs, drawings, illustrations, work of art); streams of numeric data (satellite information, cosmological data); digitised sound and moving visual images and 3D representations (holograms).

In the context of Digital Imaging, librarians face greater challenges in capturing, storing, formatting, retrieval and reproduction of non-textual information. Because, it is a new area of developing sources of information and experiences are few. In particular, the technical aspects of digital imaging are far beyond the scope of most of our libraries. The digitization and handling of data require specialized knowledge and computer hardware/ software unavailable to most of us.

As the arrival of Digital Libraries is imminent, librarians are forced to re-educate themselves to meet this new challenge. As Sylvia EA Piggott puts "The rapid technological developments as well as economic changes have made it clear that the familiar role of librarians as information intermediaries must undergo immense change, if the librarians are to avoid being displaced by a variety of contenders". To achieve this, the institutions need to relate the digital image projects to the fundamental collection activities such as accessing and preservation.

Digital imaging

The collections of libraries and archives, the primary repository of analog form of information constitute print (documents) image form (map & photographs) and Sound formats (records and videotapes). In other words, the principal categories of information sources are text, video and voice. The visual representation of objects, colours and shapes has always been an integral part of human culture. Hence the representation of visual phenomena through photography, motion film and video have become part of our daily lives. For information to be communicated broadly, it needs to be stored outside the human memory. Today, we have moved beyond text and language, into the storage and communication of images of this visual world.

Let us now consider the imaging aspects of non-textual data. Looking back, recording of original non-textual (image) data was manual until the development of photography. The invention of silver based film and photographic process added a new dimension to information acquisition, as it was possible to accurately capture complex visual images. Later on, electromagnetic media opened up new possibilities in capturing information through video tapes.

Image information stored in these analog formats could not be processed easily and this led to the birth of magnetic and optical media. Modern information systems are now able to represent the information electronically (as digital signals) and to manipulate automatically at high speeds. Such information represented digitally, in two states, or binary form is often referred to as DIGITAL INFORMATION. Magnetic tapes (serial access), magnetic disks (direct access), and optical disks form the basic recording and storage media in digital forms.

The capture of data for electronic storage and digital processing is accomplished by manual (keyboard) and automatic (image processing) techniques. Interestingly, it is observed that two thirds of the information cannot be digitised by keyboard transcription because they contain drawings, signature, images, etc. or because keying-in would be highly uneconomical. Hence imaging process becomes the primary modes of converting analog image data into computer readable digital format.

An image database

It has been more complicated to develop hardware and software which would handle images as easily as figures and text. Only a few years ago the resolution and quality of digital images over-passed the domestic T.V. reference (SVGA, 800×600).

Now with true colour 24 bits, CD ROMS can bring images of very high quality. An image database seems a near perfect replacement for traditional methods of access, which required the handling of original non-textual formats. With numerous advantages it is clear that digital image databases will be used to greater extent in the future. In the building of image database — includes phases such as scanning source material, interfacing the images with a database tool or delivering the images to the user.

The power and attraction of digital image databases are attributed mainly to the synergy between the two complex technologies, namely, computerised search/ retrieval system and digital imaging. Each of these disciplines — cataloging on one hand, imaging science on the other hand has long been a speciality of its own. Digitizing often becomes challenging as the materials (such as coins, stamps) very in size and resolution, but the images have to be recorded on a single file format, named JTIP.

A typical image database, as conceptualised by Jean F. Barda is given in Figure 1. Generated image files are stored to be set online with a magnetic disk pack (of RAID technology) for image retrieval, together with the indexation data. Apart from numbering, documentary fields need to be defined clearly. Image retrieval as shown in Figure 1, could be achieved through screen display, printout, CDROM edition, file export, etc.

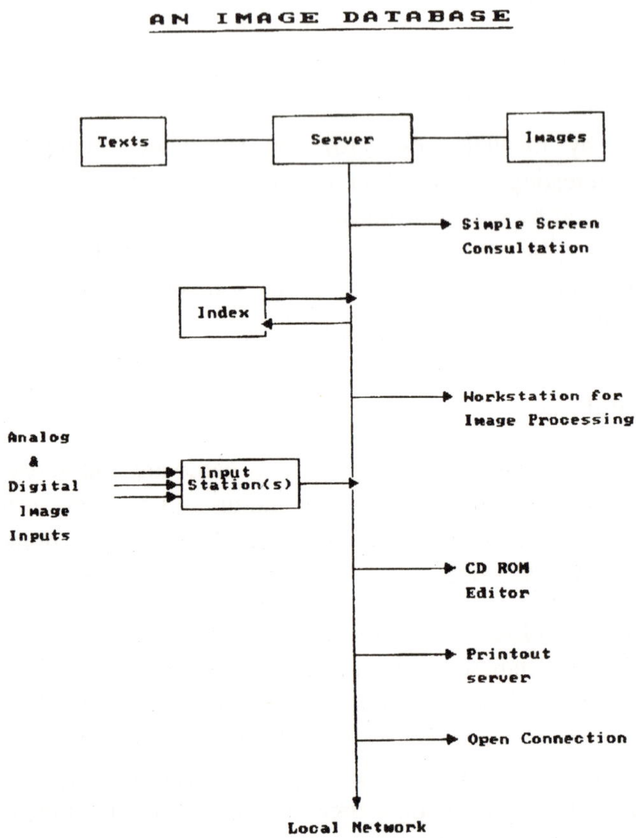

Figure 1

Image capture and processing

Image processing involves the use of high resolution scanning cameras. But how does a camera record and transform a 'document page' into a 'digital page' which can be read and manipulated by a computer? To generate a digital representation of a document page, cameras divide the page into minute areas called picture elements (pixels) and produce an array of binary digits, each representing the brightness of a pixel. The resulting stream of bits is enhanced, compressed and stored in high density storage media such as microfilm, PCMCIA card, optical disks, etc.

It is estimated that a document page of 2500 characters require 45,000 bytes of space, while uncompressed. A PCMCIA card can hold upto 60-80 sharp but compressed pictures or document pages. These cards are re-usable after loading the images on to computers are often erasing them.

Digital cameras use special silicon chip incorporating electronic sensors such as Charged Couple Devices (CCD's). The image scanner digitises the entire page into series of 'ones' and 'zeroes' and display an image as it does not recognise characters and words of text. In other words, the scanner senses the presence of photons (light) rather than the electrical signals as in video cameras. After the picture is digitised the camera transforms it into one of the industry standard image file formats as per MPEG system or its equivalents such as TIFF, JPEG, EPS and DAVIC.

The widespread deployment of digital technology is due to parallel advances in software which allow the technology to be used by persons other than computer experts. To bring up the picture on to the monitor and to manipulate (cut, crop, reduce, brighten, soften, diffuse, twist, emboss, etc) a host of software packages such as Photoplus, Photo finish, Image Assistant, etc are available. These softwares does all these things in seconds that would have taken hours in the conventional wet process. This aspect is considered as the real strength of digital imaging.

Even though the principle of digital imaging is decade old, digital cameras have emerged stronger, only in the recent 3-4 years. Industry leaders like Kodak and Canon and computer companies like Apple have found a new common ground. Some of the leading cameras are given in Table 1, with their special features.

Digital cameras are available today with resolutions from 320 × 240 pixels to 4096 × 4096 pixels. An ordinary digital camera may cost between $1000 and $5000, but it may go up to $28,000 as in the case of NIKON N90 model, which runs high resolution (3060 × 2036 pixel) images. Nikon and Fuji have jointly developed SLR cameras which can record compressed as well as non-compressed data. It is assumed that the future will provide more opportunities to libraries, as digital cameras improve their speed and performances, users gain more experiences and the cost comes down further.

Data compression

Multimedia research has mainly focussed on real time data capturing and display, combined with compression storages and transmission of data. The concept of video compression is driven by many of the new applications in

Table 1 Some leading cameras and their special features

Popular digital cameras	
Make / model	Features
CASIO QC - 10	On board memory for 95 shots.
KODAK DCS 420 C	Picture stored on computer chips. Can take 48 shots. Cost $8,000. Camera with NIKON SLR. Image can be directly sent to the printer.
NIKON E-2	Imaging censor with 1.3 million pixels. Sharp pictures. Cost $1,000.
SONY	3 chip action camera.
SINAR E/Leaf 493.62	Large format, heavy duty and multiple operations.
RICOH DC - 1	Can record sound also. Detachable LCD screen for instant playback Cost $2,000.
APPLE Quick Take 150	Stores 32 Std a 16 high resolution pictures can download on to MAC or IBM PC's. Cost $1,000.

multimedia, image databases, video conferencing, interactive training, broadcast service, medical imaging and the national information infrastructure. Compressions means removing of unnecessary data such as spaces, which is restored when the data is decompressed. The analogy of 'removing water from frozen juice as the compression portion' fits in very aptly here.

Any digital application is by nature band-width consuming. According to Texas Instruments, transmitting un-compressed data require about 216 megabits per second (mbps) compared to 6 mbps required to send the same amount of data when compressed. Due to economic reasons, the bandwidth available in most of the networks is limited and this demands data to be compressed before it is transmitted across such a media.

Any digital compression algorithm will normally have the capabilities, such as random access, audio, video and textual synchronization, searchability, editability, scalability linked with network quality of service, Asymmetric compression and Security and copyright protection.

MPEG (Moving Picture Expert Group) of the ISO has standardised the system for representing compression algorithms. MPEG-2 is the digital video compression system and by far the most accepted and functional choice for multimedia application. MPEG is defined in 3 parts — System, Video and Audio. ISO/IEC-13818 (Generic Coding of Moving pictures and Associated Audio) is another equivalent standard for MPEG-2.

MPEG-2 uses inter frame coding, which operates on each video frame individually and provides a compression ratio of about 8:1. However high volume multimedia application need higher compression level varying between 20:1 and 30:1. Texas instruments have demonstrated a new algorithm that allows better use of MPEG-2 method of compression and will allow more digital data to be packed into an existing space and in real time. For the compression of still images, ISO's Joint Photographic Experts Group (JPEG) Standard is widely used.

The 'new media'

According to Dimitris Anastassiou of Columbia University, two major technological developments will revolutionize the was information is created, processed and distributed in the coming decade. They are (a) the gradual implementation of the National Information Infrastructure, and (b) full digitization of all information services. As a result not only professionals but also individual users will be empowered with several unprecedented capabilities to access, digital information from a variety of sources including large multi-media databases around the globe.

There is an evolving shared vision of the 'New Information' world. It is defined as a world of ubiquitous, reasonably priced digital information in any and all media available to everyone from a computer, TV, palm or wrist, as predictable, ordinary and universal as a toaster.

Technology has created a communality of approaches which is assumed to have lead into the convergence, even across what has traditionally been a strongly marked boundary. Experts feel that the adaptation of new technologies as an universal tool of information storage and retrieval has made it difficult and perhaps futile to attempt a fence around the information profession.

This new media as represented in Fig.2 is the means of representation and communication of information using the forthcoming digital infrastructure. It

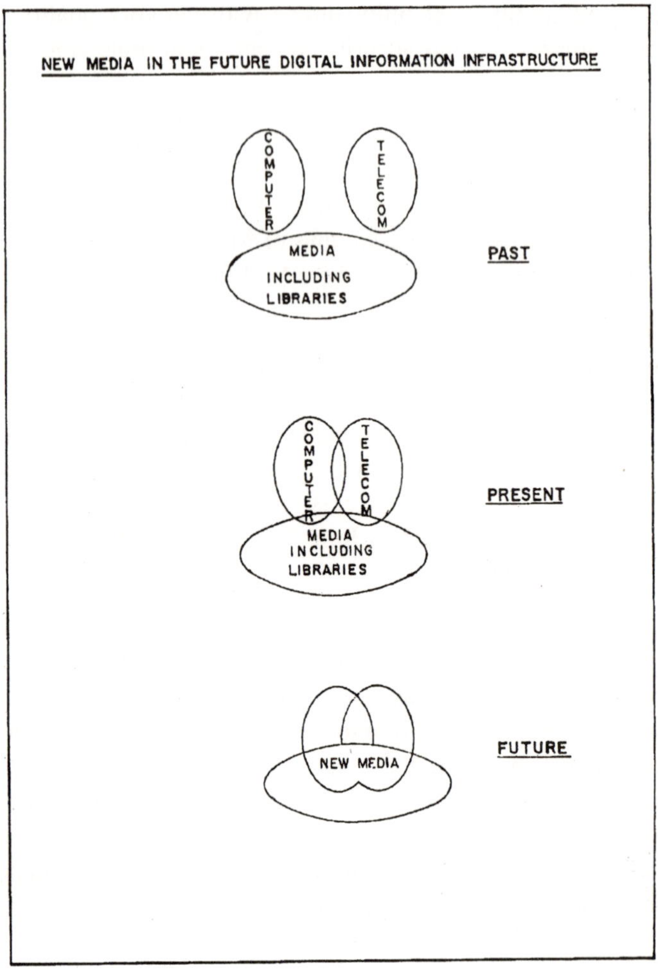

Figure 2

allows interactive, multipoint communication in which computer, telecom and media (including libraries) tend to be integrated. This convergence is obviously catalysed by the advancements in Imaging Science and Technology (IST).

Merits and challenges

Compared to the analog form of graphic representation, digital imaging stands out as a wonder tool in the hands of the information technologists due to the following merits.

- It permits direct and exact controls of numerous parameters, right on the monitor.
- It has essentially abandoned film technology in document copying, colour reproduction, microfilm duplicating and graphic arts.
- It produces detailed image information for immediate utilization.
- With 1 to 3 million pixel CCD's (charged couple devices) digital cameras provide high quality pictures.
- Digital reconstruction of faded photographs, maps, manuscripts and other library materials of archival value is much easier.
- It is a powerful teaching tool; prototype could be presented by simulation which helps to visualise the actual process.
- It has the capability to integrate different forms of data into new form of representation.

The digital imaging technology is not without limitations. As this is a newly emerging field, it is facing a few challenges and some of them mentioned below:

- Digital imaging is not likely to replace conventional film based methods completely.
- The technology faces more difficulty with moving objects and this is being addressed, constantly.
- The reformatting projects in libraries currently involve high cost and labour.
- Digital imaging consumes higher band width which is limited in most of the networks. This factor restricts easy transport of data while networking.
- Digital imaging emerged so quickly, that the technical and quality issues need to be addressed further.
- It offers limited capabilities for demanding applications such as high speed; high resolution; and continuous tone imaging unlike in silver based photographic systems.
- The extent of usage of digital databases depends on the power of cataloging/indexing system, which is still a concern.
- The hardware and software becomes obsolete so fast that the preservation of digital images require a constant file refreshing and migration.
- Digitised video consumes large quantities of computer power (processing & storage) as each minute of digital video represents a large depository of data.

- It is temporarily inhibited by cost, performance, user experience and supporting systems.

Conclusion

As indicated earlier digital imaging technology is still new and is changing fast. So rapid is the pace of revolution that it is difficult to assess its true state of development or to gain an overview of its impact on other fields. But as this field is concerned with the visualization of our knowledge, culture, arts and literature, we must recognise that advances in imaging science will inevitably improve quality of our lives in general and the efficiency of our libraries in particular.

The multimedia, through imaging technology and networking can be effectively used for library management, database transportation and collection exhibition. Libraries and museums should recognise this potential of digital imaging for enhancing the coverage and improving the efficiency of their user service.

Initially it looks like the invasion of all these technologies will make the services of library professionals redundant, especially in the context of less paper (if not paperless!) libraries. To quote Kurzweil Raymond, "the virtual library is still an institution and clearly will require administration. As with all institutions, computers will continue to facilitate the efficiency of administration, but this human directed function will not get away".

Librarians will continue to play a crucial role in collecting, cataloging, indexing and retrieving of information, despite the pattern of information transfer and processing becoming complex. Further it is foreseen that until such time as computers are capable of matching human intelligence, and until such time as all the information required is delivered at an affordable price, the role of librarian will remain central.

The information personnel will have to increasingly familiarise with the machine readable formats and refine their knowledge of vocabularies query language and indexing techniques. In addition their traditional library skills has to be enhanced to allow for effective exploitation of this new technology in keeping with their organizational strategy for information delivery. The competencies of the staff has to be reviewed and training needs to be identified.

Finally let us see what Mr.Louis Rosetto editor of 'Wired' magazine has said: "Technology is not a trend. It's not even a Zeitgeist. This is a phreaking....revolution". Further he warns that "the digital revolution is whipping through our lives like a Bengali typhoon". While we can clearly foresee the great benefits of digital imaging, the learning process and experience are certainly needed to get from here to there.

Acknowledgements

The author gratefully acknowledges the support given and permission granted by the Management of Hindustan Photo Films Mfg.Co.Ltd. for presenting this paper.

References

1. Arthur S Diamond (Ed): Handbook of Imaging Materials. Marcel Dekker Inc. N.Y. 1991.

2. Dimitris Anastassiou. Image Technology for New Media. IS&T'S 48th Annual Conference on Imaging on the Information Super Highway. (May 7-11, 1995), Washington DC, USA.

3. Jean F Barda. Olympic Museum: Compression storage and pyramidal tiling. IS&T'S 48th Annual Conference on Imaging on the Information Super Highway (May 7-11, 1995), Washington DC, USA.

4. John Feather. The Information Society: A Study of Continuity and Change. Library Association. London, 1994.

5. John R Garrett. Digital Libraries: The grand challenges. *Educom*, July/ August 1993, pp.17-21.

6. Joshi S.C. Role of Information in the 21st Century. *Annals of Library and Documentation*, 39(2) 1992, pp.94-100.

7. Paul Keegan. Brave New World of the Digerati. *Span*, November 1995 pp.2-9, 48.

8. Philip W. Goetz. (Ed): The New Encyclopedia Britannica; Vol 21. Encyclopedia Britanica, Inc. Chicago, 1991. pp.558-565.

9. Sylvia E.A. Piggot. The Virtual Library: Almost there ..... *Special Libraries*, Fall 1993, pp.206-212.

10. Sinar A.G. Photographers and their cameras. Sinar AG Ch-8245. Fenerthalen/Switzerland 1995.

SIS–96, 18–20, Jan. '96, Bangalore

Design and implementation of a visual browser for digital image libraries

M.A. MALINI AND C.E. PRAKASH
Supercomputer Education and Research Centre, Indian Institute of Science , Bangalore-560 012

Abstract

Visual browser is an interactive browser of 2D images and 3D volume data. Libraries of 2D images and 3D volume data are very common in scientific and enginerring applications. Given a collection of files, efficient organization, visual search, visualization and manipulation is a challenging task. This paper describes the design and implementation of a MOTIF based Visual Browser system which helps to navigate a library of 2D images and 3D volume data.

Introduction

A common application for a library of 2D images is medical imaging. Hundreds of CT scans, MRI images, X-rays and so on are acquired from scanning devices. With the availability of 3D scanners, 3D scans or volume scanned data (volume data) are also now widely used for medical analysis.

There is a lot of interest currently underway to build virtual museums and art galleries with a collection of images or textures. The collection of such images/textures forms an effective learning tool from the user's desktop instead of the user visiting the gallery. Also, computer artists can quickly browse through textures and create new palettes with combination of existing textures. The Internet is another mine of images which is very difficult to browse currently.

Another potential area is satellite imagery. The satellites send images to ground stations and we have to interpret the data. A typical case is the study of ozone layer depletion by analysing satellite images. Similar problem also arises in image comparisons in forensic sciences. With the current explosion of credit and other cards, photo identity becomes a must, whether the person needs to use a bank facility or to cast a vote. The inspector in such a situation has to quickly search for the identity of a particular individual.

The problem with these systems are that :

- large number of files are to be handled

- the size of each image is more than a megabyte
- volume of data can be several megabytes
- data is acquired from several modalities
- data is acquired over a period of several months or years.

The problem in such a system is the difficulty in locating a particular image and to visualize the data in it. So there is a need for a tool to browse volumes of 2D or 3D data. Our contribution here is the design of the GUI for efficient navigation in an ocean of 2D and 3D data.

GUI design

In this section, we describe the design goals for the development of visual browser and the ways to achieve these design goals.

1. Handling 2D and 3D data: Currently we have the need for a system which handles 2D images. But in the near future an information explosion with widespred use of 3D data is predicted. We solved this problem by obtaining a projection of the 3D data which is a 2D image. However our system can also be extended to handle other oblique projection.
2. A visual browser: The data or images should be presented in visual form. A picture is worth thousand words and the user can understand the information much faster than reading a file or other text information about the image. We still provide a textual information display to augment the interpretation.
3. Easy navigation: Navigation across directories should be possible and if the location of an image is available it should be possible to access the information immediately. This has been achieved by a dialog interface where key words on the image can be supplied by the user.
4. Portable: Any system should support and run on multiple vendor platforms. This has been achieved by the use of MOTIF GUI and X-Windows library.

A MOTIF based GUI has been provided for this application. The input for this application will be the path containing the image files. A search is done and the image files present in that directory will be displayed as a pixmap. These pixmaps are then aligned as a set of tiles in a scrollable window. The user can use the scroll bar to scroll the window to view all the images. The pixmap has been pasted on a pushbutton to give it a 3D look. The user can click on the desired image to view a fullscreen image and may also view the histogram of that particular image. The directory organization currently used in our implementation is same as in the UNIX operating system.

Implementation and results

The program has been implmented on an SGI Indigo system with Extreme Graphics and uses the X-Windows and MOTIF portable graphics libraries. The implementation runs on any UNIX workstation that supports X-Windows and MOTIF. The image file is read into a character buffer and then converted into *XImage* format using the function *XCreateImage*. The data in the *XImage* format is then converted to a pixmap. The figure shows the main window of the visual browser.

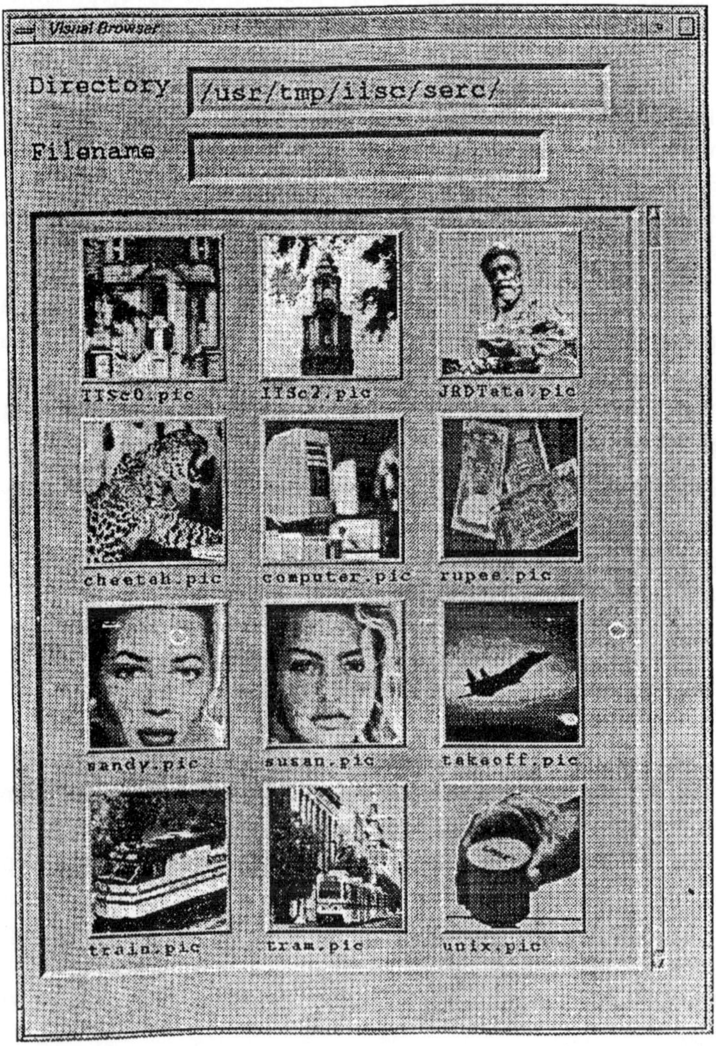

Future work

Currently we have limited our implementation to handle raw images and rgb images. Tools exist which quickly convert popular image formats such as GIF, TIFF, PICT, PCX, BMP, etc. formats to *Xpixmap* format the integration of which is our next phase of work. The ultimate goal is to make this application a full fledged software package with different options to cater to all scientific and engineering applications. Work is also in progress to develop software to handle a library of digital audio and video files.

SIS–96, 18–20, Jan. '96, Bangalore

Digital information delivery

T.N. PRAKASH
Aeronautical Development Agency, Bangalore - 560 017

Abstract

The paper discusses digital information delivery, its improved data quality, speed of access, reduction in cost, etc., compared to the traditional document delivery. The document delivery system comprises of three components: a document strores, delivery and receiving which in digital context are digitized archieve, telcom systems and receiving station respectively. Each of these components are dicussed particularly for transmission of large drawings etc.

Introduction

The technology for electronic transfer of information is developing rapidly; electronic publishing, electronic storage, processing and delivery of information including text and images are all feasible and operational. Presently most of the information are produced on paper. The legibility of documents which are reproduced is poor, the transmission of the same to other users is difficult, and it requires a large amount of storage space. We are now moving towards paperless information. This will include digitization of information, drawings etc, their electronic transmission, electronic ordering, payment etc., This will improve data quality, speed up data access and reduce data storage costs. Presently, most designs, engineering and manufacturing are aided by Computer Aided Design (CAD), Computer Aided Engineering (CAE), and Computer Aided Manufacturing (CAM) without relying on paper. Added to this the CAD is designed to allow three dimensional representations, and to allow them to be viewed from different perspectives at users command. Thus, printing a CAD representation does not provide a complete picture. In electronic media, there will be no loss of clarity, irrespective of its number of usage and reproduction. The multiplication is easy and quick which results in substantial savings in both time and money. The U.S. Airforce will save $135 million annually just in the cost of updating their manuals.

Documents

A document may be defined as a structured data set of which there is a lasting independent record for the purpose of transferring information or knowledge between human beings.

Typical examples of documents are: books, journal articles, letters, memos, forms, stored voice messages, photographs and films.

The fact that different document data sets have different structures, has important consequences for the design of IT systems.

Analysis of various common document data structures is significant for the definition of appropriate standards for document storage, transmission and management.

The data structures to note are: text, tabular data, pictures, moving pictures, and sound recordings.

Moreover, document data set structures come in two broad kinds: physical, mainly concerned with visualization on screen or page, and logical, mainly concerned with how the information is to be processed in IT systems.

The data structures are made of data compression/decompression and encryption. The former is applied to save storage and, particularly, transmission costs. The latter scrambles the original data set and usually increase its size. Both these techniques need recognition by hands and machines for transformations.

The physical supports in common use for document storage are: paper, magnetic media (tape, diskette, winchester, etc.), optical media — (CD-ROM, WORM etc.), static semiconductor (ROM), engravings (plastic records, stone tablets, etc.).

Choice of physical support depends upon the use to be made of documents and cost. Perhaps this may be the reason why the paperless office is not yet in view despite IT's progress.

Document delivery systems

At its basic, a document delivery system comprises just three components: a document store or archive (a sending station), a means of delivery, i.e. transmission/telecoms systems, a receiving station. We are concentrating on digital document delivery between computers via networks.

It is worth noting, that postal services are still the only means of delivering certain types of documents where the physical characteristics of the supporting medium are considered to be essential, and also that postal services can be combined successfully with electronic delivery means for optional quality of service.

Document store or archive

First, we shall consider the main physical modules and functions of the document store or archive. Typically an archive can be: a basic, minimal storage telecopier; a PC with a data communications interface to either a wide area network or a local area network; or a mainframe with data communication hardware and software.

Operating system

Regarding operating systems, we are still in the era of MS-DOS, and UNIX. Indeed, UNIX, could become the de facto standard.

The interesting feature of UNIX is that it is a multi-tasking, multi-user operating system, whereas MS-DOS is designed only for handling a single task at a time for a single user although it can do better. This can be important for document archives which are likely to be required to support many local administrative jobs concurrently with sending documents and receiving online requests, for documents to be delivered.

Local input/output

The system administrator and/or document delivery service operator needs a terminal consisting of a keyboard, a screen and a pointer, e.g. a mouse. It is preferable that a complete A4, or even an A3 page can be visualized on the screen; with windowing, this facilitates the operator interface when dealing with complicated document management procedures.

The pointing device is convenient for using dialogue menus of the graphical user interface.

In order to digitize documents from paper, a scanner is needed; it may be advisable to be able to scan A3 and A4 formats as well as B4 and to be able to transform A3 to A4 and B4 to A4. Resolution should be selectable from 200, 300, 400 or 600 pixels per inch and scan speed from six to eight pages per minute. Automatic sheet feeding is also a useful feature.

The scanned image can be compressed using a hardware coder. For documents containing only text, if storage is at a premium, software for performing optical character recognition and identifying page layout may be used to transform the scanned image into an appropriate text processor format.

A printer width 200, 300, 400, or 600 pixels per inch resolution is the other physical device requirement, a decoder doing decompression when necessary.

Document storage

Memory is of course required to store documents. It is not that important whether it is magnetic or optical, but it should be optical large enough to hold, at least for the time needed, a sufficient number of documents, and have access times and transfer rates that are adequately fast.

Communications

Insertion of digital representations of documents into telecommunications networks for delivery requires one or more communications modules in the document archive.

A link with the public switched telephone network is useful because of its wide geographical coverage; however its data transmission speed leaves much to be desired: 300 bits/s-2400 bits/s recommended, with group 3 telecopier systems going up to 9600 bits/s, giving transmission times of about 20-40 secs for a page at 200 pixels per inch resolution.

In addition to the public telephone network, packet switched data networks and circuit switched networks can be used at intermediate data rates, say 9600-48000 bits/s.

In the near future ISDN connections will be available with basic rate access (64, 144 Kbits/s)

Functional requirements

The document archive has to provide the functions for operations i.e. (i) control of requests and deliveries; (ii) delivery of references and abstracts; (iii) control of local interfaces; (iv) creation, editing and deletion of document files; (v) optional security, confidentiality when necessary.

And functions for administration purposes i.e. (i) billing, (ii) user file record so that documents are sent in receivable form, (iii) user and system statistics, (iv) directory and distribution list management are the major functions that have to be implemented in the archive.

The document receiving station

Typically, a document receiving station will be a desktop computer with a suitable operator interface (keyboard, screen, pointer), a 300 pixels per inch printer, a memory buffer and of course the telecomms interface necessary to receive documents.

The applications software should have an attractive, easy-to-use graphical user interface. Since documents may be received in character-coded, facsimile or mixed mode, the document terminal must be capable of handling all these document file formats.

Also, in many instances the document terminal is likely to be incorporated into a local computing environment which may include a local area network. Since the organization may wish to forward the document electronically, to recipients who use other terminals, the document terminal will be required either to provide file transfer across the local area network or to incorporate a distributed file server or to offer mailbox facilities. It is to be noted that only the last named is an international standard.

Networks and services

Setting aside the telex network, which, although useful for the purpose we are discussing, namely, document delivery, is so restricted in speed, character set and lay-out possibilities that it will almost certainly be superseded in the coming years. Let us briefly consider the chief characteristics of five network types i.e. public switched telephone; circuit switched data; packet switched data; integrated services digital and satellite.

Public switched telephone network

In addition to its main purpose, namely, telephony, certain data services have for many years used this network; access to databases, facsimile, videotex, teletex, electronic messaging are well-known examples. Data rates, from 300 to 2400, 4800 and even 9600 bits/second.

Circuit switched data networks

A few national public switched data networks have been implemented and a number of private international organizations, have built their own. Data rates can be high (e.g. 2Mbits/second). They are not sufficiently widespread to be used as a vehicle for electronic document delivery except within those organizations which can afford them.

Packet switched data network

Packet switching is a viable technology for transmitting character-coded documents between two access points of a packet switched data network. However, to use such a network to transfer a document of the same size in facsimile mode because it is on paper only, not stored in a machine or treatable with OCR, is less attractive.

Integrated services digital network

As is widely recognized we have witnessed in the last 15 years a technological convergence of the computer and telecomms business into the telematics one. A catalyst for this process has been the parallel evolution toward digital processing and the use of integrated circuit components in computers and communications switching and transmission equipment.

Satellites

Document delivery services sometimes require more bandwidth and geographical coverage provided by existing wide area data networks. ISDN will eventually satisfy these needs, but there will be an extended transitional phase lasting until the early part of the 21st century during which satellite networks will be the most effective means of transmission at narrowband (64Kbits/sec.) or broadband (2Mbits/sec.) data rates.

The advantages of satellites for telecomms services are: (i) wide geographical coverage, (ii) broadcast and multicast mode of use, (iii) distance-independent tariff, and (iv) high data rates.

Satellite networks for document delivery services either have one central hub station near to the source of documents and several or many receive-only stations. Thus they allow several transmitting stations located near to document sources (archives) and many receive-only stations. These configurations are well suited to document delivery applications in which one or a few centres are the source of documents to be distributed to many widely dispersed receiving locations. This is not the case for ordinary electronic mail but does apply to publishing, libraries, manufacturer/dealer networks, software distribution, etc.

Standards

Since document delivery is required between organizations which have different suppliers of computer systems, standards are essential for the interworking of the equipment.

Some important standards are File Transfer Access and Management (ISO 8571), Directory (ISO 9594, CCITT X.500) and Message Handling System (ISO 8505, CCITT X.400).

Conclusions

Documents have been considered as a broad range of entities that hold permanent information for the purpose of transferring knowledge. Their structural variety is complex, but information technology is steadily evolving towards the time when document preparation and local management will become more efficient.

References

1. AGARD-CP-466. Electronic transfer of information and its impact on Aerospace and Defence Research and Development. AGARD, France, 1990

2. AGARD-CP-487. Bridging the communication Gap. AGARD, France, 1991

3. Digital Libraries. *Communications of the ACM*. April 1995, 38(4).

4. Gaylasch, Alexander. Effective Database Management, New Jersey, Prentice Hall, 1988.

Three

Cataloguing, Indexing, Processing

SIS–96, 18–20, Jan. '96, Bangalore

Common communication format for online ordering : A proposal for book trade and libraries

M. M. KASHYAP
201 Kadambari Apartments, Sector IX, Plot XIX, Rohini, Delhi-110 085

Abstract

In the context of digital libraries, most of the information is digitized, information that is stored, transmitted, accessed and used. In the very near future, many libraries and book trade agencies, even in India will carry their business transaction on line. Hence, they have to evolve or establish protocols and conventions to enable them to carry out their digitized and on line business transactions with ease and speed. The paper proposes for creating standards to generate compatible bibliographic databases by the book trade and the libraries in India. The CCF with slight modification and addition can be used to create databases for entity — types other than bibliographic entity—types. The book trade and librarians can identify the entity — types, mostly commonly associated with their database systems, and bring out an extended version of the CCF. Such an extended version is discussed in detail

Introduction

Today book trade enterprises (publishers and booksellers) and libraries in developing countries, like India, are in the threshold of building and maintaining the catalogues of their publications or collections electronically. It is possible that in near future the basic bibliographic data about the published documents shall be made available electronically by many Indian publishers and book sellers prior to the publication of documents.

The availability of book trade online catalogues will enable the libraries to select and order documents electronically (also named as teleordering, online purchase and online acquisition), that is, by following the process of sending purchase orders directly through telecommunication networks. Under the circumstances it is necessary that we must examine:

(a) Up to what extent the need of libraries for placing orders or creating the bibliographic databases can be met through the data included by the publishers and book sellers in their database records?

(b) In what way the bibliographic information generated by the book trade can be made compatible enough to be downloaded and used by libraries for creating their own catalogues?

(c) What standard practices book trade and libraries need to follow to make their databases records compatible, to be able to transfer data and communicate with each other without any difficulty?

(d) What need to be done in this domain, in addition to what has been done so far?

Further, for online transmission of book orders, supply bills and other communications, the book trade agencies and libraries must lay down certain norms, standards or protocols for common application by mutual agreement to provide reliable communication among them and their computer systems. The existence of such standard practices will also prove helpful to the users of computerised information systems, both lay and professionals, to search the online bibliographic databases of various commercial online bibliographic databases, with ease.

These and other protocols may be laid down according to guidelines laid down by OSI reference manual, also known as Open System Interconnections or OSIs. [ISO : 7]

The term "open" implies mutual acceptance and implementation of protocols or communication standards about the different layers ranging from the lowest physical layer, which covers standards about the electric and physical connections between devices, to the seventh (7th) uppermost application layer [Bishop: 9; Kashyap: 8, p.118-23]. The top seventh (7th) layer provides support to the applications and it is the one area with which we are most concerned.

Different application employ different applications layer protocols and different library networks may employ different application level protocols. Some protocols about this layer and concerning library applications area are: ISO 2709 [6]; CCF/B Format [3; 16-19]; CCF/F Format [4; 5]; and, UNIMARC [13]. Some OSI application protocols developed in the area of electronic delivery systems are: X.400 — message handling system; X.500, ISO-95911 — ILL (Inter Library Loan) protocols also fall in this category. [Turner, 21 ; Swain and Cleveland, 20]. In electronic ordering (also named as teleordering, online purchase and online acquisition); that is, process of sending purchase orders directly by communication network, we have standards developed by the Book Industry Advisory Committee and Serial Industry Advisory Committee, known as BISAC and SISAC protocols for electronic transfer of purchase order invoices and report information between libraries and vendors. [Bullard, 2; Kelly, 12 ; Sabosik, 15].

These protocols should be pragmatic, functional and easy to implement uniformly and consistently by all concerned. It is also necessary that the agreed upon protocols or standard practices are implemented unfailingly, within the limits of tolerable variations, by all concerned.

Keeping in view the issues mentioned above, some suggestions are put forward in this paper for creating standards to generate compatible bibliographic databases by the book trade and the libraries in India.

The use of the CCF for creating library and book trade databases

To facilitate the methodical and practical construction and operation of library information systems the library profession and other agencies (Unesco, IFLA) have developed certain tools, techniques and standards to provide a detailed and structured method for recording mandatory and optional data elements in computer-readable bibliographic record for exchange purpose between two or more computer-based systems. The book trade can also make use these tools, techniques and standards to design and develop their information systems databases.

The Unesco has developed the CCF: The common Communication format, as standard format for the exchange of bibliographic records between group of libraries and abstracting and indexing services. It specifies all the data elements essential to describe a bibliographic entity — a monograph, a serial, or a part of a serial (an article) or a monograph including their content designator or tags and subfields identifiers. By providing the list of these data elements it serves as a basis for defining a format for an agency's own bibliographic database. This format can be used with certain addition both by book trade and libraries as a protocol for exchange of bibliographic data and electronic transfer of purchase orders, invoices and reports between libraries and book trade.

The CCF is designed as a standard code to provide a detailed and structured method for recording number of mandatory and optional data elements in a computer-readable bibliographic record for exchanging data between two or more computer-based systems. Nevertheless, its design is such that it meets the requirements of all type of libraries and other institutions for local implementation. With the availability of very efficient CDS/ISIS database management system developed by Unesco, this format is being increasingly used by libraries in India and abroad for creating their database systems.

Further, the CCF with slight modification and addition can also be used to create databases for entity-types other than bibliographic entity-types, say for creating databases of users, and/or staff members of a library [Kashyap, 8-11].

Recently, the Unesco has now brought out a companion volume of the Common Communication Format for Bibliographic Information (CCF/B) entitled CCF/F: the Common Communication Format for Factual Information [3-5]. CCF/F provide a list of data elements for recording information about projects, persons, institutions, "though other categories of factual information is likely to be added in future" [5: p6].

It is recommended that the CCF may be accepted by mutual agreement, both by the book trade and libraries in India for developing their databases and as a common communication format for online ordering and supply of publications.

This standard, however, can only be used with certain additions for the purpose of designing and developing a computerised information system covering all library and book trade functional activities. For example, It does not provide some essential and mandatory data elements pertaining to entity types order, bill, and so on. We need to include data elements of these entity types in its framework to implement electronic book ordering, book supply, bill supply and payment and related functions in the systems.

The book trade and librarians can identify the entity types, mostly commonly associated with the book trade and library systems, and bring out an extended version of the CCF by including them within its framework by:

(a) describing the entity types or objects such as documents, bills, orders etc. about which information is to be collected for use and transactions processing.

(b) specifying the mandatory and optional data elements and their unique names which are required to create unambiguous records of the defined entity types.

(c) assigning unique codes, also called content designator, comprising field tags, indicators, and sub-fields codes and serve as means of identifying data elements or values of fields or subfields in a machine readable record.

Some of the data element types including relationship type data elements of the entity types commonly associated with the library system and book trade are identified and defined for inclusion in the CCF, in the next part of the paper.

The proposed group to be responsible to define and approve the common protocols or standard for library systems and book trade can use this approach to further identify and defining the common entity types, and their relationships types and attribute types (or data elements) for inclusion in the extended CCF standard format.

Definition of data elements of entity types commonly associated with the library and book trade

As stated earlier the CCF has been primarily designed to define the attributes and relationships (relationships are the natural associations with one or more entities) or the data elements of the bibliographic entity types and associated entity types, in connection with the design, development and exchange of bibliographic databases.

Some of the relationships types attributes, namely — AUTHOR(-OF), PUBLISHER(-OF), DISTRIBUTOR(-OF) associated with the bibliographic entity type — DOCUMENT or its sub-categories, namely— MONOGRAPH, MULTI-VOLUME MONOGRAPH, SERIAL, COMPONENT PART Of A SERIAL, COMPONENT PART OF A MONOGRAPH or a MULTI-VOLUME MONOGRAPH, as defined in CCF, are listed below:

ENTITY TYPES Treated as RELATIONSHIPS TYPES DATA ELEMENTS OF A DOCUMENT	Field tag	
PERSONAL AUTHOR(S)	300	Name of Person(s): The name identifying a person(s) associated with an entity
CORPORATE AUTHOR		
CORPORATE BODY	310	Name of corporate body
SPONSOR	310	Name of corporate body
CONFERENCE	320	Name of meeting associated with an bibliographic entity
PUBLISHER	400	Place of publication and publisher associated with a bibliographic entity
DISTRIBUTOR	420	Place and name of distributor book-seller, vendor associated with an entity
LOCATION or ADDRESS	430	The location of an entity in a form suitable for postal purpose
AGENCY — LIBRARY ONLINE DATABASE VENDOR	020	Source of record, agency preparing the database record

We find that between a library system and book trade in addition to the exchange of bibliographic data, the data about entity types orders, bills, requisitions and like also take place. We must, therefore, identify and define the attributes and relationship types between these entity type and the bibliographic entity types for inclusion within the CCF's framework.

To identify the attributes and relationships of entity types orders, invoices, requisitions and like, we must examine the purpose, and role or function of these entity types.

A communication, a message, a memorandum, a request, an order, an invoice, or a report is an incoming or out-going TRANSACTION or EVENT that occur within an organisation. Transactions or events are entities which trigger processes in a system, and two types of transaction-processing occur in a system. The most common is the processing of input transactions, such as user requests for procurement of books or reservation of books, membership registrations, vendor bills, customer orders, customer bill payments. All these transactions input new data into the information system of an organisation. For example, a request for purchase of an item — an input (the input data may consist of a AUTHOR(S), NAME(S), TITLE, and EDITION etc.) triggers selection process and subsequently order process resulting into an output — order of the items to a vendor.

Another type is output transaction. Output transactions trigger responses from or confirm actions to those who eventually receive those transactions. Example of output transactions are book orders (to vendors), book lists or current awareness bulletins (to readers). In each of such cases the output transaction triggers a response or confirm an action. From example, from vendor acknowledgement of the order or from a library the item requested or suggested by a member has been ordered.

If we examine a transaction processing system, as illustrated above, we find that an entity type ORDER is associated with one or more entities - type ITEM as well as the entity — type VENDOR. Thus, an Order has a relationship with an item or items as well as with a vendor. Alternatively, we can also consider it as a single entity — Vendor's Order (containing Items), depending the design of a database record structure.

With the help of a database management system like CDS/ISIS we create an output for a Vendor's Order or list of Ordered item(s) with vendors two ways. We can generate distinct records for each entity types ITEM, ORDER and VENDOR and create an output by linking three types of records for a Vendor's Order. Alternatively treating or defining Order of item(s) with

Vendor as a relationship attributes or data elements for a ITEM-ORDER-VENDOR RELATIONSHIP TYPE record structure we can generate records of Ordered Items with a vendor. (CDS/ISIS database management system allows us to form both types of entity records or databases).

Some of the relationship type attributes data, such as — a requisition (i.e., a written or a telephonic message) say for the purchase of a monograph may form an input to a transaction processing system (Book Selection and Approval System in this case). Another relationship type attribute or data element, such as — Order Date or the date when an order for the item(s) is forwarded to a vendor, may be generated as an output of a transaction processing system (Book Ordering System in this case). Such a data element forms an input to another system (Book Supply System of a Book-Seller in this case).

On the basis of above analysis, we will now define some entity types not covered by the CCF and on which data need to be kept in library and book trade information systems to maintain and process data about online purchase and supply transactions.

Entity types associated with online purchase and supply transactions processing

An illustrative list of entity types, whose data elements do not figure in the CCF and on which data need to be kept in library and book trade information systems for electronic ordering and supply, is given below:

(1) **PURCHASE REQUEST/QUERY (In)** (an event): A named (or numbered) and dated purchase request is generated by a user and forwarded or given to the library. The receipt of request is recorded in correspondence receipt register and the receipt number and date of receipt is entered on the request in the Correspondence Section. The letter or form is then forwarded to the dealing unit for further action. The request is received in the section on a particular date which takes appropriate action. The necessary reply is forwarded to the sender of communication by post or some way through the despatch section. The recommendation for order may be also be forwarded to the Order Section.

(2) **PURCHASE REQUEST REPLY (out)** (an event): A named (or numbered) and dated reply is generated by the library and forwarded to the member. The reply is forwarded to the despatch section on a particular date for onward despatch to the member by post or by

messenger after recording the despatch number and date of despatch on it.

(3) **ORDER Out** (an event): A named (or numbered) and dated order is generated and placed with a supplier for an item or items, in response to the instructions or approval given by an appropriate authority of the organisation for purchase. The order is forwarded to the despatch section on a particular date for onward transmission to the vendor, to post/hand after recording despatch number and date of despatch on the letter.

(4) **ORDER In** (an event): A named or numbered and dated order is received by a supplier's for the item or items ordered by a library. The receipt of order is recorded in correspondence receipt register and the receipt number and date is inscribed on the order in the Correspondence Section and latter forwarded to the supply unit for further action.

(5) **INVOICE Out** (an event): A named (numbered) and dated invoice is generated by a supplier in response to a shipped or partially shipped order to the organisation or individual, who placed the order.

(6) **SUPPLY MEMO and SUPPLY Out** (an event): A named (numbered) and dated supply memo is prepared by the Supplier's Store Unit for item(s) and forwarded to correspondence Section with the invoice and item(s) for onward transmission. The Correspondence Section makes an entry in the despatch register, the despatch no and date is recorded on the supply memo and on the bill and the supply memo, bill and item(s) are forwarded to the library placing the order

(7) **SUPPLY MEMO and SUPPLY In** (an event): A named or numbered, dated supply memo and supply is received by the Library's Correspondence Section. The supply memo and item's receipt is recorded in the register. After recording the receipt no and date on the supply memo, the supply memo and item(s) are forwarded to the purchase section for further action.

(8) **INVOICE Out** (an event): A named (numbered) and dated invoice is received by the Library's Correspondence Section, very often with the supply. The receipt of bill is recorded in the correspondence register and bill is forwarded to finance section for further action. The bill is then registered in the bill receipt register and forwarded to order section by appending Bill Receipt No and date on the bill for further action.

The description of some of the fields (data elements) of the entity types mentioned above along with their proposed tags is given below:

	FIELD (RELATIONSHIP)	TAG	DEFINITION
(a)	SELECTION, or PROCUREMENT REQUEST — of Item	720	Selection components (data elements) associated with an entity.
(b)	ORDER (Order Out) SUPPLY, ORDER (Order In), GIFT or EXCHANGE REQUEST — of Item	730	Acquisition, purchase order components (data elements) associated with an entity
(c)	SUPPLY (Out, In) — of Item(s)	740	Supply components (data elements) associated with an entity (Monograph).
(d)	SUPPLY (In, Out) — of Item(s)	741	Supply components (data elements) associated with an entity (Serial).
(e)	BILL (Out, In) — of Item(s)	750	The bill forwarding and receipt components (data elements) associated with an entity
(f)	BILL PAYMENT (Out, In) — of item(s)	751	Bill payment components (data elements) associated with an entity
(g)	ITEM'S TECHNICAL OPERATIONS	760	Classification and cataloguing components (data elements) associated with an entity
(h)	QUERY — about or REQUISITION — of Item(s)	770	Query or requisition components (data elements) associated with an entity.
(i)	SEARCH — of item(s)	771	Search, retrieval, location components (data elements) associated with an entity
(j)	CIRCULATION — of LOAN OUT LOAN RETURN	780	Charging and discharging components (data elements) associated with an entity.
(k)	BORROWING or LOAN REQUEST — of Item	781	Inter-Library Borrowing: Loan Request components (data elements) associated with an entity.

(l)	BORROWED ITEM IN HOUSE CONSULTATION-of	782	Inter-Library Borrowing: Consultation components (data elements) associated with an entity
(m)	BORROWED ITEM RETURN — of	783	Inter-Library Borrowing: Return components (data element) associated with an entity

An example of detailed description of a field, as provided in the CCF, including the following information about the field and its subfields, is presented below:

(a) The three-digit code or identification tag followed by the name of data field.

(b) Definition of the data field.

(c) The form in which data field is to be represented.

(d) About the data field use, whether it is mandatory or optional.

(e) Note or comments, if any.

(f) The description of subfields that form elements within field.

FIELD 720

PROCUREMENT OR SELECTION COMMUNICATION

DEFINITION	The identification number of query or communication associated with an entity — Request for purchase, In house selection for purchase, request for gift or exchange, indent for item/ items
USE	Mandatory. Not repeatable.
REPRESENTATION	In accordance with the practice of the agency preparing the record.
SUBFIELD A	Entry Element
DEF	The identification name or number of the communication.
REP	In accordance with the practice of the agency preparing the record.
USE	Mandatory. Repeatable.
SUBFIELD B	Date(s)
DEF	A date or dates relating to communication (e.g., its date of origin, communication forwarding date).
REP	In accordance with the practice of the agency preparing the record.
USE	Mandatory. Repeatable.

SUBFIELD C	Source of communication.
DEF	Name of source and/or sender as an additional information to identify the communication.
REP	In abbreviated form when possible. In accordance with the practice of the agency preparing the record.
USE	Optional. Repeatable for different kind of additional elements
SUBFIELD D	Form of communication.
DEF	Additional information to identify the communication, e.g., form of massage — telephonic message, fax, electronic, urgent, or secret communication
REP	In abbreviated form, when possible, in accordance with the practice of the agency preparing the record.
USE	Optional. Repeatable for different kind of additional elements.
SUBFIELD E	Receiver of communication (coded)
DEF	Name of receiver, to whom the communication is forwarded.
REP	In abbreviated form when possible. In accordance with the practice of the agency preparing the record.
USE	Mandatory. Not repeatable
SUBFIELD F	Receiver of communication (Non-coded)
DEF	Name of receiver, to whom the communication is forwarded or received.
REP	In abbreviated form when possible. In accordance with the practice of the agency preparing the record.
USE	Mandatory. Not repeatable
SUBFIELD G	Registration number of in communication
DEF	Number of registration when the communication is received by receiver.
REP	In accordance with the practice of the agency preparing the record.
USE	Mandatory. Not repeatable
SUBFIELD H	Date of receipt
DEF	Date when the communication is received and recorded in receipt register by the receiver.
REP	In accordance with the practice of the agency preparing the record.
USE	Mandatory. Not repeatable

SUBFIELD I	Receiver of communication within an organisation.
DEF	Name of section or person to whom the communication is forwarded for action.
REP	In abbreviated form when possible. In accordance with the practice of the agency preparing the record.
USE	Mandatory. Not Repeatable
SUBFIELD J	Date forwarded and/or receipt of communication
DEF	Date the communication is forwarded and/or received by the section or person
REP	In accordance with the practice of the agency preparing the record
USE	Mandatory. Repeatable
SUBFIELD K	Status of communication
DEF	An indication the status of a communication: whether under process, in abeyance, disposed and note what action has been finally taken and like.
REP	In accordance with the practice of the agency preparing the record
USE	Mandatory. Not repeatable

Rendering of the names of authors in direct form as heading

The known authors or collaborators of works have always been considered as key access elements and given leading position in a bibliographic reference or a record. To represent the name of an author in a standard form in an entry or to render it in standard form as heading, various rules and guideline are provide in the cataloguing codes. Libraries maintain authority files of such names for maintaining consistency in the records of bibliographic items in their catalogues.

However, we find that the names of authors (persons and corporate bodies) and collaborators are represented and accessed in varying forms in various situations. The cataloguing codes (e.g. AACR-II and CCC [1, 14]), have different rules for the choice of the entry element and the form and order of presentation of other name elements. libraries often differ drastically from each other in the choice of entry element, and the form and order of representing the other name elements of authors (persons or corporate bodies) and collaborators as heading. This happens, even when two libraries are using the same catalogue code to catalogue their documents.

In case of book trade agencies the situation could be more unsatisfactory as usually they do not use any code or standard for choice of entry element, and the form and order of presentation of name elements in a bibliography record.

Under the circumstances, to achieve standardisation or one to one correspondence in the description of bibliographic information, and in the choice and rendering of headings in the bibliographic records created by various agencies the following courses of action are suggested:

The libraries and book trade, by mutual agreement must agree to follow strictly the "Canon of Ascertainabilty" [Ranganathan: 14, p.34-35] to render or describe the contents of the field and subfields; that is, to follow the practice of describing the data elements or contents of the fields and subfields of bibliographic items as found in the title page of a document and its over-flow of pages.

In the CCF an additional subfield namely Heading Field may be defined to represent the names elements of authors (both personal, corporate authors) and collaborators exactly in the form and sequence shown on the document, adding the terms after their names, by, ed. by, comp. by and like, indicating the statement of responsibility or the function of the persons or corporate body in relation to the creation of the intellectual or artistic contents of the work (document) or its realization. The name of a persons and corporate bodies also be displayed in the direct form in the bibliographic references or printed communication when used as Heading.

This subfield may include the name of the author and one joint author (Personal or Corporate Author). If the name of author or joint authors is not given on the title page then the name of collaborator and one joint collaborator (i.e., the name of editor(s), in absence of editor(s) the name compiler(s)) is to be used as the Heading. Descriptive element indication of the role of the collaborator(s) (ed., Comp., and like) is to be added thereafter.

The various other approaches and methods for defining an entry element, and the forms and sequence of representation of name elements used to generate various access points or added entries, may be covered by using the following three repeatable fields defined in the CCF: (1) Field 300: Name of Person, (2) Field 310: Name of Corporate Body, and (3) Field 320: Name of Meeting.

If we follow this practice at the data input stage, in the heading field, no distortion shall take place, as no decision is involved about the choice of entry element, form and sequence of presentation of other data elements according to the rules of a cataloguing code. The variation in the access constituent of a name, as seen in different situations, could be implemented by the various agencies, according to the rules of a cataloguing code, or the practices or conventions followed by them. The name of authors can be rendered to meet the local, regional as well as national practices. Further, by manipulating the order of the subfields with the help of DBMS, the agencies can also generate alternative outputs.

Conclusion

I think, most of you attending this conference will agree that in the very near future many libraries and book trade agencies in India will carry their business transactions online. For this purpose, they must deliberate and evolve or establish protocols and conventions to enable them to carry out their online business transactions with ease. It is also hoped that the above proposal will set the ball rolling in right direction.

References

1. *Anglo-American Cataloguing Rules*. Ed. by Michael Gorman and Paul W. Winkler. Second Edition Revised. 1988. American Library Association, Chicago.

2. Bullard, Scott R. Standards for automate acquisition system BISAC and SISAC considerations. *Library Acquisition Practice and Theory*, 11, 4; 1987, pp.357-58.

3. Hopkinson, Alan, *Comp. Implementation notes for users of the Common Communication Format (CCF)*, 1990. Paris, Unesco.

4. Hopkinson, Alan. Comp. *Implementation notes for users of the Common Communication Format for factual information: CCF/F*. 1992. Paris, Unesco.

5. Hopkinson, Alan and Simmons, Peter. *Ed. CCF/F: The Common Communication Format for factual information*, 1992. Unesco, Paris.

6. ISO 2709-1981. Format for bibliographic interchange on magnetic tape. International Organisation of Standardisation (ISO), Geneva.

7. ISO 7498-1986. *Open system Interconnection — Basic reference manual.* 1986. International Organisation of Standardisation (ISO), Geneva.

8. Kashyap, M.M. *Database system: Design and development.* 1994 (Reprint). Sterling Publishers, New Delhi.

9. Kashyap, M.M. Design and development of computerized information system for the Ratan Tata Library, University of Delhi with the aid of CDS/ISIS software. *Library Herald,* 28, 1989; pp.72-117.6.

10. Kashyap, M.M. Integrated database design for a Library system: Employing library techniques developed by Ranganathan and CDS/ISIS DBMS. *Journal of Library and Information Science (India)*, 18, 2; 1993; pp.82-141.

11. Kashyap, M.M. Standard bibliographic data designating system and communication format for Indian libraries and information organisations. *I L A Bulletin*, 25, 3, 1989, pp.111-23

12. Kelly (Glen J). Exploring costs of electronically transmitting in formation between a library and a vendor. *Information Technology and Libraries*. 9; March,1990, pp.53- 65.

13. International Federation of Library Association and Institutions. *UNIMARC: Universal MARC Format.* 2nd Rev ed. IFLA International Office for OBC, London.

14. Ranganathan, S.R. *Classified catalogue code, with additional rules for dictionary catalogue code*. Ed 5. 1988. Sarda Ranganathan Endowment, Bangalore.

15. Sabosik, Patricia. "SISAC: Standardizes format for serials. *Information Technology and Libraries,* 5, June, 1986, pp.149-54.

16. Simmons, Peter. Applying database management concepts to bibliographic records. *Annals of Library Science,* 1988, 35, 1, pp.1-10.

17. Simmons, Peter. Using CCF: the Common Communication Format. *Information Technology and Libraries*, 5, 2, 1986, pp.285-94.

18. Simmons, P. Ed. *Proceedings of the first CCF users meeting (Geneva) (1989)*, 1990. (PGI-90/WS/4). Unesco, General information Program and UNISIST, Paris

19. Simmons, Peter and Hopkinson, Alan. *Ed. CCF: the common communication format*. Ed 2. 1988. (PGI-88/WS/2). Unesco, Paris.

20. Swain, Leigh and Cleveland, Leigh. Library document delivery and libraries: Technologies, strategies, and issues. *Journal of Library and Information Science,* 16, 1, 1992, pp.70-4.

21. TURNER (F). The inter library loan protocol: an OSI solution to ILL massaging. *Library Hi Tech.,* 8, 4, 1990, pp.73-82.

SIS–96, 18–20, Jan. '96, Bangalore

Noun phrases for query formulation

K.T. ANURADHA AND W.B. CROFT*
National Center for Science Information, Indian Institute of Science;
Bangalore 560 012, India
(Email: kta@ncsi.iisc.ernet.in)

*Center for Intelligent Information Retrieval (CIIR), University of Massachusetts,
Amherst, MA 01003, USA
(Email: croft@cs.umass.edu)

Abstract

The recent developments in telecommunication and data storage techniques have changed the way in which information is stored, accessed, searched and retrieved. Searching for and retrieving of relevant information for a specific query even by an experienced searcher is a difficult task because of the uncertainty in document and query representaions. Also, there is no definite methodology to perform these tasks. Many database producers encourage end user searching. Their goal is satisfied only when user need based, user friendly interface is provided. This study is directed towards developing a browser file containing noun phrases selected from natural language processing techniques. The browser file can be considered as a user dedicated concept dictionary and can be used at the time of query formulation.

Introduction

A huge amount of data stored on publicly available online databases. In addition to online services, one can access databases through stand-alone and networked CD-ROMs, and locally mounted databases available over networks. Apart from this, through Internet a whole range of resources can be accessed. Hence, database searchers in their quest for information, are faced with a wealth of resources on a variety of media. They must also confront a bewildering number of command languages, file loading techniques, system features, system responses, data element designators, print formats, access protocols, system designators on different telecommunication networks. Even proficient searcher of one system alone finds it difficult to retrieve relevant information from the database. It is believed that less use is made of these databases than could or should be since searching these databases is a complicated process.

However, in recent days many database providers have started encouraging end user searching. Their effort is going to be successful only when user need based, user friendly interface is provided.

Computer user interfaces range from systems that require rigid query formats to systems that allow (pseudo) natural language query. Since the user should directly be able to interrogate a retrieval system with a minimum of prior instruction and learning, it is important that these systems recognise the vocabulary of the user, thereby eliminating the need for the user to learn a query format. The systems based on natural language queries usually use complex descriptors like phrases to describe or index the query.

An attempt is made here to identify noun phrases in free text using natural language processing techniques and normalize the noun phrases based on co-occurrence frequency of compound terms in the noun phrase corpus file and internal syntax of the terms. The normalized noun phrases can be used as an aid in concept identification at the query formulation stage. The preliminary results of this study are quite encouraging but more work has to be carried out to arrive at a standard methodology.

An overview of information retrieval system (IRS)

In an IRS, documents and queries are represented by means of some indexing language. The relationship between documents and queries is established by some matching function which matches document representations with that of query representations or vise versa. This matching function is called the retrieval engine. Hence in the existing Information Retrieval (IR) models, documents and queries are conceived as two different entities and symmetry between them is brought out by the retrieval engine. The relevance relation is the relation between documents and queries. In many existing systems this is not defined, and, if defined, it is the function of the system to predict this relation which is usually calculated apriori based on term frequency. An interface (human or machanised) can be considered as part of the retrieval engine which serves as a kind of translator or layer between the capabilities of the system and the user who wants to exploit these capabilities. The retrieval engine and interface together form access software. The very idea of using retrieval engine directly would be roughly equivalent to using assembly language for word processing.

The critical component in information system design is document and query indexing. Although the technologies to process information have become more sophisticated, there is no well defined indexing method which satisfies all users because indexing is charecterised as:

- Subjective: depends on human judgement and thus not an inherent characteristic of information or a document

- Cognitive: depends on human knowledge and perception
- Situational: relates to information problem of individual user
- Multidimensional: Influenced by many factors
- Dynamic: constantly changes over time
- Measurable and observable at a single point of time[3].

User interface for IR

Conceptually, IR process can be divided into two broad categories viz., mechanical operations and intellectual operations. Mechanical operations include connecting to the network, sending password, loading CD-ROM disk, uploading the stored search commands or profiles, displaying the results, downloading the references, and e-mailing the reference. Intellectual operations include analysing and conceptualising search topic, structuring search logic, formulating search tactics, selecting database, browsing inverted file for concept matching, interpreting search results, reformulating search logic structure. While many of the mechanical operations are automated, the intellectual operations are untouched. An interface may be invoked at a number of points in the intellectual process to achieve the following aims:

- Establish the context of the query
- Choose appropriate database
- Offer user friendly facilities to express an information requirement
- Facilitate the user to express query in his/her words
- Formulate the query using the database vocabulary
- Express the query as a search statement
- Reformulate the query by changing search term or search statement
- Answer presentation based on relevance[4].

Among these, query formulation is the most intellectually demanding aspect. The basic characteristic of indexing has made this a complicated process. Also, query formulation process is not very well understood and hence it is very difficult to automate this process. At query formulation stage, the user first represents his/her request using key term(s) or key phrase(s) which represents the underlying concepts in his/her request. It is then submitted to the system in a language which is understood by the system. Based on the results obtained, an attempt is made to reformulate the initial query to improve the final outcome. The query formulation and reformulation is done manually by the user or the user with the assistance of the system or by the system with the assistance of the user or by the system automatically.

Interface for query formulation

The present automatic indexing systems use words and word stems as document and query descriptors. In these systems, documents and queries are represented as an unstructured collection of simple descriptors and is based on explicit subject information in the documents and queries. The syntactic or semantic relationships among the terms is not considered and thus it reduces the overall efficiency of the system. To overcome such inefficiency in the indexing system, many retrieval systems provide syntactic tools called proximity operators such as 'near', 'with', 'adjacent' in the retrieval engine. Since these tools are not precise enough a number of other methods such as probabilistic term dependency model, statistical association models and recognition of syntactic relationships as basis for identifying phrases for use as content indicators have been developed[1].

The phrase relationship is primarily dependent on the grammatical structure of the text in which the words occur and is referred as syntagmatic relation. Though both noun phrases and verb phrases are content indicators, the syntactic analysis of full-text concentrates on noun phrases. IRS based on linguistic syntactic components have the following problems:

Noun phrase recognition: Noun phrases can appear in different forms and contain either only nouns or a combination of nouns and adjectives. For example, air pollution and agricultural pollution both are noun phrases. This association is called first order association or semantically compatible relation. Air pollution can also be represented as pollution of air and this association is called second order association or interchangeable relation.

Noun phrase selection: After defining and recognizing noun phrases, the next step is to decide which noun phrases or which part of noun phrases have to be selected. The selected noun phrases should represent document content and should be used by the users to represent the concepts in their queries.

Noun phrase normalization: After defining and selecting the noun phrases, the noun phrases have to be normalized i.e. all appropriate canonical forms of the noun phrases have to be considered so as to cover all possible formulations.

Noun phrase matching: The retrieval engine has to match the normalized noun phrases in the query with that in the document.

Ranking reference with noun phrase: If the retrieval engine ranks the retrieved references, then it has to account for the partial matches of the noun phrases for ranking purpose.

In this paper, we propose an algorithm for noun phrase selection and normalisation. The normalised noun phrase file can be used as an aid in concept identification at query formulation stage. This is implemented on a SUN workstation using LEX, AWK and C.

Methodology adopted

Subject domain: Since the terminology and term relationship is highly dependent on the subject, we restricted our study for a specific subject. About 1000 references are retrieved on 'pollution' from a database of Department of Energy, USA [DOE] and Dissertation Abstract [DA] database.

Phrases from abstracts and titles: Noun phrases were extracted from titles and abstracts of the references retrieved from the above databases. Since title and abstract represent document content and are similar to the user requests, we restricted noun phrase extraction only for these fields. Moreover, full text retrieval experiments have revealed that retrieval at the passage level yields good results.

Definition of noun phrase: Noun phrase is defined as the phrase having nouns only or combination of adjectives and nouns. Since head and modifiers are the smallest possible contexts of the terms which are semantically compatible, an analysis of semantically compatible relation is considered. If we get better results with first order association, we can extend this to second order associations. A corpus file of noun phrases with frequency count in the domain document file is created. These noun phrases were identified with part of speech tagger developed at the computer science department, University of Masschusetts, Amherst, USA, which is based on quantitative approach exemplified by Church's part program[2].

The noun phrases are extracted from titles and abstracts separately. Since titles are more precise than abstracts, it is interesting to compare the occurrence of noun phrases in the titles with that of the abstracts. However, the DOE file has only abstracts.

Table 1 gives total number of unique phrases extracted from the two files

Table 1 Noun phrases occurrence frequency in the domain files

File name	# unique phrases	# phrases/abstract
DOE file	12184	about 12
DAABS file	17927	about 18
DA TIT file	2250	about 2

This was compared with the controlled vocabulary used by the 'Pollution Abstracts' which has 1490 concepts.

Noun phrase modification: After extraction of the noun phrases, acronyms which are usually represented in capital letters are separated. This led to deletion of some chemical names which are also represented in capital letters. To avoid deletion of such terms, a list of standard chemical names can be used which can be consulted before the terms with capital letters are removed. Also, words starting with upper case is changed to lower case and plural form is converted to singular form.

Common words in the front of the noun phrase which do not add meaning to the phrase are deleted. Since these are corpus dependent, 94 such words are selected manually by going through the noun phrase corpus file. The following list is a sample of such words:

above	adequate	available
absolute	adjacent	average
acceptable	alternative	basic
accepted	annual	better
accurate	application	best
actual	appropriate	both
acute	attempt	broad
additional	availability	brief
capability	greatest	possible
capacity	higher	primary
common	highest	recent
complete	important	relevant
continued	improved	separate
continuous	individual	separated
constant	initial	severe
considerable	large	serious
convenient	late	short
corresponding	later	significant
critical	Latest	similar
detailed	little	sinple

different	lower	simple
direct	major	small
effective	marked	special
efficient	new	specific
fundamental	numerous	strong
further	old	subsequent
future	original	substantial
general	overall	total
good	own	type
great	particular	upper
greater	poor	various

The deletion of the above common words resulted in many single terms occurring only once in the noun phrase corpus file, which are noise words. Hence all the single terms with unit frequency are deleted from the corpus file. The total number of unique phrases in the files after making these deletions and modifications is given in table 2. Table 3 shows frequency distribution of phrases with different word combinations in the corpus file.

Table 2 Noun phrase occurrence frequency after word modification and deletion

File name	# phrases after deletion	% deduction
DOE file	10209	20%
DAABS file	15197	20%
DA TIT file	2213	1.6%

Table.3 Frequency distribution of phrases in the noun phrase corpus file

File name	# words in a phrase							
	one	two	three	four	five	six	seven	eight
DOE	267	6964	2310	514	124	25	3	2
DABAS file	302	9979	3716	936	204	54	4	2
DA TIT file	9	1320	455	122	16	7	1	0

Noun phrase normalization : Usually, the noun phrases are normalised by grouping head and modifiers. In two word phrases it is easy to identify this relationship. The first word modifies the last word. However, in multiple word phrases it is difficult to identify this relationship. If permutation and combination of all the words in these phrases is considered, then the size of the inverted file will grow enormously. Also, term order variation leads to many concepts with a totally different meaning. To decide which part of the noun phrase is to be the head, the term association from left to right in a phrase is compared with the distribution frequency of the compound terms in the corpus file. The head is considered as that part of noun phrase which has the highest frequency of occurrence in the corpus file. Table 4 gives some examples of noun phrases and their corresponding head/modifiers.

Table 4 Noun phrases and their corresponding head/modifiers with their respective occurrence frequencies

Phrase	Count	Head	Modifier
air pollution	54		
air	5		
pollution	15	air pollution	—
polluted air	5		
polluted	0		
air	5	polluted air	—
air toxics	4		
air	5		
toxics	1	air	—
air emission	4		
air	5		
emission	17	emission	air
air pollution control	5		
air pollution	54		
pollution control	28	air pollution	control
wastewater treatment plant	6		
wastewater treatment	2		
treatment plant	1	wastewater	
wetland wastewater treatment system	1		
wetland wastewater	0		
wetland wastewater treatment	3		
wastewater treatment	2		
wastewater treatment system	4		
treatment system	3	wastewater treatment	wetland

This is based on the assumption that if a concept or a phrase is well established in a subject area, authors tend to use that concept or phrase to express their ideas and hence those phrases with more frequency become standard terms. Since an information generator is also an information user, the possibility of a user using the same term is high. Hence for a phrase with $t_1, t_2, \ldots t_n$ terms, Etn n=1,n–1 combinations can be considered and among these, the head is the one which has the highest frequency of occurrence in the corpus collection.

Arranging terms within the same head: For the same head, modifiers which are adjectives and nouns are grouped. Thus, to generate head/modifier relation, term co-occurrence frequency in the corpus noun phrase file is considered which is 'external observation of phrase' and to organise modifiers for a head 'internal syntax of terms' is considered.

The following is a list of modifiers for the noun phrase 'air pollutant'. NN is the tag for noun phrase, JJ is the tag for adjectives. The number in bracket is the occurrence frequency of the head in the corpus file.

air/NN pollutant/NN (118) carbon/NN monoxide/NN
air/NN pollutant/NN (118) gas/NN releases/NN
air/NN pollutant/NN (118) individual/NN
air/NN pollutant/NN (118) sulphur dioxide/NN
air/NN pollutant/NN (118) ,acidifying/JJ
air/NN pollutant/NN (118) ,ambient/JJ
air/NN pollutant/NN (118) ,different/JJ
air/NN pollutant/NN (118) ,gaseous/JJ
air/NN pollutant/NN (118) ,hazardous/JJ
air/NN pollutant/NN (118) ,important/JJ
air/NN pollutant/NN (118) ,indoor-generated/JJ
air/NN pollutant/NN (118) ,indoor/JJ
air/NN pollutant/NN (118) ,inhalable/JJ
air/NN pollutant/NN (118) ,inorganic/JJ particulate/JJ

Total number of unique heads generated is given in Table 5.

Table.5 Total number of unique heads and frequency distribution of phrases in the noun head file

File	# unique head	# of words in a phrase head						
		1	2	3	4	5	6	7
DOE file	5588	267	3620	1405	247	40	7	2
DA ABS file	9094	302	5647	2518	517	92	18	0
DA TIT file	1930	9	1320	455	122	16	7	1

This number is compared with the controlled vocabulary used by the 'Pollution Abstracts', an abstracting journal published by Cambridge Scientific Abstract, which has 1661 concepts.

An analysis of head phrases occurring in the three files indicates that the noun phrases from titles are highly structured and good content indicators. The figures in Table 1 and Table 2 for title file also confirm this fact. Table 6 gives total number of common phrases occurring in the three files.

Table 6 Number of common phrase heads occurring in DOE, DA ABS and DA TIT files

File name	# of common noun phrases
DOE file	677
DA ABS file	215
DA TIT file	533

Conclusions

This study has shown that by normalising first order phrase associations complex descriptors which are document and query representations can be identified and structured. However, many problems relating to phrase normalisation remain unsolved. The following issues can be tested to obtain better descriptors.

Words in a phrase can occur in a number of different types of strings such as hyphenated words, words with special characters like -, \, /, punctuations like ',', '.', numbers, capital letters (as in proper nouns, acronyms, chemical names).

Different forms of words which occur in a phrase have to be identified, defined and their relation with other words in the phrase and other phrases have to be considered.

Conversion of plural forms of words to singular forms and stemming of adjectives and nouns can be considered.

Phrase normalisation is performed by word/phrase deletion, word/phrase modification, word/phrase insertion techniques. To carry out these operations in a more systematic way, a weighing scheme has to be developed based on detailed statistical, syntactic and lexical analysis of word-word relation within a phrase, among phrases and among other terms in the domain database.

Table 3 and 5 indicate that two worded and three worded phrases occur more frequently than others. To increase the frequence of occurrence of two worded and three worded phrases in the normalised noun phrase file, co-occurrence frequency of terms within a phrase i.e. substsring of a phrase can be considered.

Table 4 shows that two worded and three worded phrases occur more frequently than others. To increase the frequency of occurrence of two worded and three worded phrases in the normalised noun phrase file, cooccurrence frequency of terms within a phrase i.e. substring of a phrase can be considered.

To identify semantically similar terms such as synonyms and antonyms correlation analysis of head and modifier relation can be considered.

Acknowledgements

This study is carried out as a part of Fulbright grant awarded to the first author (Sep '94-Mar '95). She is highly thankful to Prof. Bruce Croft for being the academic advisor and to her sponsors United States Information Agency, USA, Institute of International Education, USA and United States Education Foundation in India, India. Also, thanks to Mr. Moris Hirsch, ACSIOM, University of Massachusetts, CIIR, University of Massachusetts, Amherst, USA, for his programming support in creating the noun phrase corpus file.

References

1. Fagan, J.L. The effectiveness of a nonsyntactic approach to automatic phrase indexing for document retrieval. *Journal of American Society for Information Science,* 40(2), 115-132, 1989.
2. Jinxi Xu, Broglio J. and Croft, W.B. The design and implementation of a part of speech tagger for English. Internal report No. Compsci TR 94-26, Computer Science Department, University of Massachusetts, Amherst, USA.
3. Schamber, Linda. Relevance and Information Behavior. *Annual Review of Information Science and Technology,* 29, 4-48, 1994.
4. Vickery B. and Vickery A. Online search interfaces. *Journal of Documentation.* 49(2), 103-187, 1993.

SIS–96, 18–20, Jan. '96, Bangalore

Verbal representations of specialised material: Case study on paintings

A.Y. ASUNDI
Deptt. of Library and Information Science, Bangalore University, Bangalore-560 056

Abstract

Digital library includes digitized information regarding all types of matetrial including special material such as; sound, image and video. The 'paintings' is one such type where man's ingenuous creativity is seen. The paper suggests a unified scheme at macro level based on the verbal representation for the contents of 'paintings' from the five Bibliographic Classification Schemes, CC, DDC, UDC, Britannica, and World Book.

Background

Indications of large scale digitising activity of contents of libraries to create full text databases call for development of coding scheme for variety of information forms and to represent them in machine environment. The Library of Congress by the year 2000 A.D. proposes to digitise the most important material in its collection[1]. The library has large collection of illustrated material too and that would also go in digitised form. For the precise retrieval of information about such material, a uniform verbal scheme representing the contents of such material is a pre-requisite.

Digital libraries of text and sound, images and videos and other data are rapidly growing in size and availability. Further it is emphasised that the contents of libraries are diverse, tools for accessing digitised contents are still in their infancy and when data are not text, rather sound and image or video, then generating labels is considered more difficult[2].

The heterogeneous sources or 'source heterogeneity' in libraries limit the effectiveness of information access, with conventional retrieval interfaces. In this context user has to be provided with a tool to access multiple contents of sources, with different characteristics of content forms and provenances[3].

There is a need for a uniform scheme for representing patterns for specialised material and especially as pointed out for images and sound, content based retrieval systems are essential[4].

The proposal

Taking into consideration these background references which express content based retrieval systems for specialised material, a semantic scheme is proposed in this paper taking "PAINTINGS" as an example of specialised sources in general and libraries in particular. The scheme based on Bibliographic Classification Systems has potentiality to represent, store and retrieve such material by their content relationship.

A set of sources are selected that enumerate 'verbal representation' for the contents of "Paintings" as library and general materials. After a close comparison of these schemes, it is observed that a scheme can be generated deriving good points from each one of them. The unified scheme at macro level is derived from the combined verbal representations drawn from: Colon Classification, Decimal Classification, Universal Decimal Classification, New Encyclopaedia Britannica and the World Book Encyclopedia.

To arrive at a compatible scheme more than one scheme is examined as each source document has shown certain variations and inadequacies.

Class structure "paintings" in five sources

The table presents the class structure for "Paintings" as enumerated in the five source documents.

CC	DDC	UDC	Britannica	World Book
Figure	Materials	Materials	Techniques & Methods	People
Human Figure	Surfaces	Foundations	Mediums	Religious
Equestrian	Pigments	Wood	Tempera	Landscapes
Bust	Mediums	Canvas	Fresco	Seascapes
Nature	Fixatives	Metal	Oil	Still Life
Earth	Coatings		Water Colour	History &
Mountain	Techniques & Procedures	Fabric	Ink	Mythology
Water	Colour		Gouache	Social
Sky	Water	Color	Encaustic	Expression
Plant	Ink	Paints	Casein	Painting in
Animal	Acrylic	Varnishes	Synthetic	Decoration
Sculpture	Tempre	Pigments	Medium	Colour
Effigy	Fresco	Oils	Mixed	Line
Cartoon	Oil	Water	Medium	Man
Iconography	Encaustic	Inks	Forms of	Space
Material	Mosaic	Pastels	Painting	Texture
Wood	Finger	Cryons	Mural	Material &
Paper	Sand	Charcoal	Miniature	Techniques
Fresco	Collage	Encaustic	Scroll	Material
Stone	Forms	Fresco	Screen	Wood
Metals	Murals	Tempera	Panaroma	Fabric
	Panaroma	Styles & Periods	Modern forms	
	Scenic	Subjects	Imagery	
	Miniature	Human Form	Subjects	
		Activity	Symbolism	
			Devotional	

CC	DDC	UDC	Britannica	World Book
Materls (contd.) Canvas Ivory Concrete Colour Oil Water Distemper Encaustic	Abstraction Allegory Mythology Legend Symbolism Religious Symbolism Genre Human Figure Erotica Miniature Portraits According to attire Nude Draped Figure Men Women Children Groups of figure Other subjects Landscapes Marinescapes Animal Life Plant Life Industrial & Technical Subjects Architectural subjects & Cityscapes	Genre Animal Life Historical Ceremonial Epic Landscapes Townscapes Still Life Murals Miniature Portraits The Nude Nature Landscape Animal Heraldic	Allegorical Narrative Folk & Tradition	Metal Plastic Fresco Water Colour Encaustic Pastels Tempera Oils SyntheticResins History Primitive Renaissance Later Renaissance Modern

The comparative study of the five sources shows variations in them hence the proposal for creating a unified scheme is attempted here and presented in two levels.

The unified scheme:

LEVEL 1

1. Forms and Subjects
2. Materials
3. Techniques and Procedures
4. Styles
5. Periods and Phases

The level 1 is expanded with some examples in each and presented as Level 2.

1.1 Forms and Subjects
- Human Figure
- Nature
- Historical
- Mythological
- Religious
- Folk and Tradition
- Genre
- Symbolic
- Narrative

1.2 Material
- Foundation/Surfaces
  - Textile/Fabric
  - Canvas
  - Mediums
  - Coatings

1.3 Techniques & Procedures
- Colour
  - Oil
  - Water
  - Ink
- Charcoal/Cryons
- Encaustic

1.4 Styles & Schools
- Egyptian
- Indian
- Japanese
- Islamic
- Chinese
- Greek

1.5 Periods and Phases
- Prehistoric/Primitive/Aboriginals/Indigenous
- Renaissance,
- Later Renaissance
- Modern

Conclusions

The paper has demonstrated how classification schemes can be utilised for developing verbal schemes for representing illustrated materials especially paintings in this case. The author also feels such a scheme has potentiality to use in hypertext and suggests similar attempts be made to other kinds of illustrated materials that are part of any library. The digitised contents of these specialised materials need to be accessed contentwise hence linear schemes are not suitable for such material.

References

1. Virtual Library: News Track. *Communications of the ACM*, 37(11), Nov. 1994.
2. Picard, R.W. and Minka, T.P. Vision texture for annotation. *Communications of the ACM*, 37(11), Nov. 1994.

3. Rajashekar, T.B. Review of the Special Issue on Digital Libraries. April 1995, p.3.

4. Desai, A.Narasimhalu. Special section on content based retrieval: Guest editorial. *Multimedia Systems*, 3(1), 1995, pp.3-14.

SIS–96, 18–20, Jan. '96, Bangalore

Creating a hyper-catalogue using World Wide Web (WWW) at Indian Institute of Technology, Kharagpur

KAMALENDU MAJUMDAR AND A.K. KATNA
Indian Institute of Technology, Kharagpur

Abstract

Hypertext facilities offered by the World Wide Web are exploited to develop a hypercatalogue. The paper attempts to describe the concepts used in the experimental development of a hypercatalogue of books by the faculty of IIT, Kharagpur. The hypercatalogue may be made available for use at ERNET/INTERNET sites. Paper describes how a hypercatalogue may be developed and used by interested libraries and information centres and possible benefits that may accrue by adopting such technology.

The World Wide Web

The World Wide Web popularly called WWW or W3 is one of the recent modes of information retrieval services on the Internet. This also provides hypertext links between textual documents of related files. A link may be necessary to explain or define a chosen word or where an explanation is required, through a text or picture stored or written in another paper or document. Links may also be required to explore definitions occurring in the linked-up documents. With this method, users can click on a highlighted word or words in the text to get additional information about the selected word(s). Users can also access graphic pictures, images, audio clips, or even full-motion video through hypermedia, an extension of hypertext. The hyper-catalogue is similarly able to provide linked information to the chosen elements while making a catalogue search.

The World Wide Web Project was started by CERN (European Laboratory for Particle Physics), Switzerland in an attempt to build distributed hypermedia system. The system can co-ordinate among several protocols. The system uses a network protocol with a markup language which every client is required to understand. Users may access WWW through a "browser program" that can read and fetch documents locally as well as from sites around the world via the Internet. Browsers access files using FTP, NNTP, Gopher, and several other Internet-based protocols, browser clients can also search remote documents and databases if the associated server at that site has built-in search capabilities. It supports the idea of a boundless information world in which any item out of the available knowledge to mankind may be retrieved instantantaneously. Browser program can be line oriented or graphics oriented. One of the most graphics oriented browser program is Mosaic which is developed by the National Center for Supercomputing Applications, University of California also provided a facility to use with Unix with X-Window called as Xmosaic. So Mosaic is a system for wide area distributed hypermedia based information discovery and retrieval.

What is hypertext?

The word hypertext (HT) means the combination of natural language text with embedded links enabling non-linear information access and navigation. A large number of information fragments, chunks such as text, graphics and images linked together electronically forming a multi-faceted indefinite shaped database in which one can write and read the information non-linearly.

The term HT also describes a medium wherein the reader can study a particular document and if encountered with a word or phrases that he or she does not understand, wishes to browse another document that may provide further elaborations over the same text.

What is hypertext transfer protocol?

Hypertext Transfer Protocol (HTTP) refers to the protocol enabling retrieval of information pointed to by the hypertext link. This protocol can transfer plain text file, hypertext or even images from the server end to the user's end. HTTP is an internal requirement of WWW and is often referred to as client server protocol. In the process the client (who is a user of hypertext document) may ask a query to the server (the WWW machine) and the server makes available the required information in a format, which is interpreted by a WWW browser like Mosaic or Netscape.

What is hypertext markup language?

Nowadays many of the formats for electronic distribution embody the restrictions of the printed page documents which are broken into a sequence of fixed pages and pages are described in terms of various symbols marked at specified positions of rows and columns. This has prevented true communication, transmission and interchangeability of informations over the networks.

The Standard Generalized Markup Language (SGML) was invented as a solution to such problems. By focusing on the logical elements in a document, the recipient of information is freed from the oftcn inappropriate choices of the originator. Hypertext Markup Language (HTML) was developed as a simple non-proprietary delivery format for global hypertext, based on SGML. These include text flow around floating figures, fill-out forms, tables and mathematical equations.

The hyper-catalogue project at IIT, Kharagpur

Library automation in IIT, Kharagpur has been a prime activity. While placing this library gopher on Internet our system analyst explored the benefits of WWW. At an experimental level it was decided to create a hyper-catalogue. It was perceived that the users would be able to browse through major title keywords and their connotations, more information on authors and similar facets. These facets were introduced or supposed to serve at various levels of links. Therefore our definition of hyper-catalogue means adding hypertext links (using HTML) to our existing computerised catalogue of book collection. For example, think of a user searching the author index. By choosing a particular name one can link to books authored by him at the first level on the computer screen. At the second level one may seek out his affiliation, at the third level his field of specialization, at fourth level his bio-data, photograph and so on.

To make a modest beginning we took up the task of creating hyper-catalogue for the collection of publications by our own faculty. This is called as Faculty Publications. At the initial level only author links are being developed. The users may get the information about the works of a particular faculty within one go without quitting from the working screen. This is possible due to the hyper-links between the author index and the database. The search string may be a text word and the name of the author or any word related to the database. The linking and retrieval of images or the photographs is possible with the facilities of 'Windows' or 'X-Windows' only.

Nowadays the information providers may create HTML documents by developing macros in their preferred editor such as edlin, vi or Emacs, or word processor to convert documents to HTML format. They may use simple, easy-to-use authoring tools, typically with a graphical user interface. Authoring tools currently available, including HTML Hyper Edit, HTML Assistant, etc.

We have created the hypertext catalogue by using a standard text editor (vi in a Unix environment) in a plain text format. Although HTML code is a tedious language to work with, some software tools can convert plain text to HTML automatically. We provide hereunder an overlook on how to develop a hyper-link for a document in Annexure 1 and to browse the hypercatalogue (over the network) in Annexure 2.

Hypertext may be used as a powerful tool in a library scenario as it can connect text at various levels of information. This may also as well serve to link up any machine in the world.

Experience and prospects

Libraries in developed countries are gradually changing from print to full text databases and titles available solely electronically in remarkably short span although the facilities like possessing good computing machines, data in electronic/digital formats and networking active links are rarely available in the Indian scene. IIT, Kharagpur having had this advantage has been constantly exploiting technological benefits and has been among the first to accomplish such activities at practical level to the best of the knowledge of the authors. We are eager to exploit the generation of new services and receive co-ordination and comments from any librarians involved in similar exercise.

The benefits of this high technological marvel is being slowly impregnated to our library users. We are quite pleased to see users' happiness over the ease of availability of information, although we also encounter frustration whenever links or communication lines do not work or interrupt mid-way.

Acknowledgment

The authors are indebted to Prof. S. Parthan, and Mr. S. Raguraman, Mr. Rohil Muktibodh for their guidance and expertise.

Annexure 1

Librarians interested to develop hyper-link facilities should have the following :

1. A computer with 486 or higher configuration operating with UNIX or compatible system with 8 MB RAM and 256 byte cache memory.

2. The computer should be equipped with a network card and connection to an Internet service provided like NICNET, ERNET or VSNL.

3. Networking software like TCP/IP loaded on Unix, X-Window system will give facility of catalogue access.

4. Download the WWW public domain software and set up the server on this computer.

5. Create HTML files linking to desire documents (in our case faculty publications).

Annexure 2

The librarians interested in hooking-up to IIT, Kharagpur library catalogue may do so if an active network site is available to them. One can use the IP address of 144.16.192.17

or by using the command as under:

$ telnet library@library.iitkgp.ernet.in

if the connection is successful then the login screen of IIT, Kharagpur library will be displayed. To use hypercatalogue the login of "www" is to be used. The permission to use this login and the password may be sought from library authorities.

At the prompt the COMMAND ww should be entered. Then WWW will take care to link the hypercatalogue of faculty publication and the following screen would be displayed.

IIT KHARAGPUR

CENTRAL LIBRARY

Welcome to the Central Library library.iitkgp.ernet.in, Hyper Catalogue

This is an experimental setup.

Central Library Information Services [1]

Faculty Publication(s) [2]

INDIAN Resources on the INTERNET [3]

If the user wants to browse item [2] then this hyperlink will display another screen like this:

Author Link [1]
Title Link
[End]

If the user now selects [1] then this hyperlink will display another screen like this:

ABRAHAM, K P	[1]	[2]
ADHIKARI, B		[3]
AGARWAL, J P		[4]
BANERJEE, DHARMAPADA		[5]

If the user now press [5] then this hyperlink will hook up the catalogue card of the book written by the author.

BANERJEE, DHARMAPADA
MECHANICAL WORKING PROCESSES: IIT. METALLURGICAL FACULTY PUBLICATION. 671.3 BAN.M 159208

The search session may be ended by using instructions from the Help Menu displayed at the bottom of the screen.

Four

Networking Systems and Electronic Access

SIS–96, 18–20, Jan. '96, Bangalore

Impact of information technology on library science

N. BALAKRISHNAN
National Centre for Science Information, Indian Institute of Science, Bangalore-560 012

Abstract

The impact of information technology has been all pervading. However, the largest impact seems to have been made on library science. It has changed the way we perceive of and disseminate information and has even threatened the traditional approaches to library and librarianship. In this paper a brief overview of the impact of information technology is presented.

Introduction

The performance of the microprocessors has increased by a factor of 25,000 since its birth in 1971 and it is currently doubling every eighteen months. Simultaneously, the communication turned digital and has also shown equally stunning growth. These two revolutions — in computers and in communications — have transformed the computer from a mere number crunching device to one that is used for information access and have become synonymous with information technology.

The impact of information technology has been all pervading. However, the largest impact seems to have been made on library science. It has changed the way we perceive of and disseminate information and has even threatened the traditional approaches to library and librarianship. In this paper a brief overview of the impact of information technology is presented.

Information storage and transmission

Traditionally, transmission and storage of information have been by paper documents. In the past few decades there have been two parallel developments that have taken place in apparently diverse fields such as digitisation of information and image processing. First, the advent of low cost computers and the easy-to-use word processing software has resulted in increasingly larger share of documents originating on the computer, paving the way for "digitised information". The emergence of the machine-readable bibliographic database in the '60s as a spin-off from computer- controlled photocomposition procedures for printing large indexing and abstracting journals, is distinctly different from the current developments. However, this spearheaded intense research efforts in information retrieval techniques involving Boolean queries based on keyword occurrences and document similarity measures based on word frequencies. These techniques depend heavily on the fact that the data is available in ASCII form and they are now sufficiently sophisticated and refined to take advantage of the full-text documents and databases available today.

The birth of fast Fourier transform in the mid 1960's and the subsequent maturity of computer based image processing techniques have made it possible to process textual and non-textual information with equal ease. This has motivated the shift in the information paradigm from textual to multimedia — data consisting of images of text, digitised speech and video.

The storage and transmission of library information thus shifted from volume-limiting paper form to a limitless multimedia digital form, that is fit enough to exploit the advances in computers and communication.

The communication revolution and information explosion

Information in isolated pockets is static and does not grow. Democratic accessing and sharing of information contributes to its further growth and its multiplier effect results in the information explosion. Thus the communication revolution that contributed to a reliable and easily affordable mode of information interchange is the single most important factor in the growth of digital library. The ease of communication has made a significant shift in the information use paradigm from the need to know basis to that of information being available when and where you need it. This also avoids massive replication of information and has shrunk the world for one to imagine a global library.

One of the manifestations of the information revolution is the Internet — the network of networks. The advanced search engines available on the net allow one to navigate effectively through trillions of bytes of data store on diverse computers located across continents. The global network of telecommunication provide a very cost effective global library.

Library in the digital world

The library is often associated with large buildings filled with massive rows of storage racks for printed books and journals. The library continuously goes through an exercise of acquiring to keep abreast of advances in the fields of relevance and organising for ease of use for the readers and preserving collections. Weeding out useless and outdated information is a librarian's nightmare. A conventional library is gauged by the number of titles that it holds and by the number of journals that it subscribes. With ever increasing cost of printed journals and books, it is next to impossible for any library to maintain the same rate of growth in terms of its collection, let alone grow exponentially in time with the information revolution.

The modern Digital Library will be a sleek array of computer based information systems. This library will be gauged by the number of access made rather than by the number of titles it holds. Weeding out of outdated information and adding of current information will be tasks that would be too simple. Sharing of information across continents would become a rule than an exception. The modern digital library will be tested for collecting quantitative statistics that will ultimately decide the quality and worth of information that the library possesses.

Librarian in the digital world

The librarian in the digital world would become the guardian of information and would be the vehicle to preserve democratic access to information. His role will be increasingly towards offering consultancy to the users in their efforts in navigating through the web of documents that span the global library. He would be the integrating link between the computer scientists and the information seekers and he would require a common language that links the lingo of computer scientists and the users. He will be the embodiment of an information broker who would ensure that the wares that he has, are used effectively and with ease.

The future

The interaction of the users with multiple disparate information sources provided by a digital library would continue to be a serious focus of the future. The mythical "paperless office" is still a debatable distant dream. The paper since its invention, has served as one of our primary communication medium. In spite of its second class citizen status in the electronic world, its inherent physical properties make it easy to use, transport and store and is cheap. The recent trend has been to use both paper- based and electronic information in an integrated way. In other words, paper would be readable by both computer and people. In the digital library, paper may continue to form the user interface medium.

The need to develop better work spaces for retrieving, visualising and manipulating large volumes of data has been one of major thrust areas in information technology. These call for more than that would be possible with WIMP (Windows, Icons, Mouse, Pointers). The path breaking efforts in interactive graphics and animation technology are finding applications in visualising and disseminating large volumes of data. This is based on the pretext that much of the complex cognitive tasks are better performed by the human perceptual system.

The navigation tools of the future would tend to integrate with the human assisted information retrieval and provide a virtual landscape that reflects the structure of the networked universe and would support rapid information navigation and precision retrieval.

In this new world, the librarian's role will be that of a continuous learner, an alert user and an expert consultant, all rolled into one.

SIS–96, 18–20, Jan. '96, Bangalore

Entering a new civilization: Digital libraries and its social impact

ARCHANA KAKODKAR
Centre for Latin American Studies, Goa University, Goa

Abstract

The idea of this title is taken from Alvin and Heidi Toffler's recent work "Creating a New Civilization" (1993). This paper discusses the issues such as: Why digital libraries? Internet CD-ROM/; Electronic publishing references documents (ERDS) with special references to maps and contemporary archives; electronic translations; copyright and digital technology; digital networks and Indian scenario; role of the librarian in digital technology.

Why digital libraries?

In 1990 Alvin Toffler estimated in his book, "Powershift" that in one year the United States runs out 1.3 trillion documents sufficient according to some calculations to "Wallpaper" the Grand Canyon 107 times. By now the number of documents has risen to four trillion. According to BIS Strategic Decisions, a market research and consultancy firm in Norwell, Mass, U.S.A. all but 5% of this is still in paper[1]. Estimates indicate that there are close to 50,000 periodicals in science and technology and this number is steadily increasing at a compound rate of 2 to 4 percent per year. Considering an average of 40 papers per periodical title per year, there are about two million journal papers published every year. To this one has to add other publications like reports, conference proceedings, thesis, patents etc.[2] This is the result of the information explosion. The impact of all this is telling on a scientist of today. He spends about ten percent of his working time in "Keeping up with the literature" and this proportion is the same as in 1990 as it was in 1980, yet twice as much published in 1990 as in 1980. This means scientists either ignores some currently available services or takes the help of technical tools.[3]

This information explosion is also taking place in Social Sciences, Huamanities and other areas. The best example is a recently held Womens Conference at Beijing, China in September 1995 for two weeks. There were 500 Seminars/Conferences/Discussions/Debates over different issues, facing women, from the entire globe. Even if every seminar has produced only twenty papers, the total number of papers presented is 10,000 on different themes and from different countries pertaining to only women's issues.[4]

The standard library methods of information transfer are incapable of handling such large data, and servicing users effectively. One more factor that aggravated the situation is the soaring prices of printed matter. The most severe price increase occurred in reference manuals (Abstracts, Indexes, etc.) Chemical Abstracts rose from $ 12 in 1940 to $ 16,350 in 1994. Resource sharing became an essential component of library service. Therefore librarians had no alternative but to adopt new information technology which has come to the rescue of the librarians and library users and computerisation of databases became the need of the hour.[5]

Development of computer industry and also the parallel developments in telecommunications have thrown open new vistas for provision of data processing, data storage, data transmission and of course better library services. Databases became the in thing in library and information field. Databases sprang up all over the world. DIALOG, BRS, ORBIT, PERGAMON/INFOLINE, ESA/IRS, STN International are some of the well known online service provides using databases.

The amount of information that is stored in electronic databases is mind boggling. Literally trillions of words, all of them minutely cross referenced. Even with this high capacity, the amount of information that becomes available every day is simply too much to computerise and store.

For example, it is estimated that to store the 1.5 terabytes of data on DIALOG, you need approximately 7,50,000 home computers, to transfer the data from DIALOG to base computers using 1200 baud modems, you need to transmit 24 hours a day for about 375 years.[7]

So friends, even textual databases are also not going to serve our purpose of compact storage and transmission effectively. Hence, the modern scene is to digitise the information (To make it more compact). Digital technology is able to handle other media elements such as sound, graphics, pictures, colours etc. which is the wider advantage of going digital.

Internet

It is the world's first digital information utility, an all purpose network that lets anybody send particularly anything digital to almost anyone anywhere. Without argument, Internet is the most famous network ever evolved. Computer libraries in 77 countries now have access to Internet. Nobody owns Internet. It knows no geographical boundaries. All its growth has come spontaneously. From 32 million computers around the world, the Internet is expected to swell over 100 million machines by the end of this century. The number of users will cross two millions by 1997. Thus INTERNET is heading a new fully wired digital society.

CD-ROM

Previously all the PC's were restricted to only one medium, that is text. Whereas the latest ones are able to handle other media elements such as text, sound, graphics, pictures, colours etc. Today CD-ROM's are one of the largest data memories available for a commercial PC application.[8] "CD-ROM will change the world" a sentiment that Microsoft Press used to quote on every CD-ROM they published and that prediction is coming true. There was a recent Wall Street journal article about how CD-ROM has revolutionised educational publishing. A 650 MB CD-ROM disc can store more than 2,50,000 pages of information or the entire Encyclopedia Britannica, with some more space left.[11] Digital delivery of reference information is growing increasingly popular. CD-ROM's electronic publishing (ERD) lets you build, circulate and enhance your library treasures into knowledge base with greater speed and flexibility than ever was possible with papers. Paper is easy to read but often impossible to find, a week or year later. With an electronic document, database you can search and retrieve document in a few seconds using common indexing and retrieval software.[12]

ERD's assist learning process in a very different way from most multimedia documents, in that their primary role is to give you fast access to data, so that you can solve problem efficiently, plus ERDS offer a variety of features that are beyond the ability of hard copy.

In one window you can browse through the table of contents. While "Synchronized" companion window presents the next of the section under your cursor. Others offer graphical access tool to help to locate information. While with a careful analysis you can tailor an ERD to the specific needs of your users.[13]

Digital documents

Document production is only a small part of the overall process of gathering digital documents, while the time that must be spent on searching, writing, reviewing, revising the contents of long printed documents constitute as 80 to 90 percent of the process. The time that is spent for formatting them for delivery constitute perhaps only 10 percent of the process, given the speed with which you can devise EDS, the purely mechanical task of building and formatting.

In India, NISSAT has established sectoral information centres (SICS) with the object of creating information awareness and to meet the information needs of Indian scientific community and decision makers. Out of the ten SICS "NICDROM" caters to institutions providing information on CD-ROM references, collection of books and journals on CD-ROM, technical specifications, choice and information regarding cost of CD-ROM equipment, CD-ROM databases and services. NICDROM services are national in character and the host institution is National Aeronautical Laboratory, Bangalore. CD-ROM's market is 900 million disc per year. Compact DISC India Limited is planning to set up the CD Project in India.[14]

The main benefits of CD-ROM for the library are :

- CD-ROM offers on-disk access to bibiographic database without connect time costs and communication fees.
- CD-ROM is physically portable and can be even mailed.
- No telecommunication facilities essential.
- The physical specifications are standardized (ISO 9660 International Standard)
- Less storage needed for print products because of its high storage capacity.
- More service to the end user with all search options and browsability. It is user friendly (search indexes are available).
- CD-ROM database are more cost effective.
- Pre-mastering is possible.
- Printing and downloading to hard disk or floppy disk is feasible.
- CD-ROM networking helps to share resources through Local Area Networks (LAN).

CD-ROM systems resolve many of the retrieval issues of preservation, access, storage and security of libraries and information centres. Since these systems are expensive and beyond the budget of individuals, libraries must make it possible for people to use and become familiar with this.

Electronic mail

Electronic Mail is the most used service of the computer networks in India. ERNET is mail service established by DOE during (1986-91) to provide academic and research Institutions with electronic mail facility. It is currently used by DSIR labs, IITs, and Academic & Research Institutions. E-mail does not require the presence of other party at the other end.

File transfer is the second most common service. Bulletin Board System allows users to post news and receive news from a central database.[15]

INFLIBNET

On June 20, 1995 the INFLIBNET announced the opening of the Union Catalogue of about 25,000 periodicals and 45,000 thesis holdings received from about 60 universities/institutions in the country.[16]

Indian National Oceanographic Data Centre (INODOC)

It is situated at National Institute of Oceanography (NIO), Goa. A powerful and efficient computer system is installed for scientists and researchers working in this field.[17]

Examples of digitised maps and contemporary archives

INFO TEC, Hyderabad (1991) has digitized map of India for Hindustan Lever. This map has the following features:

— Digitization upto taluka level with a complete road and railway network.

— Towns and villages digitized whose population extends 1000.

— Number of households.

INFO TEC has designed a software by which management of drawings and engineering systems (MODES) can be digitized. It is also working on a project which entails the conversion of atlas paper based information into digital form.[18]

Antarctic Digital Database Project

Antarctic digital database project: A new tool for Antartic environmental science and management. Harris, C.M. (Scott Polar Res. Inst. Univ. Cambridge, Cambridge CB2 1ER, UK) POLAR REC., Vol.27 No.162, July 1991, pp.260-261. En.

Antartic science and management require up-to-date geographic map as a basis for analysing and displaying a wide variety of environmental data. Until now scientists had to rely on many sources for this geographic framework, mostly in the form of paper maps of variable quality at a variety of scales. The Antartic digital database project (ADDP), which was officially launched at the

Royal Geographical Society in London on 9 May 1991, aims to improve this situation by providing a single, comprehensive geographic framework of the Antartic continent and its surrounding islands, stored in digital form on CD-ROM. The database is intended to be available by the end of the year. Sponsored by British Petroleum (BP), the ADDP is a joint venture between British Antartic Survey (BAS), Scott Polar Research Institute (SPRI), the World Conservation and Monitoring Centre (WCMC — Jointly established by IUCN, UNEP and WWF), and the Scientific Committee on Antartic Research (SCAR).

Keeping contemporary archives

It is a monthly records of world events, published since 1931. Each issue contains information on published situation world wide. Over the years this has built up into a valuable archive of contemporary historical information. Cartermill International's growing electro portfolio are now offering the years from 1960-1994 on CD-ROM. This user folio views search software giving instant access to over 15.5 million words. Any significant political event in any country in the world over the last 34 years can be referred to simply by keeping an appropriate search term.

Thesaurus of names that are covered over the period on the CD-ROM makes life easier too. The value of this electronic option is to go directly to the answer of your question. You can build up to major world events, or follow their effects, follow the careers of public figures or watch the development of International Organisations. It is cost effective too.

Machine translations (MT)

Never before in history has there been a more urgent need to topple linguistic barriers, that divide the people of the world. The process of converting information from one language into another with a computer, MT is an information technology. Being able to tap into MT from your desktop, has several advantages, for example you can use OCR (Optical Character Recognition), CD-ROM and internal modems and faxes to capture text and graphics download databases and exchange electronic files with libraries anywhere in the world.[21] Many databases offer information other than English, for example you might search other countries patents or body of legal decisions or scientists can upgrade his knowledge of latest Japanese advances in superconductivity.[22]

In information gathering operations, the input of documents usually come from a wide range of sources and are available in hard copy.

The cost of converting the input into a electronic file may be prohibitive. And the use of OCR in combination with automatic processing and human monitoring might not make enough of a difference to warrant the introduction of MT. However, what is making MT more feasible for information gathering purposes is the widespread availability of that in digital form. MT will help international economic and political stability, trade, economy and well being, for these are dependent on shared information. This will help in the formation of Global Village.

Intellectual property rights: Copyright

Defining property rights in knowledge, information or reputation is a capitalist innovation. International property rights cover trade marks and copyrights.[24] Now the issue that we will be dealing with will be for on-line services. The real question is what is the appropriate analogy for on-line service providers? Are they like telephone companies? Which are not responsible for what goes over their wires? Or at the other extremes, are they like publishers, and responsible for everything? Or are they more like a book stores or leading libraries, which can be held responsible for distributed pirated goods, only if it can be shown that they know that the goods were pirated.[25] A computer programme is infringed by making a floppy disk.[26]

In 1993 December, Playboy Magazine won an injunction against an obscure computerised bulletin board, TEC's WARF HOUSE BBS — which was using its bulletin board to distribute thousands of unauthorised copies of 170 Playboy Photoplay.[27] The most important charge which U.S. Patent & Tradesmark Commissioner, Bruce Lehman could suggest to Clinton administration is, he would make it illegal to "Create technological devices designed to defeat anticopying measures". Paul Goldstein, a Stanford University legal scholar and author of "Copyrights Highway" says, nearly 200 years ago Thomas Jefferson wrote to his friend Samuel Kercheval "I am not an advocate of frequent charges in Laws and Constitutions, But laws & institutions must go hand in hand with the progress of humankind". That sums up the challenge of the US copyrights.[28]

Bons Marcque former French civil servant in the Ministry of Culture now campaigning for globalisation of European System of CR, felt that the Indian CR laws did not give the rights of author and other performers much importance, unlike the European System, which incorporated moral right. This disadvantage should be removed from Indian CRs. There is a need to universalise the intellectual property rights, the need to protect the legal and moral rights of the creator. This was unanimously accepted at the Euro-Asian

Seminar on Intellectual Property Rights, Culture and Industry in Asia.[29] With all kinds of intellectual property now floating around in Cyberspace, U.S. copyrights need updating, along with the entire globe.[30] U.S has to do the job of policing Cyberspace.

Digital networks and Indian scenario

The Indian information highway is slowly being built, but universal excess to it is still only a distant dream.

VSNL: Charter is to provide Indian users with gateways to foreign telecom network. But it has now become a service provider itself at rates more than 100 times higher than other networks, and trying to prevent others from breaking its monopoly.

NICNET: An independent high-capacity satellite-linked information highway, meant to link government organisations, has been set up on this network, connecting 70 cities and towns. But VSNL and the DOT are fighting to prevent it from offering business services.

E-mail networks: Privately run, they pay whopping licence fees to the DOT, but they're not allowed to connect with one another. No private networks are allowed direct access to the Internet, so they can't offer the flash the World Wide Web.

I-Net: The public data communication network is only linked to nine cities, instead of the 89 it was to be hooked to by 1994. And the telecom standards used by I-Net are useful only for low use volumes like e-mail and credit-card verification.

ERNET: India's first provider of full access to the Internet. Links 300 research and educational institutions nationwide, and increasingly, business-related groups. But cheap connections to business have prompted protests from VSNL and the DOT.

Cellular and pager networks: Both face problems of getting their calls through on the creaky main lines of the DOT, which they have to use for call routing. Limited allocation of telecom frequencies could soon overburden the networks as they add on subscribers.

VSAT Networks: Sats are mushrooming all over India to provide business with reliable data transmission links, an alternative to leasing unreliable DOT lines. But these networks are not allowed to connect with the DOT's lines.

Any information highway needs a fibre-optic backbone to carry voice, data and video. DOT's trunk routes are 80% fibre, but antiquated exchanges and poorly maintained equipment are major blocks to building a seamless national information highway.

Librarian in the age of digital libraries

Our mission is to: Work towards meeting the information needs of people by providing high quality information systems, services, products, based on the recorded human knowledge of the world, through the utilization of current and emerging information technologies, i.e. digital technology. To be an active player in the international information industry. To participate in educational training and development programmes that leads to better utilisation of information resources by the beneficiaries of our services at large.

Besides, library and information service management is entering a new age of accountability, and the provision of information even in a more traditional or modern library setting is no longer accepted by funding authorities as inherently good. Library and information professionals who are not willing to learn the modern technological advances must justify their existence as the basic concept of quality management is to be applied to library and information service units with success. Responsibility, performance and control are as essential for the successful libraries and information services agencies as they are for any other enterprise.

Technology alone cannot help bring about the required changes, attitudes, practices and policies need to be changed, if the librarians in India are to benefit themselves and their community of users by the application of new technologies.[31] Digital information environment is going to be part of our day-to-day professional activities, in the next couple of years, simply, the way we carry out research, teaching and learning is not going to be the same at all[32]. Computers do cataloguing now, but the librarians who navigate the internet will survive. Others will become history. If you want to be called 'Cybernarians' learn to dabble with Cyberspace technology. The exchange structure of the digital data types lets you leverage the information content in your data in ways you never imagined. But exchanging data across platforms requires lots of hard work.[33]

Irrespective of whether we are working in the public, academic or research libraries, the developing areas of multimedia interactive digital communications and visualisation needs to be studied and mastered, to play a role in the emerging application areas on the information superhighway. Exciting learning opportunities exist, for all of us. Those who are already in bigger research libraries, even more opportunities await them. New entrants need to prepare themselves with the most of new skills, so that they can play a meaningful and leading role in the information society that will register a new millennium while entering a new civilization.

References

1. Refkin, Glenn. The future of the document. *Furbes AP,* Oct. 9, 1995.
2. Rajashekhar, T.B. Information support for scientific research. Evolving a National Information Transfer System in Science in Society Education by Yashpal Kapoor and others New Delhi, 1994, pp.150.
3. Opcit, pp.152
4. Martins, Sabina. Womens Conference at Beijing. *Navhind Times*, Goa, 30th Sept' 1995.
5. Parekh, Harsha. Social science literature; Use, Pattern and Biographic Services, *EPW*, Aug' 28, 1982.
6. Sharma, S.K. Computer networks for library development in Preparing Libraries for the 21st Century, Delhi, ILA, 1995, pp. 13.
7. Mulvey, Katrie. U and I: *A Newsletter for Informatic,* 1(2), Feb' 1994.
8. Ramaiah, C.K. CD-ROM Networking: State of the Art. Preparing Libraries for the 21st Century, pp.374-392.
9. Selvi, M.G. Current Technology in the Library: CD-ROM in New Horizons in Library and Information Science Education by C.P. Vashista, Madras, T.R. Publications, 1994, pp.230.
10. *Byte*. Sept' 1993, pp.230.
11. Rajashekhar, T.B., Opcit pp.155.
12. Murry, C. Philip. Documentation goes digital. *Byte*, Sept' 1993, pp.123.
13. Opcit pp.12.
14. Selvi, M.G., Opcit pp.558.
15. Rajashekhar, T.B., Opcit, pp.157.
16. INFLIBNET, June 20, 1995 (*Newsletter* from Ahmedabad).
17. Aquatic Science and Fisheries Abstracts, - (ASFA-2), 22(3), March' 1992, pp.2.
18. *Dataquest,* F6-28, Feb' 95. pp.61.

19. *ASFA* 2, Opcit.

20. Keeping record of World Events, CD-ROM

21. *Byte*, Jan' 1993, pp.156.

22. Opcit pp.158.

23. Opcit. pp.164.

24. Bagchi, A.K. International property rights and technology charge in follower countries. Opcit, No.2.

25. Noer, Michael, Policing Cyberspace. *Furbes,* April 10, 1995, pp.50-52.

26. Punkshe, S. The management of intellectual property. Pune, Author, 1991, pp.298.

27. *Furbes*, April 10, 1995, pp.50-52.

28. Opcit, pp.50-52.

29. Times of India, Bombay, 26 Nov. 1995.

30. Opcit, pp.50-52.

31. Haravu, L.J. Library automation and networking in India: An overview of recent developments. Opcit No.10, pp.505.

32. Rajashekhar, T.B., *Communications of the ACM*, Special issue on Digital Libraries, April' 1995, pp.2.

33. Randall, Crunk, Unlocking data content, *Byte,* Sept'19 93, pp.111.

SIS–96, 18–20, Jan. '96, Bangalore

The Implications of Internet on Indian library network system

S.I. FAZZULUDIN AND CHIKKAMALLAIAH
Indian Institute of Management, Bangalore

Abstract

This paper reviews the basic functions related to Indian library network link with Internet library services. The components, services and the facilities of Internet with respect to library services are discussed. Implications of the library network functions, future expandability of library in India, proper management, support functions and the role of Internet services are studied. An attempt is made to co-relate the Indian library network system and the Internet library services available at the higher educational institutes and the universities around the world.

Introduction

In India more than 180 universities and over 6000 colleges use the library services for their academic and research activities and depend on the resources available in their libraries. Currently the technical, scientific and management institute libraries are functioning in isolation and there is no mechanism for the dissemination of valuUable information available in these institutes. Library network system will enable the universities and the higher learning institutes to share and electronically transmit the information resources among them. The information sharing through computer networks and document delivery in the form of electronic media are helpful to the research scholars and the teaching faculties. Internet, the network of networks in the world referred to as the information superhighway, is growing at a very fast rate of 10 percent every month, connected with more than 500,000 networks, interlinked with approximately 2 million computers (hosts) having about 40 million users. Through the Internet one can access vast reservoir of information like the U.S. Library of Congress. The Internet user can also send e-mail to various places, access remote servers and download data and software from remote hosts. In India till recently Internet was accessible to a small group of academic and government users through the Educational and Research Network (ERNET) and National Informatics Network (NICNET). With VSNL (Videsh Sanchar Nigam Limited) opening the flood gates of the Internet on August, 1995 there is going to be a drastic increase in the number of Internet users. Internet connectivity will be handy to access the electronic journals, bibliographic and full-text resources and to answer the reference questions which will help the Internet users in general and the Indian community in particular.

Information network systems in India

Information and Library Network (INFLIBNET) was setup in 1993 by UGC to computerise and network the libraries of the universities and higher education institutes in India. DELNET, BONET, CALIBNET, MALIBNET, HYDLIBNET & BALNET under the auspices of NISSAT were initiated to interconnect the libraries located at Delhi, Bombay, Calcutta, Madras, Hyderabad and Bangalore respectively. Table 1 gives the details of information/library network systems in India.

National Informatics Centre (NIC) is playing a catalytic role in ushering in computer consciousness and promoting systematic approach in data collection, organisation, processing, analysis and accessibility.

The following databases are available on the NICNET NEC system:

GIST	General Information to Public
CEN	Census Data
ECO	Economic Data
IMF	Member Countries Data
TECH	Technology Data
ANAL	Analyst S/W

ERNET (Education and Research Network) in India is connected to Internet via National Centre for Software Technology (NCST), Bombay. This network is providing e-mail, FTP (File Transfer Protocol), and Telnet modes of access to various resources and services available on the Internet.

Internet services and tools

The Internet is the world's largest network of electronic mail users. All that is needed to send mail to anyone else on the Internet is their mail address (in RFC 822 format) and access to a mail system connected to the Internet.

Internet addressing

Mail addresses for the Internet can appear in one of the two forms, the modern Internet (or RFC 822) format and older UUCP format. UUCP is a means of sending mail from one site to another, where no direct connection exists between the sites. Messages are instead forwarded from one site to another in a 'bucket brigade' fashion, until they reach a site which can communicate with the site where their eventual recipients are located — at which point the mail message is delivered.

Table 1 Information and Scientific Networks in India

Networks	Network used by	Controlled by
NICNET	Government departments and agencies	Planning Commission
ERNET	Institutions working in frontier areas of science and technology	Department of Electronics
CALIBNET	Libraries in Calcutta	Under the auspices of NISSAT
DELNET	Libraries in Delhi	Under the auspices of NISSAT
BOMNET	Libraries in Bombay	Under the auspices of NISSAT
MALIBNET	Libraries in Madras	Under the auspices of NISSAT
HYDLIBNET	Libraries in Hyderabad	Under the auspices of NISSAT
BALNET	Libraries in Bangalore	
BTISNET	Academic and research biotechnology institutions	Department of Science & Technology
INFLIBNET	University libraries and specialised R & D institutions	U.G.C.
DESINET	Defence science laboratories	Department of Defence
SIRNET	Laboratories under the C.S.I.R.	C.S.I.R.

RFC 822 addresses

An Internet address has two main parts, the user's name, and the Internet site at which they receive their mail. The address is written and used in the form:

user@machine.site.domain.topdomain

e.g.:spride@cix.compulink.co.uk

Starting from the right hand side, the identifiers signify:

'uk'	the particular site is located in the portion of the Internet which includes the UK
'co'	indicates that the site is a commercial organization (the other main domain identifier you will see is 'ac' for academic sites)
'compulink'	identifies Compulink Information Exchange as the site to which the mail should be sent
'cix'	identifies the particular part of all Compulink's systems
'at',	the @ sign links the user name on CIX to the address information
'Spride'	the user name.

The second level domains list and the types of Internet connections are given in Tables 2 and 3.

Table 2 Second-Level Domains

Domain abbrevi-ation	Meaning	Exmaple
.edu	Educational institution	University, community college, educational institution
.com	Commercial site	Business, professional organiza-tion, commercial access provider
.net	Network sites that pass e-mail to the Internet using a gateway	Uunet
.gov	Government site	The White House, National Institution of Health
.mil	Military	Military bases
.org	Organization that does not neatly fit into the other categories; used also for noncommercial gateways	The Open Software Foundation, the ISOC, FIDOnet-Internet gateway

Table 3 Types of Internet Connections

Connection	Availability	Account or System on Internet	Applications
Direct	Constant	System jim @cam.com	All available
Dial-up	Only when dialed up	Account on access provider's system jim @panix.com	Only applications supported by access provider
Dial-up SLIP/PPP	Only when dialed up	System jim @cam.com	All available
Dedicated SLIP/PPP	Constant	System jim @cam.com	All available
UUCP	Only when dialed up	Not considered a true internet connection	E-mail and newsgroups only

Internet services for journals and newsletters

Another important development is the emergence of electronic journals and newsletters on the computer networks. Many of these are available on various gophers, bulletin boards and anonymous FTP sites also <PACS Review> <PACS News> and <Current Cites> are the three examples of this phenomenon. *PACS Review* and *PACS News* are published from Houston and *Current Cites* is published from Berkeley in the U.S.A. *PACS Review* is a peer-reviewed journal, *Current Cites* is an abstracting journal, but *PACS News* is simply a newsletter. There are many more e-journals and newsletters. The above three publications can be subscribed by sending the following e-mail message to:

<listserv@uhupvm1.bitnet>

Internet commercial services

Now-a-days, commercial publishers have also started publishing electronic journals on the Internet. Elsevier, Springer-Verlag and Meckler Corporation are the three such examples.

It is possible to order Meckler books via Internet now. To access the MC2 service telnet to: <nicol.jvnc.net> and type <nicol> at the login prompt. To subscribe freely to the Meckjournal, send the following e-mail message to :

<meckler@jvne.net>
<subscribe Meckjournal your name>

Other commercial databases available on the Internet are as under:

BRS <Bibliographic Retrieval Service>
<telnet brs.com>
Dat-Star <telnet reserve. rs.ch>
Dialog/knowledge <telnet dialog, com or 192. 132.3.254>
EPIC/First Search <telnet epic.oclc. org or 132.174.100.2>
ESA-IRS <telnet 192.106.252. 1>
MEDLARS <telnet medlars. nim.nih.gov>
LEXIX/NEXIS (Mead Data General) <telnet lexis.meaddata.com or 192.73.216.20 or 192.73.216.21>
ORBIT <telnet orbit.com>
RLIN (Research Libraries Information Net-work) <telnet rlg. Stanford.edu or 36.54.0.10 or rlin. stanford. edu or 36.54.0.19
STN <telnet stnc.cas.org or 143.243.5.32>

The list of commercial databases is also expanding on the Internet. These databases can be accessed Via NISS gateway and other routes also. But to get latest information on these databases, send e-mail message to Tom Keays at: <libht@suv.bitnet or libhtk@suvm. syr.edu>.

HYTELNET and library resources

HYTELNET is the basic tool for getting around the library system. Keeping HYTELNET ready for use as one engages in a Telnet session with a remote library may be one of the best moves one can make. It is hard to imagine taking full advantage of the Internet's library resources without. HYTELNET was created for library catalogs. The main menu item, Library Catalogs <SITES>, takes us to a submenu offering a choice of libraries in America, Europe, Scandinavia, Asia, Pacific, and South Africa. Within each, the library listings are broken down by country, as shown:

Europe/Scandinavia

<ATOOO>	Austria	<ILOOO>	Israel
<BEOOO>	Belgium	<ITOOO>	Italy
<DKOOO>	Denmark	<NLOOO>	Netherlands
<FIOOO>	Finland	<NOOOO>	Norway
<FROOO>	France	<ESOOO>	Spain
<DEOOO>	Germany	<SEOOO>	Sweden
<HUOOO>	Hungary	<CHOOO>	Switzerland
<ISOOO>	Iceland	<UKOOO>	United Kingdom
<IEOOO>	Ireland		

Pressing RETURN on one of these items produces site information for various systems.

To exit, hit Telnet escape key.

Title searches: To search for a particular title, use the t=search command followed by the title.
Example: t=foundation

Author searches: To search for a particular author, use the a= search command followed by the author's name
Example: a=asimov

Subject searches: To search for a particular subject, use the s=search command followed by the subject.
Example: s=tennis

Keyword searches: To search for a particular keyword, use the k= search command followed by a string.
Example: k=cry wolf
You may use the logical operator (AND,OR< NOT) and parenthesis to group the operators. Also, $ is a wildcard character.

Example: k=car and fast
k=computer and not ibm
k=comps and (toy or game)

Using HYTELINE through Gopher

The Gopher implementation of HYTELNET is helpful because it brings a search capability into play that HYTELNET would otherwise lack. A helpful implementation of it through Gopher is available at Washington and Lee University. The address is liberty.us.wlu.edu.

LIBTEL — an on-line library resource

LIBTEL was developed by Dan Mahone, of the University of New Mexico in Albuquerque. It is available in UNIX and VMS versions, as well as through a Telnet connection. LIBS comes from Mark Mesmer at Sonoma State University in California.

Using LIBS to search remote libraries

LIBS (Library Internet Browsing Software) is a Telnet-based network access tool that helps users find and log on to library catalog systems. The Program became available in June, 1991. The system also grew in size, connecting to numerous on-line library catalogs as well as campus wide information systems (CWIS), information services, and a variety of databases. Examples are shown in Table 4.

Table 4 The Telnet connections available for LIBS

Address	Site	Login
nic.csu.net	California State University	libs
nessie.wwu.edu	Western Washington University	libs
rsl.ox.ac.uk	Menuegesteuerter hierarchischer Bibliothekszugang	libs
garam.kreonet. re.kr	KREONet, Republic of Korea	liba
info.anu.edu.au	Electronic Library Information Service, Australian National University	library
oavax.csuchico. edu	CSU Chico LIBS Information Service	libs

The screen will look as below and the standard login for a LIBS system is 'libs'. After using Telnet to reach one of these sites, and entering libs at the login prompt, you will see a menu like this one:

Libs - Internet Access Software v2.0

Mark Resmer, Sonoma State University, Dec 1992 WWU rev. 10/11/93

On-line service available through the Internet:

United States Library catalogs
Library catalogs in other countries
Campus-wide information systems
Databases and information services
Wide-area information services
Information for first time users
Special Internet connection list

Press RETURN alone to exit now or

Press Control-C Q <RETURN> to Exit at any time

Enter the number of your choice.

Internet at Indian environment

Digital information available on the Internet is expanding very rapidly. Scientific and Industrial Research Network (SIRNET) of INSDOC has been created with the objective to link S&T establishments throughout India. It has its network management centers at Delhi, Bangalore, Calcutta, and Madras.

Among Indian organisations which have put up home pages, which are virtually electronic storefronts, are the State Bank of India, the Center for Monitoring of Indian Economy (CMIE) and *The Hindu* newspaper. A number of Indian publications, including *India Today, Express Computer* and *Dataquest*, have also gone online, which means that their latest edition can be viewed by users of the Net on their computer screens.

It is not as if Indians never had access to the Internet before. Scientific and educational institutions have already got on to the Net through various dedicated networks like ERNET and NICNET. However, Videsh Sanchar Nigam Ltd. (VSNL) has done a great service now by opening its Gateway Internet Access Service (GAIS) in August 1995 to make the Net instantly accessible by anyone who has a computer, a modem and a telephone connection.

Internet library network system proposals

The Internet Library Network System with reference to Indian environment may have the following proposals:

- To establish the core facilities of e-mail for communication among Indian Library Networks and generation of user services.
- To conduct user-education workshops for Indian library staff.
- To constitute expert committees to evolve the standards, compatibility and procedure for information science applications.
- To acquire and install the necessary hardware and software for the access of international databases through Internet.
- To provide and share the information among the experts of Indian and Internet Users community around the world.

Conclusion

Internet based resources and services are very valuable particularly for the developing countries since the printed sources of information are not easily available in time from the developed countries. The network awareness and culture in India is growing with a fast speed. The Departments of Electronics, Telecommunications, Human Resource Development, CSIR, STPs and U.G.C. and similar other government organizations are taking a lead in this direction. More workshops, seminars and short-term training courses are required to develop and promote the Internet services in India. Internet services and access to it should be fully exploited to integrate the network-based resources and services by the Indian users community. Most of the valuable bibliographic databases are accessible through network only. Internet services can be used effectively for library applications by down-loading the information from remote databases. Currently every library lack funds and resource sharing among the libraries is the only answer. LAN, WAN & Internet connectivity will improve this situation to a great extent. Special concessions and permission to be given to the Indian libraries to establish and connect to Internet services.

References

1. Varhol, D. Peter. E-mail: Achieving Local & Global Communications, Computer Technology Research Corporation, 1994.
2. Camlron, Deb. The Internet: A global business opportunity, Computer Technology Research Corporation, 1995.
3. Pride, Simon. E-mail for librarians, *ASLIB*, 1994.
4. Corrall, Sheila. Strategic Planning for Library and Information Services, *ASLIB*, 1994.
5. Nagaraj, M.N., Kapoor, S.K. and Chatterjee, Amitabha. Networking of Libraries: Problems and Prospects, Indian Association of Special Libraries & Information Centers, 1994.
6. Lahiri Abhijit. An Indian Model for Database Services, Publications & Information Directorate, New Delhi, 1991.
7. Jocobson L., Robert. Desk Top Libraries, *The Chronicle of Higher Education*, November 10, 1995.
8. Bazzewski, Philip et al. Tricks of the Internet Gurus, Sams Publishing, 1994.
9. Gilster, Paul. Finding it on the Internet, John Wiley & Sons, Inc., 1994.
10. Suryadevra Sanjay. The Internet — Joining the Global Information Super Highway, *Business Standard*, Aug 19, 1995.

SIS–96, 18–20, Jan. '96, Bangalore

Use of digital libraries available on national and international networks — its status and relevance

D.B. RAMESH AND J.R. SAHU
Library & Documentation, Regional Research Laboratory, Bhubaneswar-751 013

Abstract

Gives a brief account on some of the proposed/operational national and international computer and library networks. Use and relevance of digital libraries available on these networks for providing and improving some of the library and information services is presented.

Introduction

Digital libraries aim to provide ready access to the storehouse of humanity's information. Majority of the digital libraries specialises in storing a particular subject field of information which will be interwoven together with the other participating libraries. Digital libraries combine technology and information source and allow remote access of its resources to other libraries by breaking down the physical barriers through national and international computer networks.

Digital libraries rest upon — (i) Basic human need for timely and relevant information, (ii) Accumulation of information and all the supporting infrastructure which includes users, professional associations, library and information centres and publishers; and (iii) Advances made in networking, information science, information storage & retrieval, hypermedia, human-computer interaction, artificial intelligence, etc.

Components of a digital library system

As described in a report on a Workshop on Intellectual Property Rights in a Digital Library System (1989) convened by the Corporation for National Research Initiatives (CNRI), the components of a digital library system may include — (i) Personal library system for the users, (ii) Organisational library system for serving groups of individuals or activities, (iii) New as well as existing local or distant databases, (iv) Database servers to handle remote requests, and (v) a variety of system functions to coordinate and manage the entry and retrieval of data.

Networked digital libraries

Networks implies putting together sub-sets of information centres and libraries in order to act in a cooperative manner with a predetermined obligation. It offers potential for increased access to larger resources and for a greater measure of service than the sum of all the constituent parts.

Network concept is an old one found throughout the world popularly in the form of inter-library loans and centralised cataloguing. But now there is a widespread interest in the possibility of improving operations interconnecting information systems and services, as well as inter-library operations. Networked digital libraries means a formal organisation of group of digital libraries following common pattern or design for information exchange and communication with a view to improve efficiency and effect economy in an overall manner. Digital library networking concept is a cooperative venture of all the participating libraries and transmit the data on short and long distance lines from one library to another.

National networks

Following are some of the national digital library networks which are in operation/implementation stage in the country:

INFLIBNET

In 1986, a national policy on library and information system was formulated wherein it was recommended that the national libraries should form an integrated system for a better coordination of their activities and services. The Planning Commission had set up a working group on modernisation of library and information services for the 7th Plan to suggest measures to network important libraries in the country so that their resources could be shared for optimum utilisation. UGC, under the chairmanship of Prof. Yash Pal, formulated the plan in 1988 on Information and Library Network (INFLIBNET) which proposed a mechanism to establish a network connecting libraries in universities, colleges, and institutions affiliated to the CSIR, ICMR, ICAR, DRDO and government departments. When fulfledged, it is envisaged that INFLIBNET will network 184 universities and 23 institutions, deemed to be universities, 6100 colleges and over 200 libraries affiliated to other organisations. It is designed to operate at national, regional, sectoral and local levels as a multi-service network to provide catalogue-based services, access to databases and document supply services and facilities for computer mediated communication such as e-mail, bulletin boards, etc.

NICNET

It is designed primarily to be a government information network to promote the collection, storage, analysis, transmission and exchange of data at districts, state headquarters and central ministries and departments at New Delhi for use in planning, management and monitoring of projects and government sponsored programmes. NICNET provides dial-up access to CDROM databases of the US National Library of Medicine, MEDLINE, Biotechnology Abstracts, COMPENDEX etc.

INDONET

It is a commercial distributed computer network to provide access to the computing power and software resources of CMC Ltd. to users who cannot afford. INDONET has three IBM mainframes at Calcutta, Bombay and Madras and smaller computers at Delhi and Hyderabad. The Bombay node is connected to VSNL's GPSS (Videsh Sanchar Nigham Limited/Gateway Packet Switched Services) enabling computer-to-computer communication via networks abroad. The primary objective of the project is the establishment of a network of computing centres accessible from remote parts of the country so as to deliver the benefits of information resources management to a wider section of users in the country.

I-NET

The Department of Telecommunications has established during the year 1992 a nation-wide Public Packet Switched Data Network (PSDN) called I-NET which will have nodes in 8 cities connected through high-speed links. Databases when mounted on I-NET hosts are of great interest to the library community.

SIRNET (Scientific and Industrial Research Network)

It is proposed to interconnect all the CSIR laboratories (22 laboratories have already been connected) and other R&D institutions in India. It is to harness the vast S&T information resources available with national laboratories and inculcate the habit of resources sharing among them. The ultimate aim of the SIRNET is to link the entire scientific community of the nation with the national library system and the international links to achieve efficient scientific communication. The services proposed to be available on SIRNET are — E-mail, file transfer, document transfer, access to indigenous and international databases. INSDOC, New Delhi node of SIRNET has established access to over 1800 international databases on 15 different hosts through VSNL's GPSS facility. SIRNET operates through I-NET which is the main national data network.

ERNET

It was initiated by the Department of Electronics (DOE) during the 7th Plan as a thrust area for setting up a computer network, as a part of UNDP project, for academic and research community with initial participation from 5 IIT's (Delhi, Madras, Bombay, Kanpur & Kharagpur), IISc, NCST, and DOE. The development objective of ERNET is to enhance national capabilities in the areas of design, development, research, education and training on state-of-the-art concepts of computer networking and related emerging technologies. Over 300 institutions in the country reporting a cross section of universities, government societies, R&D organisations, research institutes are already using it extensively; over 20,000 users throughout the country. Services available on the network are — e-mail, database access, file transfer, remote login, information retrieval tools etc.

DELNET (Delhi Libraries Network)

The main objectives of DELNET are optimum utilisation of funds through sharing of resources, creation of commonly usable databases and communication between libraries with the help of automation and networking. It will network 35 libraries in Delhi area. A packet switched network is envisaged with each cluster of libraries being serviced by a packet switching exchange. All databases created cooperatively are expected to reside on a central computer system and dial-up access will be provided to all participating libraries. This network will have e-mail, file transfer, union catalogue of serials, database of holdings of individual libraries, bulletin board facilities etc.

CALIBNET (Calcutta Library Network)

It is envisaged to cover 38 science and technology libraries in Calcutta metropolitan area. It will have access to the VSNL, Bombay through Indian Public Switched Data Network (PSDN). Each of the participating libraries is expected to automate their book acquisitions, cataloguing, serials control, fund accounting and circulation control. The network centre will provide on-line access to the networks union catalogue, current awareness services and inter-library loan facilities.

MALIBNET (Madras Library Network)

It has become operational since May 1993. Currently six major academic institutions are directly linked to the MALIBNET host system. Two online databases namely; Current Serials in Madras database covering 300 libraries and Contents Database covering articles published in 300 journals available in Madras libraries have been created utilising the resources available in Madras libraries. MALIBNET will offer: current serials acquired in about 50 libraries, full journal holdings of about 50 libraries, contents information of about 400 important journals, specialised databases giving abstract of articles, e-mail including international connectivity, document delivery, etc.

BSN (Business Subscribers Network)

It is being planned for providing integrated and reliable facilities to business and industrial users. Initially 500 subscribers will be connected to this network. Services to be provided include — voice and facsimile transfer, teletex, videotex, e-mail and access to remote databases. The central nodes will be at Bombay, Calcutta, Madras and Delhi and secondary nodes are proposed to be at Ahmedabad, Bangalore, Hyderabad, Kanpur/Lucknow and Pune.

RABMN (The Remote Area Business Message Network)

It has been established by the Department of Telecommunications in 1991 to facilitate exchange of messages in chosen user groups. The satellite based star network has master earth station at Sikanderabad near Delhi and Very Small Aperture Terminal (VSAT) at user premises.

BITSNET

Under the BITS programme, Microvax-II system in 1C specialised information centres in genetic engineering, cell culture, virology, plant tissue culture, immunology, bioprocessing engineering, etc. are being linked through micro-earth station and X.25 protocols.

Many more networks are likely to emerge in the near future. For instance, Defence Science, Information Network (DESINET), VIKRAM (by the Department of Telecommunications), Oil and Natural Gas Commission Network (ONGC), Bombay Library Network (BONET), Pune, Library network (PUNENET), Transportation Information Service Network (TISNET), Network for Business Commission, PAILET, COALNET, OILNET, BANKNET SAILNET, TIFACLINE, etc.

International network

Given below are some of the leading international computer and digital library networks which are in operation in the world over :

Internet

It is an international network spread over a large number of sites all over the world. The three basic Internet applications are — e-mail, remote login, and file transfer. Services such as mailing lists, directory, enquiry, usernet news, etc. TELENET, TYMNET, UNINET, BITNET (based in USA) and EURONET & DIANE (based in Europe) are some of the leading international networks which offers e-mail, remote login and file transfer services. A wide variety of public domain (free) and commercial information sources are currently available on Internet, with new sources being announced every day. These include, bibliographical/full text databases, table of contents of journals, discussion forums, preprints, technical reports, directories, teaching and training material, data archives (software, numeric data, documents), library catalogues etc.

OCLC'S Online Computer Library Centre, Inc., Ohio, USA

It is the largest computer and telecommunications network of 14,000 libraries and information centres in the world, contains about 25 million records and nearly 2 million records are added each year. OCLC provides a full range of online products and services. Its main purpose is to build the world's preeminent bibliographic database and computerised network to compile and share the world's knowledge. Libraries, all over the world, are using this vast database to catalogue 8,00 titles and borrow 10,000 books a day. Through this network libraries benefit from reduction in operational cost as well as increase in access to library materials held in other libraries. Most of the participating libraries in OCLC system are also required to be the members of regional networks the NELINET for obtaining the necessary services. It provides: rapid searching of the OCLC databases, online cataloguing of library materials, location for inter-library loans, preparation of computer output accession list, catalogue conversion, etc.

OLC (Oakland Library Consortium)

It is a consortium of three libraries located in Pittsburgh (Carnegie Mellon University Libraries, University of Pittsburgh Libraries and Carnegie Public Library). It provides online access to collections of these libraries.

LIS (Library Information System)

LIS of Carnegie Mellon University Libraries, Pittsburgh provides fast and easy access to university owned library materials as well as to commercially leased indexes and full text databases on CDROM. A simple search begins at the search window. Many work stations are scattered through out the libraries for the use of its readers.

ILLINET (Illinois Library Network)

It provides access to OCLC and other databases for Illinois libraries as well as coordinating other cooperative programs. It allows participation libraries to borrow books through resource sharing arrangement.

NELINET (New England Library Information Network)

About 200 libraries are participating in this network. It also provides OCLC services.

AGLINET (World Network of Agricultural Libraries)

It consists of a chain of major agricultural libraries in each region or country of the world within the framework of the International Association of Agricultural Libraries and Documentalists (IAALD). The main objective of the AGLINET is to promote mutual and rational exploitation of library resources for the benefit of the world's agricultural development through systematic collaboration among agricultural libraries for the efficient provision for inter-library loan services and bibliographic information.

ISONET (International Standards Organisation Network)

It is a network comprising the National Standards Information Centres and the links between them. It includes the ISO Information Centre in Geneva which has the responsibility to collect, organise, index, and disseminate information for international standardising documents similar to the national responsibility for national documents.

ChIN (International Chemical Information Network)

It was launched during 1990 with the support from UNESCO and UNIDO hosted by the International Centre for Chemical Studies of the University of Edward Kardelj Ljubljana, Yugoslovakia. The main objectives of ChIN are — to bring awareness about new developments and applications in databases, information systems and software in chemistry and related fields, to promote the development and use of chemical information systems and services; to encourage cooperation in information among chemists and chemical engineers and to develop goal oriented programmes.

DEVINSA (Development Information Network on South Asia)

It is a project conceived in 1981 by the Committee on Studies for Cooperation and Development in South Asia, an organisation of scholars representing 6 South Asian countries (India, Sri Lanka, Bangladesh, Pakistan, Nepal and Maldives) to provide information on current development activities and socio-economic research through dissemination and document delivery and thereby help avoid or reduce duplication of research.

APINES (Asia-Pacific Information Network in Social Sciences)

It is presently based at UNESCO's Regional Unit for Social and Human Sciences in Asia and the Pacific, Bangkok. This network will disseminate information to the scholars doing research in the field of social sciences in the region in order to enrich them with the pool of universe of knowledge.

RINAP (Regional Informatics Network for Asia and the Pacific)

A project proposal was worked out in joint cooperation with NIC, Government of India and RINSEAP (Regional Information Network for South East Asia and the Pacific) to evolve a low cost RINAP with computer linkages and access to mutually agreed upon national and international databases.

TIPS (Technology Information Pilot System)

It is an UNDP's information network which disseminates commercial data, business and investment opportunities, the latest prices and availability of certain equipments, and offers for joint collaboration. It has 6,000 subscribers and 50.00 entries on technology and trade information, making it one of the biggest databases in the world on trade and technology opportunities in the world. TIPS international operation centre is based in Rome with regional offices in Manila for Asia, and Caracas for Latin America.

DIALOG Information Services Inc., Palo Alto, California, USA

It provides online access to vast sources of information covering most of the published literature of the world. It offers online access to more than 450 databases from a broad scope of disciplines.

STN (Scientific & Technical Information Network)

STN International is a computerised scientific & technical information network offered jointly by the American Chemical Society and the Fachinformation Szentrum Energie, Physik, Mathematik GmbH (Fiz Karlsruhe). The Japan Information Centre of Science & Technology (JICST) will be part of this network in the future. STN offers direct access to number of databases that are located on different continents.

BLAISE (British Library Automated Information Service), ESA/IRS (European Space Agency Information Retrieval Service), etc. are some of the leading agencies also offers online access to various databases.

Relevance of these Networks to Library & Information Centres

The following functions of the library & informations centres can be improved/benefited by using the services of some of the above mentioned computer as well a digital library networks.

Library Activities

Inter-library loan, reference & referral service, circulation, document consultation, acquisition of library documents, technical processing (cataloguing & classification), collection development, preparation of union catalogues, photocopying & document delivery.

Documentation Services

Current awareness and SDI services, list of latest additions, literature searching.

Specialised Services

Access to bibliographical databases (in-house & international), distribution of CD-ROM databases, distribution of in-house databases, participation in international databases by inputting domestic information, electronic transmission of full text, tele-conferencing.

Library Management

Better utilisation of funds, continuing education for users and staff, better management of library and information centres.

Conclusion

Networked digital libraries are going to be part of our day to day professional activities in the next couple of years. In India, it is quite impossible for libraries and information centres to meet the various information needs of the present day society, escalation of the scientific field, mainly due to information explosion in one hand and the especially in the price of information on the other hand. The situation can be managed only through resource sharing which can be realised by networking of libraries and information centres. The library networking drive in India which owes its inception to the sustained efforts in recent years of NISSAT of the DSIR and NIC of DOE, DOT, Government of India. Now our country is in a position to establish, operate and manage information network to link the information resources available in the world over. We hope in the near future that all the libraries in India will be without walls and the resources of all libraries will be available to the whole user community through networked digital libraries. Whether we will be able to achieve this only time can tell.

Acknowledgements

The authors are thankful to Prof. H.S. Ray, Director, Regional Research Laboratory, Bhubaneswar for his kind permission to present this during the 15th Annual Convention & Conference of the Society for Information Science (SIS) to be held at Indian Institute of Science, Bangalore from 18-20 January, 1996.

References

1. Viswanathan, T. Library Networks in India. *Annals of Library Science and Documentation,* 38(2), 1993, pp.39-52.

2. Viswanathan, T. Application of Information Technology in Libraries. *Annals of Library Science and Documentation,* 38(1), 1993, pp.1-7.

3. Haravu, L.J. Library Automation and Networking in India — An Overview of Recent Developments. *Annals of Library Science and Documentation,* 40(1), 1993, pp.32-40.

4. Dhaka, R.P.S and Munshi, U.M. Electronic Transfer of Documents. *Annals of Library Science and Documentation,* 40(2), 1993, pp.41-47.

5. Viswanathan, T. and Raghavan J. MALIBENT: A Library Network for Madras. *Annals of Library Science and Documentation,* 41(1), 1994, pp.1-7.

6. Kaul, H.K. DELNET: An Overview. *IASLIC Bulletin,* 38(3), 1993, pp.113-122.

7. CALIBNET, *NISSAT Newsletter,* No.1, 3 (1994).

8. BONET. *NISSAT Newsletter,* No.1, 3 & 22 (1993).

9. PUNENET. *NISSAT Newsletter,* No.3, 3 (1992).

10. ERNET. *NISSAT Newsletter,* No.4. 6 (1993).

11. NISSAT. *NISSAT Newsletter,* No.1, 3 (1992).

12. Fox, E.A and Lunin, L.F. Perspectives on Digital Libraries — Introduction & Preview. *JASIS*, 44(8), 1993, pp.441-445.

13. Rajasekhar, T.B. *Communications of the ACM,* Special Issues on Digital Libraries — A review. April, 1995.

Five

Information Professionals for Digital Information Systems

SIS–96, 18–20, Jan. '96, Bangalore

Development of a curriculum for digital information systems: A learning package for library and information professionals

M.A. GOPINATH
Documentation Research and Training Centre, Indian Statistical Institute, Bangalore

Abstract

Information technology has provided new media, new modes of studies, organising, retrieving and communicating information to users of the same. The library and information professionals have to gain a comprehensive perception of the role of IT. The paper attempts to provide a modular structure for the learning of a computer based information system that is the essence of IT.

Introduction

Information technology has provided several new media, new modes of studies, organising, retrieving and communicating information to users of the same. This ability to communicate has opened up the emergence of new modes of publication from authorship through digital system for information access which is portable and transferable to any point on the globe. The role of library and information professional as a communicator of published information and processor of the same to facilitate quick retrieval, access and usage by the end users for the benefit of human development.

In order to develop in this direction, there is a need for library and information professionals to gain a comprehensive, balanced and creative perception of the role of computer communication technology. The essence of this technology is found in the understanding a computer based information system. This paper attempts to provide a modular structure for the learning of a computer based information system.

Broad structure

A basic structure of information system technology lies in its analytic approach. Here we are using the computer as a media for information. We are also using computer as an information processor — logical as well as physical. We are also looking at computer as an interface or conversational device for end-user modelling. Analytical structure is provided by the relational database management system.

Relational DBMS

There is a set of aphorisms about relational database management system. The twelve rules suggests the basic structure for information system design and development. They are structured into:

0 Foundation rule
1 The information rule
2 Guaranteed access rule
3 Systematic treatment of null values
4 Dynamic online catalogue based on the relational model
5 Comprehensive data sub-language rule
6 View updating rule
7 High level, insert, update and delete rule
8 Physical data independence
9 Logical data independence
10 Integrity independence
11 Distribution independence
12 Non-subversion rule.

Generic structure

This basic rules can be taught in modules of information system design. They can be structured into three levels, namely:

1 Information and its prospects
2 Computer system design and development
3 Interface and modelling of information for end-user.

We shall discuss these modules and analyse them.

Information

Information is a human mental product for communication of new knowledge, new happenings and new events. Information is a representation of reality — information is required for understanding, problem-solving and decision-making. Information is a strategic resource.

Systems

Actually refers to systems software. It deals with the technology of information systems. It covers what is known as hardware, computer equipment and communication equipment. We have also software technology — active and passive. Active software is the sets of instructions that tell the equipment what to do. Passive software is the data or information that is stored within, processed by and retrieved from the equipment by set of instruction.

Interface with user

Interface is an art and science. It is blend of both. It is governed by interaction of the user with a visual image or multi-media presentation. It describes the concept of information and tools used to store, organise and retrieve that information. To do this requires understanding of end-user needs, the information itself, a general familiarity with tools, technology, methods and their correlative base.

Curriculum design

Organisation of learning experiences for library and information professionals involves vertical and horizontal relationships. The vertical relationship among learning experiences is worth reference to time —the first semester, second semester etc. They build on the concept of simple to complex progression. The horizontal relationship is in terms of one area to another; for instance, the first semester talks of information and its usage; the second semester on system technology and the third semester combines both in terms of human computer interface for information access and assimilation. These shapes into a criteria of the following types namely, continuity, sequence and integration. Continuity means vertical relationship throughout the entire curriculum. Sequence means increasing breadth and depth of successive sequences. Integration means horizontal relationship of learning experiences for a unified view of the entire study programme in professional education of information personnel.

In terms of body of knowledge and intellectual content of the profession we could set a matrix of objectives, contents and performance in the learning experience of computer based information systems.

Objectives	Contents	Performance
1. Understanding the importance of being consistent in guidance	Guidance principle	Understanding cognition knowledge
2. Understand why professionals behave as they do	Reasons of Professionals ethos and behaviour	Analysis Motivation Service performance
3.Recognise and apply guidance principles	Application of guiding principles	recognition of application areas Benefits of organised team performance
4. Learn to accept the professionals Learner's rules	Professional content, Intellectual body of knowledge setting creativity	1.Innovative performance 2.Personnel motivation 3. Increased production 4.Improved quality of service
5. Recognise the importance of growth towards self-discipline	Team-growth in professionalism, systemization, recognition of change Analysis of change	Team efforts towards quality performance organisational benefit Systems development

We shall also be looking to the cognitive objectives dealing with knowledge of facets generalizations, methods processes and criteria. The types of performance to be achieved such as ability to remember, to know, to recognize, to define, to describe and to know-how. The cognitive objectives also deals with intellectual abilities and skills through which are uses the knowledge of solving problems. The abilities, skills and performance they lead to are as follows:

Intellectual Abilities and skills	Types of performance
1. Comprehension	To illustrate; to explain; to draw conclusions; to identify; to examine; to comprehend;
2. Application	To apply; to relate; to solve; to select; to use

Intellectual Abilities and skills	Types of performance
3. Analysis	To identify parts of the whole; to express relations between ideas; to analyse elements; relationships; and principles for consistency as well as discrepancy
4. Synthesis	To plan; to create; to design; to derive; abstract relations
5. Evaluation	To evaluate; to judge; to appraise, to conclude; to compare

Curriculum design: Example

As an illustration of objectives, learning experience, and generalisation.

A unit in a course: Computer-based Information Systems.

Objective	Learning Experiences for professional learning	Generalisation
1. Know what an information system is	Answer questions, observations for satisfying creativity, curiosity, doubt, and decisions	An information system is used for providing access to public knowledge
2. To recognise the inputs of thoughts, contents materials	Discussing the variety and variation of inputs, thoughts contents, their representation for retrieval, display and use	A computer-based information system consists if communication software/hardware
3. To know the use of the computer-based information systems	Discussing the users that end users should know to approach information system	An interface provision and modelling activity of end-users
4. To understand the basic principle in arranging the structure of information system	Interacting with an on-line public access catalogue	Three main stages for communication are : 4.1.1 Attraction 4.1.2 Arresting attraction 4.1.3 Communication message leading to retrieval 4.2 OPACs should be networked and easily accessible 4.3 Color of the OPAC should harmonise viewing, perceiving and absorbing information 4.4 Arrangement of the subject can follow a formal or an informal pattern.

Objective	Learning Experiences for professional learning	Generalisation
5. To select topics for inputs into computer system	Hands on experience in selecting topics for inclusion	1. The title should be crisp and short 2. The title should be expressive 3. The title should convey the meaning of display.
6. To select storage devices for information system	Identifying variety of physical storage media such as CD-ROMs, optical discs, magnetic drum Digital knowledge base	1. Elements selected should be proportional to the volume of information gathered. 2. Storage selected provide a helpful sequence 3. Storage media should harmonise with the information retrieval process
7. To prepare the materials to put in the information system	Data gathering	There is preparation of the materials to be put up on the bulletin boards should be in accordance with the theme of the system
10. To fix the background or the base for the display system	Designing windows multimedia frame work/ Browsing, filtering	The logic programming used should be flexible enough for modifications
11. To synchronise the arrangement of information system design	Provide modular logical programming	Keep display and input with economical conversion facility

Outline of course design

Paper 1

1.1 Digital information systems

Basic Structure

Importance of digital information systems

Why digital information systems are useful

International and ethical dimensions of Digital Information Systems (=DIS)

Technological and behavioural dimensions of DIS

Careers in Digital Information Systems and services

1.2 Fundamentals of Digital Information Systems

Systems concepts: Feedback and control,

Other systems characteristics

Components of a Digital Information System
Digital Information Systems components

Human Resources; Hardware resources;
Software resources

Information System Activities

Input of Date Resources
Processing of data into information
Output of information products
Storage of data resources
Control of system performance

Recognising the value/parameter
Structure of information systems

Overview of Digital Information Systems

Types of Information system

PAPER 2

Digital technology

1. Computer system concept

2. Computer system components

The central processing unit
Multiple processor
RISC processors
Computer processing speeds
Primary and secondary storage capacities

Types and trends in computers

Computer origins
Computer generations
Computer categories

Micro-computer systems
Mini computer systems
Mainframe computer systems
Networked computer systems

3. Computer peripherals
INPUT, OUTPUT AND STORAGE DEVICES

Input/Output hardware trends
Printing devices

Pen-based computers
Video input/output
Voice recognition and response
Optical and magnetic recognition
Storage trends and trade-offs
Semi-conductor memory
Magnetic disk storage
Magnetic tape storage
Optical disk storage

4. Computer software

System software/Operating system
Database management system
Telecommunication Monitors
Language transfer programme

5. Application software

Application software for users
Electronic spreadsheet packages
Database management packages
Telecommunication packages
Graphic packages
Integrated packages

6. Data Resource Management

Benefits and limitations of databases
Database Administration

7. Digital Technology Media Processing
1. Automatic test turnaround straddles Online tutorial
2. Import text by reference
3. Filter enhancements
4. Frame-viewer for electronic document distribution
5. Internet/WWW publishing support through integrated HTML document conversion tool
6. Object Team Application Systems
7. Common User Interfaces

71 Suite designed networks
72 Superior integration and automation
73 Powerful custom design tools
74 Create your own suite (Modelling)
75 Searches within hierarchical classification or domains
76 Searches against keywords or expressions containing boolean logic

77 Pervasive (network) computing model
give users easy access to information
services irrespective of their physical location
Mobility towards users' workshop

78 Building more intelligence to applications and services

8. Managewise systems

81 Asset Management
Automatic Network Discovery
Integrated Graphical Maps
Address Management

82 Server Management
Managing multiple servers
Unattended monitoring
Server optimisations
Monitor print techniques

83 Desktop management
Configuration change management
File transfer

84 Network Analysis
Traffic analysis
Detailed trouble shooting

85 Virus Protection

1. Comprehensive scanning
2. Continuous real time protection
3. Protection for mobile users
4. Automated and self-regulated maintenance

86 Macromedia Director Systems

Windows and multimedia presentation

1. Corporate presentations
2. Entertainment and educational CD-ROMs
3. Simulations
4. Visualisations
5. Digital publications
6. Kiosks
7. Electronic reference materials
8. Software demonstration disks.

PAPER 3

KNOWLEDGE BASE THROUGH DIGITAL LIBRARIES

1. Interface features

Navigation
Browsing
Filtering
Classification
Clustering
Document analysis
Searching
Mediation
Multilingual system
Visualisation Digital video
Virtuality
Multimedia system
Multimedia stream playback
Multimodal system/hypermedia
Information Retrieval/Access system
Training support.

2. Surrogation and Storage

Indexing
Abstracting
Content conversion
Database
Knowledge base
Discipline line library
Knowbots
Electronic publishing
Image processing
Intellectual property systems
Object oriented processing
Cognitive studies
Sociological study
Economic study
Repository system
Publishers library
Online archives
SGML markup

3. Management processing
   Archiving
   Digital preservation
   Digital personalisation
   Security of data
   Sustainable interaction
   Courseware presentation
   Network system
   World Wide Web
   Virtual (integration)
   Educational support

Conclusion

Digital libraries provide a new format for library and information service interface to end users. But they only lead to depth-wise structure for the classification, indexing, abstracting, annotating and reference system. They are amenable for custom-modelling and customising information services. Ultimate aim is to facilitate access to information just-in-time to the critical want of end users.

References

1. Seaman, David M. A library and apparatus of every kind: The electronic text center of University of Virginia. *Information Technology and Libraries*. March 1994, pp.15-19.

2. Warner, B.F. and Barber, David. Building the digital library: The University of Michigan's UMLIB text project. *Information Technology and Libraries*. March 1994, pp.20-24.

SIS–96, 18–20, Jan. '96, Bangalore

Hyper CAL : Design of a hypertext based computer aided learning system

SHALINI R. URS
Department of Library & Information Science, University of Mysore, Mysore-570 006

Abstract

There is a need for developing learning materials for library schools the context of new information technology. Hypercol is a project to develop learning materials using hypertext. This paper presents preliminary efforts and approaches towards developing the hyptcrcal systems.

Introduction

Recent literature and programmes and activities (workshops, conferences, and seminars) reflect a growing fascination of the profession with the computers. There has been a sharp increase in the number of conferences, seminars, and workshops on computer related issues throughout the country. By and large all of these have been devoted to the problem of computer applications to library/information work, and then its impact on education and training in library and information science (LIS). Discussions on the impact of computers to education for library and information science has been largely confined to curriculum innovations and redesigning rather than methods and media of instruction. The impact of computers, especially the inexpensive and powerful microcomputers as an innovative media for education of library and information workers has not been the focus of attention. As a matter of fact use of innovative educational media in library schools is very limited. Thus, there is a need for developing learning materials using new information technologies. Hypercal (Hypertext based Computer Aided Learning system) is a project to develop learning materials/teaching materials using the hypertext. This paper presents the preliminary efforts and approaches towards developing the Hypercal system.

Computer and teaching

Education is slowly responding to the computer age. The great educational potential of the computer has been realised and the computers have already become an essential part of school media/resource centres in the western countries. In India too, with the steady decline in the cost of computing, computers in schools and education are soon going to be a reality. The advent of microcomputer and its ready accessibility are likely to lead to a major educational revolution. A major feature of its use as a sophisticated teaching aid, a device to enhance and perhaps accelerate learning of a traditional kind, have been closely studied. Studies have indicated that there is a positive outcome and the chances of success for the individual are greater.

What is computer aided learning?

Application of computers to the process of learning and instruction is known as Computer Aided Learning. Computer Aided Instruction (CAI) and computer aided learning (CAL) are used interchangeably in the literature. Computer Aided Instruction seems to be a restrictive definition covering those areas closest to programmed instruction or strictly cognitive activities. Computer Aided Learning is often used in broader terms to embrace a wider area of learning strategies for the computer. Computer based instruction and computer based education are terms generally used to describe all aspects of the application of computer to the process of education, both instructional and managerial.

Computer Assisted Instruction Programmes are essentially tutorials in which the student responds to questions from the programme. The computer's responses vary from encouraging comments like 'very good' to explanations of why the student's response was wrong and which answer is correct. Programs 'branch out'—according to student input — in order to give practice to student's weak areas and to challenge good students. It is a logical extension of Programmed Instruction. The learner works his/her way through the instruction programme, advancing or receiving remediation depending upon their success in the exercises given.

Characteristics of CAI/CAL

The main characteristics of this sequential learning is its adaptability to learner requirements and levels. It is user paced with immediate reinforcement. The programmes are individualized and also interactive. They are also described as patient, never getting frustrated, or never tiring or irritable. Students especially appreciate these characteristics. The tactics for instruction can take many forms.

Programmed instructions can be described as: (1) drill and practice, (2) tutorial and remedial, and (3) simulations.

(1) Drill and Practice

- Programs can test, drive home or provide revision in a body of knowledge, i.e., they can test or be used to improve factual recall e.g. of scientific or historical facts, etc.
- Programmes can also be used to test particular skill.
- At a slightly higher level, a programme can be used to provide practice in using either a principle or concept, i.e., to develop 'understanding', for example by using a principle over and over again in different circumstances, or developing a concept.

In other words, drill and practice programme can provide almost endless practice in improving either factual recall, a skill, grasp of a concept or understanding and application of concepts.

(2) Tutorial

A computer programme can provide direct instruction in either factual knowledge, a concept, or a skill. This often involves breaking a learning task down in to a series of subtasks, sequencing these and providing immediate feedback to the learner at each stage. Some of the areas in which 'tutorial' type of CAI can be more effective are:

- Presenting remedial sequences.
- Providing randomly selected problems.
- Giving help if the learner asks for it or his/her responses suggest the need.
- Giving more practice at the learner's request.
- Recording the learner's responses and comments.

(3) Simulations

Simulations are based on model of a situation, usually real but sometimes imaginary. A model can be defined as simplified representation. In a simulation the model is ready-created by the programmer. The user can then alter and experiment with the external conditions and variables. affecting the model, but cannot tamper with the model itself, i.e., inter conditions. Simulations have the aim of simulating discussion, role play and sometime cooperation, of encouraging thinking, decision making and conjecture, and of developing skills, ideas and concepts in an enjoyable way.

What is hypertext

Hypertext may simply be defined as an electronic system to manage a collection of information that can be accessed non sequentially. It consists of nodes or 'chunks' of information and logical links between them. The variety of nodes and links that can be defined make hypertext a very flexible structure in which information is provided both by what is stored in each node and by the way these nodes are linked to each other. The importance of hypertext systems lies in their potential capacity to augment and amplify human intellect (Marchionini and Shneidrman, 1988).

Hypertext is an electronic writing and reading system which links together a vast network of text fragments by using the power of computer. This system allows users to traverse complex networks of information quickly. As an authoring system, hypertext enables authors to link passages, collapse or expand outlines, post notes that do not affect the main texts, and provide electronic bookmarks. From the point of view of readers, hypertext systems are more malleable than print or early text formats, as text may be accessed from multiple perspectives, for various purposes and through different search strategies.

Hypertext as a teaching/learning aid

Hypertext with its powerful, interactive nodes and associated information retrieval capabilities offers greater potential and flexibilities in the ways of presenting teaching materials. It offers great many possibilities for teaching and learning to both the teacher and the taught. The hypertext based system not only presents information on a topic but also encourages to think analytically and critically about the information from multiple perspectives. It further enables the learners to actively participate in the learning/teaching program. Another positive contribution of hypertext based system is it enables the student to develop authoring skills and add his/her views as notes, new thoughts, arguments, comments etc. Findings of several studies have provided evidence of the potential of hypertext based learning systems. For e.g.: a study at Brown University found that the students were not only able to grasp the subject quickly but also developed analytical and designing skills (Beeman, W.O. et al.).

Why CAL in library and information science?

The characteristics of library and information science education in India are:

- Given the one year duration of the dorsals (B.L.I.Sc and M.L.I.Sc), time span available for teaching/learning is short. Within this short time span of 8 to 9 months, the students have to acclimatize to the discipline and learn the skills.
- Students enter the library schools from different subject backgrounds. Hence, diversity in attitudes, knowledge, skills and levels is natural.
- Given the poor consciousness/awareness of libraries among Indians, students enter librarianship without, many a times preliminary knowledge of librarianship.
- The discipline thereby the course contents are heterogeneous in character, ranging from highly technical subjects like classification, indexing and cataloguing to purely historical and descriptive.
- It is the professional course requiring higher degree of practice orientation in teaching.

In view of the forementioned characteristics, library and information science education has to adopt multimedia approach in importing knowledge and skills. Different forms of individualized learning approaches are desirable. Conventional methods of teaching ought to be augmented with newer educational media. Computers play an important role in supporting traditional methods of teaching and training. Use of instructional systems which adopt themselves in response to learner's input is highly desirable. The educational potential of the computer and its versatility have not been fully realised in the field of Library and Information Science. CAL packages can be developed to impart skills, help to understand concepts, application of concepts and to understand principles. They can also be used for providing the necessary exercises in many practical oriented subjects like classification, cataloguing, and indexing.

Objectives of the hypercal project

The overall purpose of the project is to develop interactive Computer Aided Learning materials using the hypertext presentation system. The specific objectives from the point of view of users of the system; from a learning point of view and the designers of the package are as following:

Users point of view

It is long felt that teaching materials and teaching aught to be designed with the learner's needs and specific tabs in mind. With this in mind the following objectives for the Hypercal system were identified.

- Ease of use. The learners/users without computer background ought to be able to use the learning materials without any specific training.
- Ease of navigation. The users have to know where they are and how to reach their destination through various links.
- Various options: It is to be learner centered and learner directed and interactive.

HyperCAL - Learning system point of view

- To be a self learning tool.
- To enable understanding and application of concepts.
- To enhance grasping, factual recall and learning skills.
- To reinforce the knowledge and skills learned in the class room.
- To provide endless practice and drill.
- To provide for remedial and revision.

Designers' point of view

The objectives of the designers in undertaking this project are:

- To explore the potential of Hypertext presentation systems to developing CAI/CAL
- To gain first hand experience and insight into the design issues like annotation, display capabilities, visioning, integration, usability etc.
- To investigate the problems of implementation relating to chunking, navigation, security etc.
- To gain hands on experience in designing hypertext systems for CAI/CAL
- To hone the computing skills.

Design principles and methodology

With the above objectives in mind, the project is intended to be carried out in three phases; the first phase would involve preparing the ground for the creation of the hypertext based CAI/CAL package; in the second phase the system would be designed and prototype developed; the phase III would be testing the system with real users and incorporating modifications/changes if and as required.

Developing the knowledge base

Based on extensive literature collected on the topic and in consultation with experts in the field, the learning material in conventional form would be developed. Concepts, definitions, issues and problems along with illustrative examples would be collected and incorporated into the text.

Selection and Purchase of the Hypertext Shell

Today, as a result of considerable R&D efforts in the area of hypertext, several hypertext shell systems are commercially available. Some of the well known systems are:

- Hyper Card developed by Apple Macintosh
- Guide for IBM PC
- Hyperties developed by the University of Maryland, marketed by Cognitive Corporation, New Jersey
- Black Magic by NTERGAID
- HyperPAD developed by Brigtonbill Roberts Ltd, UK.

HyperPAD may be considered as the IBM PC version of Hyper Card and is in color and provides for visual effects and has many additional features. This can be under DOS version 2.0 or later, on all types of IBM PCs (XT, AT, PS/2, Compaq or 100% Compatible system) with any color or monochrome display or adaptor. In order to run Hyper PAD 448 KB memory is sufficient and mouse is not a necessity, as one can use keyboard without any restriction on the performance.

HyperPad is perfect for creating interactive tutorials on any topic (Boaming, 1993).

In view of the above mentioned features, especially its minimum hardware requirements and versatility, it was decided to use the HyperPAD.

Authoring the hypertext and developing the CAI /CAL package

The following design principles would be adopted during the system design and development.

Chunking

The information presented in hypertext needs to be divided into many small chunks that deal with only one topic. Every chunk works as a node in the system. The decision regarding the size of the chunk is important. If the chunks are too large, the readers may have difficulties in finding what they want to read and may also get bored by larger text. If the chunks are too small, the readers may navigate too much to arrive at the destinations and the large amount of links may make it more complicated. Therefore the optimum size of the chunk becomes crucial.

So during chunking, the original text will be divided into chunks of proper size, based on the topics. Generally, the size of chunks would be about one page (24 lines on the screen).

Links

Links are the paths that connect one node to another. Links are usually represented by words or phrases. The links may also be represented by icons. It is proposed to use icons for representing the links.

Internal links

These are links created within the learning material. The nodes at both ends of the link are located within one application.

> *Navigational links:* These are kinds of links that help readers move around the HyperCAL package. They include: Go to next page; Go to previous page; Go back to previous link; Go to home page; Quit; and many other icons.
>
> *Cross-reference links:* This kind of link brings reference information notes, relevant topics, background information to readers.

External links

This kind of links includes:

> Links between different applications of Hypertext.
>
> Links between the particular Hypertext applications and other systems.

These external links are important from the point of the possibility of integrating different CAI/CAL packages appropriately.

Screen

The basic unit of information for Hypertext is a page. One page usually occupies a full screen. Hence the design of the screen is very important to the performance of the HyperCAL package. For usability and user-friendliness, the navigation information will have to be provided on the screen.

Disorientation in a hypertext system is a common problem to the users, so navigation information is vital to an application of hypertext system.

Position Information: Disorientation usually stems from the fact that readers do not have sufficient information about their current location relative to overall structure of the text. The learning material will be structured appropriately and information about their current location is the overall structure would be indicated.

Moving around buttons: In order to enable readers to move from current screen to next destination as they like it, a set of buttons would be placed on each screen along with various icons.

Browsing

Users may be able to explore the various topics within the particular package with the help of the browsing facility. With these browsing facilities readers may be encouraged to 'travel' from one node to another looking for the information they are interested in. Keeping in view different needs of the individuals and different levels of the users, different ways for browsing like: vertical views; contents wise; facet or horizontal views may be considered and provided for.

Based on the above principles and methods the HyperCAL would be developed.

HyperCAL system architecture

The architecture of the HyperCAL system is based on the Dexter Hypertext Reference Model (Halaz & Schwartz, 1990) as shown in Fig.1. The model offers a standard hypertext terminology coupled with a formal model of the abstraction commonly found in a Wide range of hypertext systems (Conklin, 1987). The Dextel model is one of the well known proposed standards for development and comparison of hypertext systems. It is considered as a representative 'neutral' model for hypertext as it relegates to developers as many design policies as possible.

Conclusion

This project aims at developing a hypertext based Computer Aided Learning System called HyperCAL. The main objective of the project is to develop learning materials exploiting the resources and the power of the computer and the hypertext. Although hypertext offers great many opportunities for presenting and organising text in an interactive, dynamic and effective way, it also presents a whole new set of challenges for the designers to solve. Meeting these challenges and developing a prototype of HyperCAL

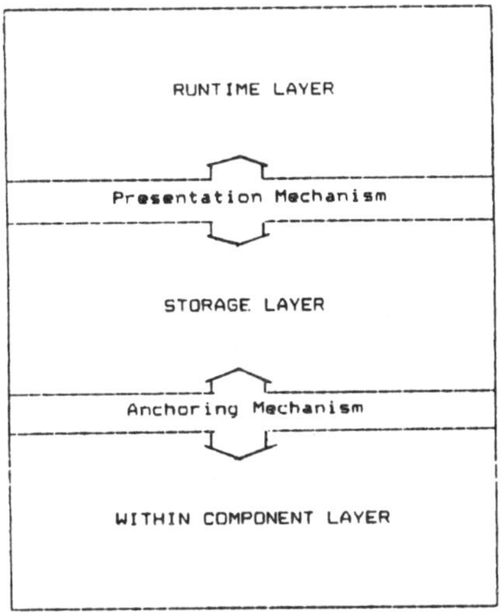

Fig 1. Dexter model layers and their interfacing mechanisms

would be an intellectually intriguing, exciting and educative experience. It is hoped that the final product HyperCAL would meet most, if not all the objectives set forth.

References

1. Akscyn, R., McCrackn, D.L. & Yodur, E.A. (1988). KMS: A distributed hypertext for managing knowledge in organizations. *Communication of the ACM*, 31(7), 820-835.
2. Beeman, W.O. et al, (1987). Intermedia — a case study of innovation in higher education, Providence, RI. Brown University.
3. Boaming, Zhang. (1993). Authoring a hypertext database —Experiences with Hyper PAD. *Aslib Proceedings*, 45(1), 19-22.
4. Conkling, J. (1987). Hypertext: An introduction and survey. *Computer*, 20, 17-41.
5. Halarz, F. and Schwartz, M. (1994). The Dexter Hypertext. *Communication of the ACM,* 37(2), 31-39.
6. Irish, P. and Trigg, R. (1989). Supporting collaboration in hypermedia: Issues and experiences. *Journal of the ASIS*, 40, 192-199.

7. Marchionini, G. (1992). Interfaces for end-user information seeking. *JASIS*, 43, 156.

8. Marchionini, G. and Shneiderman, Ben. (1988). Finding facts Vs Browsing Knowledge in Hypertext systems. *IEEE Computer*, January, pp.70-79.

9. Rada, R., Wang, W. and Birchall, A. (1993). Retrieval hierarchies in hypertext. *IPM*, 29(3), pp.359-371.

10. Raymond, D.R. and Tampa, F.W. (1988). Hypertext and the Oxford English Dictionary. *Communication of the ACM*, 31, pp.871-877.

11. Walker, J.H. and Bryan, R.E. (1988). Supporting document developed with Concordia. *Computer*, 21, 48-60.

12. Yanketovich, N., Haan, B., Meyrowitz, N. and Drucker, S. (1988). Intermedia: The concept and the construction of seamless information environment. *IEEE Computer*, 21(1), 81-96.

SIS–96, 18–20, Jan. '96, Bangalore

Towards skill development of librarians to cope with digital libraries

N.M. MALWAD
J.R.D.Tata Memorial Library, Indian Institute of Science, Bangalore-560 012

Abstract

The paper discusses the rapid technological changes brought about by the digital libraries. The acquired skills of the traditional librarians need total transformation in the changed circumstances. Considering the Indian scenario, a brief discussion is given on barriers such as economical, manpower, psychological, cultural, social and political in developing the required skills.

Introduction

The libraries have changed with time from mere static storehouses of interested collection of documents to dynamic service centres, serving all professionals and non-professionals utilising useful and need-based collection of documents. The emphasis has shifted from micro document to micro-piece of information. The medium of information storage has changed from clay tablets to paper and now to electronic and optical media of CD-ROMs. The library building is not the limit of a library, now we talk of digital library, electronic library, virtual library, and a library without walls. In such a digitised storehouse of information instead of user coming to the library, the library's vast collection is accessible and available at user's work place.

The change

As in other professions, changes have occurred for librarians too. There is one thing that does not change, and that is the phenomenon of "change" itself. Nothing is constant but "change". The changes in library catalogue codes from simple author catalogue codes to AACR2, the changes in classification schemes, the changes in institutional, organisational setups, the changes in library committee's and their suggestions, the changes in user demands for information and the user behaviour — all such changes have brought the changes in librarian's skills. Librarians have responded to the changes by adjusting or enhancing their skills.

The rapid technological changes brought about by digital libraries have opened up additional facilities, provide multiple choice of media, show improved performance and assure greater economy in time, money and effort. At the same time, there is increased complexity in selecting the right, useful, authoritative information from the vast available information sources. The user demands for information are increasing due to the knowledge of information, its availability and international competitiveness. The skills required of a librarian include acquiring information, organising it, managing it, storing it, accessing it, retrieving it, and disseminating it in the ever changing technological and social environment. The mere enhancing and adjusting the present skills of traditional librarians may not be enough. Together perhaps it requires total transformation of the skills and the way the librarians think and act.

The skills

The changes and as a response to them the skills development of librarians are summarized in Figure 1.

Librarians obtain professional knowledge through various educational courses, professional trainings and working experiences. The knowledge helps them to acquire certain professional skills that are not merely confined to mechanical skills but also include the expertise and intellectual activity. The knowledge and consequently the skills normally acquired by librarians are indicated in Table 1. It is necessary to mention here that this is an indicative summarization and should be considered as that. Infact, the knowledge and skills acquired are not mutually exclusive either in arrays and columns as indicated in the Table.

The development

The stupendous technological developments in computer, telecommunication and electronic publishing require professional skills development of librarians to acquire information, to access it, to retrieve it, and to disseminate it. The emphasis is shifting from print media to non-print electronic and multimedia. The slogans of today are 'the right to know' and free flow of information, crossing political and geographical barriers. Information is to be available and accessible to all — including poor and rich, those who can read and who cannot, literate elites and illiterate worksmen, and to blind or otherwise handicapped, to all those who need it. The knowledge comes in many forms and all forms should be accessible. Consequently, the skills required for collection, development of librarians should provide a user his right to choose from a wide range of materials in

Figure 1

Librarian's skills have changed enhancing, adjusting and transforming them to suit the timely requirement

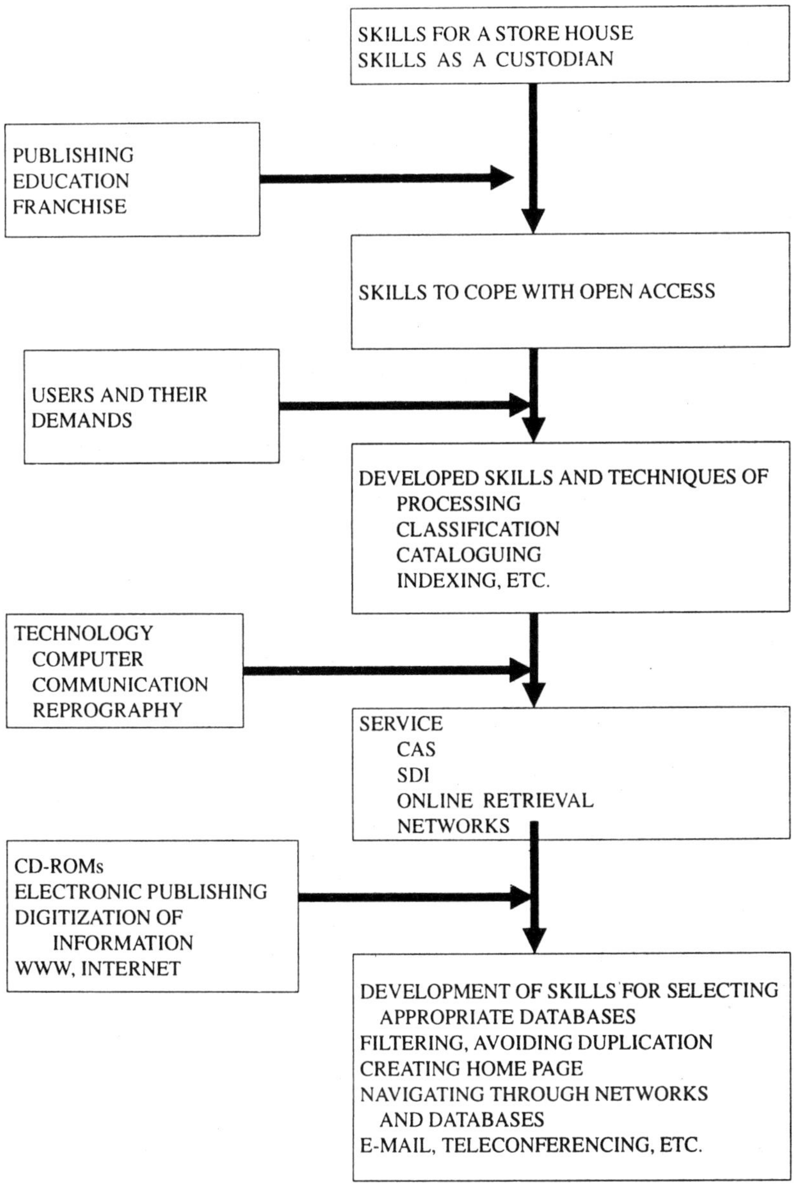

multiple formats. It should provide access to all formats and through all possible access points in the catalogues and databases.

Table 1 Professional skills normally acquired by librarians

KNOWLEDGE	SKILL ACQUIRED
Universe of knowledge, subject disciplines, their boundaries, inter-play, relationship and fusion of subjects, information-flow, channels of communication, Document — types, forms, media	Classification Cataloguing Indexing Mapping of knowledge
Document, Personnel, Users, Services, Economy, Budget	Management Administration Identification and selection of right documents, organizing them for use
Library Building	Planning, Designing, Maintenance, Economy of SPACE, TIME and MONEY
Reference/Information Sources User needs	Reference service Communication skills Public relations
Languages	Translating
Equipment, Tools, Computer, Reprographic machines Telecommunication	Systems analysis, Use of machines, Managing change
Legislation, copyright laws patent acts	Protection of rights
Writing, comprehension	Summarizing, abstracting, digesting, repackaging, information
Printing	Compiling, Editing

Electronic information

The CD-ROM, a Compact Disc Read Only Memory, of size 12 cms in diameter holds about 1,74,000 pages of A4 size print data. It is considered as a natural medium to supplement and even to replace the well known "Print on Paper". The full text in ASCII format and graphic images bring in multimedia on CD-ROM available over LAN and over WAN. The medium of CD-ROM has tremendous storage capacity for full text and graphics with user-friendly software providing easy access to its contents. The librarians need to develop skills to use CD-ROMs in saving space of library, in preserving archival material and in providing effective time saving mechanism of identifying, selecting, loading and bringing the right CD-ROM database in connection with the right user.

Electronic publishing has come to stay. An increasing number of commercial and learned societies are putting their traditional publications in electronic form. A large volume of scholarly information is increasingly becoming accessible through Internet. The Internet is an illustration of the best instances of a co-operative movement, a digitized storehouse of information, a logical global meta network of computer networks transcending political and geographical boundaries and making information available worldwide. The Internet is a physical maze and a functional wonder bringing in a worldwide testpad for scientific community.

The skills are to be developed by librarians to use e-mail effectively, to use telecommunication means economically, to use the network with fair idea of what information sources can be accessed and the skills to compile directories of information sources, services and to prepare lists of various resources.

The barriers

There are various barriers in developing adequate required professional skills by librarians in general, and in India in particular, to cope with the challenges and opportunities of digitized libraries. The specific barriers such as economic, manpower, physiological, cultural, social, political and psychological barriers are discussed briefly.

Economic barriers

A developing country such as India has the major barrier of economy in all its developmental activities. The Indian society is labour intensive and total computerisation and total digitization is hard to find full acceptability. The libraries — a larger number of them are yet to be automated, and their holdings are not available in digitized form. The libraries — even large university libraries have the problem of low availability of capital, especially, the hard currency foreign exchange. The severe budgetary constraints forced on libraries may not absorb recurring costs and expenses of international competition in developing skills to cope with digitized libraries and to provide opportunities to implement them and sustain them.

Psychological barriers

Generally, there is resistance in accepting change, due to fear of modern technology and inaccurate expectation of technology. Scientific community in the wake of digitized libraries and super highways of information still has reservations in accepting electronic information. The reasons are obvious such as doubts regarding dependable availability of electronic information, its authenticity, and integrity. The print on paper has existed and has been used for more than five hundred years. The scientific publishing and in particular, the periodicals have acquired creditability due to their well knit referring, editing and publishing system. The scientists expect the same long term and secure existence of their hard earned and scholarly work, in digitized storehouse of information.

The information seeking behaviour of users of information will continue to be similar in digitized information environment. That means the users will continue to seek information in the way they long have been doing. They seek easy access through access points they normally are familiar. They need information retrieval to be precise and prompt. The users will expect the same integrity of information from digital libraries as they are used to get from traditional libraries.

Cultural and social barriers

The cultural and social barriers include availability of a large percentage of unskilled workers, and at the same time lack of available trained personnel in the country. The library and information science schools in the country still offer inadequate and out of date curricula. There is lack of skilled technical support staff and those who are trained in modern techniques of handling information seek greener pastures and leave library jobs. There are a few facilities providing continuing education and hands on experience. In general, there seems to be low prestige attached to librarians and information professionals.

Political barriers

The political barriers in developing professional skills of librarians to cope with digitized libraries include lack of a national information policy, unstable governments and frequently changing priorities. The scientific impact is not felt at the highest levels of government. Often, there is needless tight security and secrecy of information imposed by political environment.

Barriers of existing information infra-structure

These barriers are more prominent in developing countries like India. The barriers are related to technology and availability of basic facilities. The barriers include: Poor quality of telephone service, inadequacy of postal service, unreliable power supply, stringent customs and other legal restrictions, inability to join telecommunications networks, inadequate computerization of libraries in the country, lack of library, information and technology standards, compatibility problems, lack of spare parts/ maintenance, poor library collections, absence of sufficient informal information flow.

Conclusion

Electronic information and electronic publishing have come to stay. The digital libraries have digitized collection of information at various places and not at one place. It is accessible through the use of commonly available and widely used tools. The digital library is an access environment whereas the traditional library is an ownership environment. In access environment, individual libraries need not strive to own all the collection. But still, at some place, some institution has to take the responsibility of electronic storage repository. The librarians have to develop skills to cope with the change. Their skills of classification, cataloguing, indexing, etc. are to be remoulded for data analysis, data structuring, data organization, packaging, repackaging and for providing value added services. The basics and fundamentals of librarian's skills are: to provide right information to right user at the right time. These are not going to be changed, in the environment of digital libraries. Inspite of the various barriers in the skill development, the librarians, let us hope, will acquire the timely skills, and continue to be reliable source for the information seekers.

References

1. Graham, Peter S. Requirements for the digital research library. *College & Research Libraries,* pp .331-339, July 1995.

Six

Critical Views on Efforts and Achievements

SIS–96, 18–20, Jan. '96, Bangalore

Digital libraries: Challenges and issues

I.K. RAVICHANDRA RAO AND P. SUMA
Documentation Research and Training Centre, Indian Statistical Institute, Bangalore-560 059

Abstract

Digital libraries are heterogeneous in nature with hard copies to online databases. DL calls for advanced information technologies. This paper discusses some of the issues and challenges relating to digital libraries.

Introduction

The digital revolution has altered the way societies function at the global, local and personal level. In this revolution, we have seen certain changes in information field; especially in relation to collection, storing, processing and transmitting of information. These changes have resulted into the evolution of libraries into digital libraries.

An attempt has been made in this paper to discuss scope, definition and characteristics of digital libraries, challenges and issues concerning the digital libraries and the Indian scenario.

Definition

The digital libraries may be defined as the new way of carrying out the functions of libraries encompassing new types of information resources, new approaches to acquisition (especially with move towards accessing to different library collections and their sharing); new methods of storage and preservation; new approaches to classification and cataloging; intensive use of electronic systems and networks and dramatic shifts in intellectual, organizational and electronic practices[2]. It is also known as a distributed text-based computerized information systems and services. It may have several provisions to access documents, those are of high value, mostly from outside the organization. In a simple language, we can even define digital libraries as libraries which have number of machine readable publications and facilities for remote access to several databases.

The era of digital libraries perhaps began with emergence of electronic journals. They are now becoming very popular, especially because of the fast emerging networks. The networks help us to access such electronic journals from different servers. Electronic journals are easy to distribute, less expensive and easy to search. It occupies less space, possibility of instant access, availability of the information in the multimedia environment. It can stay for many years. There are now many electronic journals; for example, AAA'S Online Journal of Current Clinical Trails, Lancet, CPSERVER, etc. In the context of digital libraries, electronic publications refer to publications of primary journals or documents in machine readable form. In the early days of electronic libraries even the machine readable databases were referred to as electronic publications.

Characteristics of digital libraries

Digital libraries (DL) require undoubtedly digital technologies. The DL is a heterogeneous library which contains hard copy to online systems. The full-fledged DL is one in which all the information is available in the digital form. This may however be difficult to achieve. Until recently, the DL consisted of mostly electronic documents which are of reference type. Now-a-days, most of the documents are primary in nature. Further, queries received and processed are again of reference type in nature. The digital records from both local and foreign databases may be used repetitively for several purposes. Thus, a considerable saving in effort, time and resources is possible.

Requirements of digital libraries

DL requires well-tested and proven information technologies including the multimedia kit. Much of the work in digital libraries is achieved through e-mail service, by participating in usernet(s), by accessing the databases or servers through networks, like Internet. Locally developed databases will contribute a lot to develop digital libraries. In other words, the components of digital libraries are[3]:

- Local library system, with adequate PCs having LAN, local databases in machine readable form, CD-ROMs etc, provision to provide e-mail service, access to servers, and to remote databases etc.
- Networks, including the network of networks.
- A variety of system functions to coordinate, manage the entry and to retrieve data.
- Well-trained man power.

Challenges and issues

The highest priority of a library, digital or any other, is to serve the research needs of clientele. The development, maintenance and extension of its collection and its technologies must be supportive as well as subordinata to this primary objective. However, in digital library environment:

Functions of authors, publishers, vendors, and users, etc. will vary. Both information professional and user will do the work of collection, storage, dissemination and organizational work. The user's work is however called as personal file collection. Any one who has access to computer in a network can easily become a publisher. An author merely by posting messages to an online discussion group, she/he becomes a publisher. In such environment, information appears in one day and can be altered or disappear in the next day. In this situation, how to give a citation? How to collect a copy of the required information? How to organize the information? These are the debatable questions?

Only digital information is disseminated; some are produced locally, and most information is obtained by remote access; most of these information are less permanent in nature. In these circumstances, it is very difficult for the professional to decide: What should be organized? Who should do it ? What standards to be followed ?

Users only locate the information; information is not usually structured, no rules or codes are followed and no one to control the information that is made available.

The data or information will be of different type. To organize these data or information, we require cataloguing practice and it calls for an appropriate data model for organizing data with standard format. The tools like Gopher, Mosaic, etc. help in cataloguing, searching and retrieval of information from these digital libraries.

Specialized technologies are needed for compressing as well as for organization of information. Database management methods whether extended relational or object oriented, not only are needed to support direct use of data collection in DL, but also will help to handle catalogues, royalty administration, security control and other services. Text analysis and information retrieval techniques are crucial for converting, indexing, representing, searching and presenting desired information.

Issues concerning intellectual property

The problems of protecting intellectual property are now being discussed for many years. Mechanisms such as copyright, patent encryption, license agreements and international treaties are being used and violated during past. In digital libraries, circumstances are such that it is inevitable for many nations to honour such mechanisms. Copyright issues are infact becoming bad to worse in DL, since copying of electronic information is easier than print copying and it can be done without human labor. In the digital world author himself becomes user as well as the publisher, and vice versa. In such circumstances, it is difficult to identify publishers, authors and users. Who are the authors? Who are users? Who are publishers? In such circumstances present laws are inadequate to handle copyright issues. Further, cost of software drops dramatically and copying the software is not worth the effort. In such cases, there is no need for any mechanism to protect intellectual property.

These mechanisms mostly designed to protect economic benefits of inventors for their R&D work. These are found inadequate to protect "information" for various reasons. Some of the reasons are:

a. Scholarly works are usually supported by the public fund and there is a public interest to have some degree of guarantee for its possible "public access", especially with a country.

b. Due to the rapid developments in information technologies, cost of reproduction becomes insignificant.

c. Protection of scholarly works may be counterproductive.

d. Rights of the one individual are considered against the rights of the many individuals.

If libraries buy a digital copy of a newly published copyrighted text for its collection and if its access to material is open to all, then first sale of digital copy will be the last sale[5]. Both authors and publishers hardly get any compensation in such situation. In this context, how can we apply the present day copyright laws?

Users may be charged for each access, downloading from servers, and or each kind of use of digital library collection. This would provide a revenue for publisher, authors and libraries. Further, to prevent serious erosion of such revenue system, one may introduce rules about what the users can do with the copies they downloaded from digital library collection.

Issues concerning the information value

The quality and performance of industrial products, professional services, such as, medical and legal services, are determined by the standards and guidelines as prescribed by the national agencies, customer's requirements and professional ethics. Industries are accordingly liable to maintain the qualities and performances.

This, however, cannot be extended to information since it is bought based on subjective evaluation of the reputation or credentials of the vendor. It is in this sense that information is inherently different from industrial products[4]. The question in this regard to be resolved is whether the user or vendor should bear the risk that the information is wrong.

Further, the value of the information is difficult to measure. In the context of DBMS, for instance, it is the owner of the database, who decides whether or not a bibliographical record should be included in the database. Authors have no role to decide whether or not it should be covered in the database. When it comes to its usage, it is again, the user (and not the author) who decides how useful it is? In fact, in the context of S & T information, value is not often measured in terms of the citations it received, its circulation, its use within a library, etc. Industries and governments decide its value purely based on the return of investments, tax returns, jobs created etc. Based only on these factors, most of the legislations for its protection are in fact introduced. Information value in general varies from time to time, country to country, depending upon users requirements. From these points of view, whatever we receive in a digital library unlikely to have the desired "value", especially when compared to traditional libraries.

Cultural and political sovereignty

Information flows in digital libraries from all over the globe. This may result into a domination of few multinational corporations in information products and services. This will have cultural implications for those who want to buy and use information. This, in turn, may lead to increased government protection of culture-based information industries (particularly in multimedia environment). Consequently, access to foreign sources of information may become difficult.

A partial solution in this regard was suggested by UNESCO[1]. It suggested that every country should have a national information infrastructure for generation, processing and for a wide distribution of information, most economically, without suppressing the national culture.

Indian scenario

Digital libraries like in other part of the world are fast emerging even in India. Due to the economic reasons, non-availability of hardware and software, absence of good number of usernets and other difficulties, we are unable to enter into DL system in a big way. The problems that are faced while entering into the digital world can be listed as follows:

- lack of adequate local and national infrastructure for handling IT and networks
- lack of well trained manpower
- non-availability of locally developed machine readable documents
- non-availability of well organized 'usernets' in different subjects both in public and private sectors
- possible control and censorship of information by the local bodies, governments or other entities
- lack of freedom to access international electronic documents.

Computer literates in India are still in less number, especially in library and information field. Even after many years of "computer talks", library automation activities are still in poor state of affairs; library networks are still in their infancy stage. Under these circumstances, handling digital libraries is extremely difficult.

Further, information requirements vary from information rich country to information poor country. The information requirements of general public that of scientists varies from each other. The existing digital libraries hardly satisfy the user's needs in India. This is primarily because of non-availability of electronic documents of local interest.

In a survey of 76 e-mail records from a bulletin service in library and information field in India, we observed that the majority of information (21.66%) received is related to simple queries and enquirers regarding addresses (where abouts?) and call for papers. The other information related to queries on CDS/ISIS and CDROMs (18.42%), software and hardware (15.79%), bibliometrics (10.53%), self promotion or individual promotion or company activities (7.89%) and miscellaneous (25%). This study further indicates one of the services of a digital library in library and information field hardly satisfy the research needs. Also this suggests that we must have a well defined and designed databases with excellent collection of records to meet the users. Without such databases, particularly primary electronic journals, digital libraries will not exist.

IConclusion

Digital libraries use of information technologies, communication technologies, online databases, CD-ROMs, multimedia databases, "usernets", e-mail services; digital libraries require access to national and international networks etc. The issues which should be dealt with before the implementation of digital libraries are information protection, property rights, privacy, relevance of information available in digital libraries as well as its value and data security. In order to have a good digital library system in our country:

- We must study and understand the transformation which are now taking place in the technology field.
- Co-operation and co-ordination among all segments of the information sector (— workers, information generators, processors, distributors, government and user).
- Must develop mechanisms for sharing of information at local, national, regional and international level.
- Must implement a comprehensive and cohesive information technologies.

References

1. Cowkell, A.E. Privacy, Security and freedom in the information Society. *Journal of Information Science*, 4(1), 1982, pp.3-8.
2. Fox, E.A. et al. Introduction to Digital Libraries. *Comm. of the ACM,* 38(4), pp.22-8.
3. Garrett, John R. and Lyons, Patrice A. Towards an Electronic Copyright Management System. *JASIS,* 44(8), pp.468-73.
4. Leaser, Barry. Information protection issues in the economy. *Bulletin of ASIS,* 14(3), pp.21-22.
5. Samuelson, Pamela. Copyright and Digital Libraries. *Comm. of the ACM,* 38(4), pp.15-21.

SIS–96, 18–20, Jan. '96, Bangalore

Digital Libraries: Attributes and architectures

T.B. RAJASHEKAR
National Centre for Science Information (NCSI), Indian Institute of Science, Bangalore-560 012
(E-Mail: raja@ncsi.iisc.ernet.in)

Abstract

Network based information provision and access, on a global scale, has become easy and convenient due to the Internet and the WWW technologies. With equally impressive developments in associated communication and computer technologies, several digital library projects have been launched in developed countries. An attempt is made in this paper to provide an understanding of digital libraries, focusing on their technical aspects. Such an understanding could be useful for librarians in India planning to embark on similar efforts. Starting with two current definitions of digital libraries, the paper provides descriptions of several digital library projects and discusses architecture of two projects in detail. An attempt is then made to indicate key attributes and technical issues considered important by workers in this area. The paper concludes with a few remarks in the Indian context.

Introduction

Electronic publishing and information access activities have become very easy and convenient today, thanks to the Internet and the World Wide Web (WWW) technologies. With parallel developments in high speed communication links, low cost digital storage solutions, powerful desk-top and workstation based servers and multi-media hardware and software technologies, the situation today is considered ripe for initiating several digital library projects. While these projects aim to develop prototypes and demonstrate variety of digital libraries through development of required technologies, they are also expected to come to grips with a number of technical and non-technical issues related to digital libraries. Efforts are also being made to formulate generalised digital library architectures[1], enabling the development and inter-networking of world wide digital libraries. Lessons from the various digital library projects are also expected to provide the impetus and inputs facilitating the emergence of a consensus digital library architecture.

In this paper focus is on technical aspects of a few ongoing digital library projects. Starting first by providing two current definitions of digital libraries, brief descriptions of several current projects are given. Architecture and hardware/software infrastructure of two digital library projects — NCSTRL (Networked Computer Science Technical Report Library) and Red Sage, a Health Science Digital Journal Library project, are then presented in some detail, with screen shots of their Web interface. An attempt is then made to indicate attributes and technical issues considered important by workers in this area. A few observations in the Indian context forms the conclusion.

What are digital libraries?

Let us consider two current definitions given by workers in this area:

Definition 1

'*Digital libraries are systems providing users with coherent access to a very large, organised repository of information and knowledge*' as defined by the Working Group of the U.S. govt's Information Infrastructure Technology and Applications (IITA)[2]

This group, which met in May 18-19, 1995, addressed several issues related to 'inter operability, scaling, and the digital libraries research agenda'. The group made several key observations: 1) digital libraries would need to span both print and digital materials, for the foreseeable future, 2) objective is to develop information systems providing access to a coherent collection of material, more and more of which will be in digital format as time goes on, and to fully exploit the opportunities that are offered by the materials that are in digital formats, 3) there would be many digital repositories, a given digital library system should provide a coherent, consistent view of as many of these repositories as possible, and 4) from the user's point of view, there should appear to be a single digital library system (integrating personal information, work group and organisational information collections and public digital libraries).

Definition 2

"*Digital library is a global virtual library — 'The Library' of thousands of networked electronic libraries*" as given by Ray R. Larson. CSTR Electronic Library project group, Univ. of California, Berkeley, 1994[3].

According to Larson, there will be a vast population of users scattered around the globe who are able to access, easily and conveniently, the complete contents of thousands of large and small repositories containing texts, images, sound recordings, videos, maps, scientific and business data, as well as hypermedia combinations of these elements. The library must, therefore be a network based distributed system with local servers responsible for maintaining individual collections of digital documents ranging from sets of electronic texts to video-on-demand services.

With these explanations as background, let us take a brief look at a few ongoing digital library projects.

Digital library projects

Several digital library projects have been undertaken since the past couple of years, mainly in U.S.A. and Europe. Chief among these are the six NSF/ARPA/NASA funded project initiatives. We discuss these and a few other projects here[4]. We focus on the *location, goal* and *content* of these projects.

NSF/ARPA/NASA digital libraries project initiatives

Funded through a joint initiative of the National Science Foundation (NSF), Department of Defense Advanced Research Projects Agency (ARPA), and the National Aeronautics and Space Administration (NASA), U.S.A., the Initiative's focus is on to dramatically advance the means to collect, store, and organize information in digital forms, and make it available for searching, retrieval, and processing via communication networks — all in user-friendly ways. It may be noted that all these projects include strong participation by external agencies from the industry (for e.g. from computer companies and publishers), and other research institutes. Total funding is about US $ 24.4 million, for a duration of 4 years.

Informedia digital video library: Located at Carnegie Mellon University (http://fuzine.mt.cs.cmu.edu/im/informedia.html), the objective of this project is to develop technologies for full-content search and retrieval from digital video libraries. The project team is creating a test bed to enable K-12 (10+2 level in India) students to access, explore, and retrieve science and mathematics materials from the digital video library, combining speech, image and natural language capabilities. It will initially contain 1,000 hours of video.

Illinois digital library project: This is located at University of Illinois, Urbana Champaign (http://www.grainger.uiuc.edu/dli). Focus here is on providing comprehensive search and display of complete contents of articles, including text, figures, equations and tables to articles from engineering and science journals, obtained in SGML format directly from the major partners in publishing industry. Some of the software and protocols used include Mosaic, BRS Search, Z39.50, etc.

Alexandria digital library project: Located at University of California, Santa Barbara (http://alexandria.sdc.ucsb.edu/), goal of this project is to provide access to collections of variety of spatial information, including digitised maps, images, air photos, and other graphical information, relating to the counties of Santa Barbara, Ventura and Los Angeles in California state. The range of users include school children, academic researchers and the general public.

University of Michigan digital library project (UMDL): The UMDL project focuses on earth and space sciences (http://sils.umich.edu/UMDL/Homepage.html). A related project, the Journal Storage Project will digitise and make available all issues from the first publication through 1990 of 10 economics journals.

University of Berkeley digital library project : The goal of this project is to develop technologies for intelligent access to massive distributed collections of multi-media documents including photographs, satellite images, videos, full text documents, comprising multiple terra byte databases (http://http.cs.berkeley.edu/~wilensky).

The Stanford digital library project: The goal of this project is to develop technologies for a single, integrated and "universal" library, composed from the large numbers of emerging individual heterogeneous repositories, ranging from personal information collections to collections in conventional libraries and large data collections shared by scientists. Technology developed in this project will provide the "glue" that will make this worldwide collection usable as a unified entity, in a scalable and economically feasible fashion (http://www-diglib.stanford.edu/diglib).

University of California CD-ROM information system: This system provides online access to a CD-ROM based database, through the Web, consisting of published federal (U.S. govt.) statistics covering 1990 census and foreign trade data, equivalent of about 260,000 books. Roughly 135 GB of data is stored on 270 CD-ROM discs, handled by 45 Pioneer 6 disc CD-ROM jukebox changers connected to 4 Sun SPARC workstations (http://cedr.lbl.gov/cdrom/doc/cdrom.html).

CORE project : This project is being carried out at Cornell University, to understand issues involved in providing access to an electronic library of primary journal articles in chemistry. The project covers five years of 20 primary journals published by the American Chemical Society, consisting of about 4,25,000 pages. The data is maintained in two forms — scanned images stored on Sony WORM juke boxes and as SGML marked up ASCII files, for each page, stored on a SUN Unix file sever. Another SUN machine is used as a print server. The system supports full text, Boolean searching. The system is on an ethernet LAN, with SVGA monitor based user terminals.

British Library's Initiative for Access: This is a program of 20 development projects, initiated in 1993, to investigate hardware and software platforms for the digitisation and subsequent networking of a range of library materials. The Patent Express Jukebox is one of the major projects — providing in-house access to over one million of the current U.K., U.S., and European patents held on 16 linked CD-ROM jukeboxes, each holding 100 discs containing 800 patents. The software searches and prints high-quality patent copies for users in under two minutes.

Digital library architecture — Case studies

NCSTRL — Networked Computer Science Technical Report Library

NCSTRL[5] is a direct descendent of two earlier systems, WATERS (Wide Area Technical Report Service), sponsored by the National Science Foundation (NSF) and Dienst CSTR (Computer Science Technical Reports) project sponsored by the Department of Defence's ARPA. WATERS and Dienst have been operational since about the middle of 1993. NCSTRL, put into operation on 1st of November 1995, combines the best of both the projects. NCSTRL provides unified access to catalogue records and complete documents of computer science technical reports stored in distributed servers around the world, through WWW. Participation in NCSTRL is open to all academic departments awarding Ph.D. in computer science/engineering and to research facilities of industry and government. Currently over 200 departments around the world are participating. NCSTRL can be accessed free of cost on Internet using any WWW browser (http://www.ncstrl.org/).

NCSTRL is aimed to provide financial and scholarly advantages to all its users and participants. Researchers can gain easy and quick access to a large body of scholarly material. Authors gain a wider audience, including those from less well-known institutions, as everyone has an equal chance of having their reports noticed. Departments get a clean, effective management system for their technical reports and eliminate much of their current copying and mailing charges. Several computer science departments are estimated to have already saved thousands of dollars.

NCSTRL allows search by author, title or abstracts, and viewing of the document as an HTML document or in PostScript. A few screen shots of the Web interface are shown in figures 2 to 8.

NCSTRL Architecture: The technology underlying NCSTRL is a network of inter-operating digital library servers. These servers provide three services: **repository** services that store and provide access to documents, **indexing** services that allow searches over bibliographic records, and **user interface** services that provide the human front-end for the other services. These services inter-operate using an open protocol, enabling development of new kinds of services (such as contents alerting services).

At individual departments, NCSTRL can be installed at two levels — **Lite** and **Standard.** Lite version is intended for sites with few resources needing lower starting investment, while Standard version will offer greater functionality. Participating sites can chose to install either of them. Lite sites need only to put their reports online (via FTP or HTTP) and edit a catalogue file with the **techrep** tool (supplied with the software). The user interface and the index service for a Lite site executes on the central NCSTRL server, which acts as an NCSTRL gateway for all the Lite sites. NCSTRL Standard software will enable full local indexing and access, including thumbnail browsing and online reading. NCSTRL architecture is shown in Fig. 1.

No matter which version is installed, the complete technical report collection will be available to all parties in a manner totally transparent to the users of NCSTRL.

Some *current and future plans* of NCSTRL include:

- Use of the handle server architecture developed at CNRI[6] (Corporation for National Research Initiatives), providing scalable, extensible location-independent naming for documents.
- Support a few digital libraries features like multi-media, annotation and storage replication.
- Adoption of an open protocol will enable NCSTRL to migrate to more advanced technologies and to emerging national/international digital library architectures.

The Red Sage digital journal library project

This is a four year project which began in 1.1.1993 at University of California, San Francisco (UCSF), dedicated to the health sciences, in collaboration with AT&T Bell Labs and about 20 publishers including

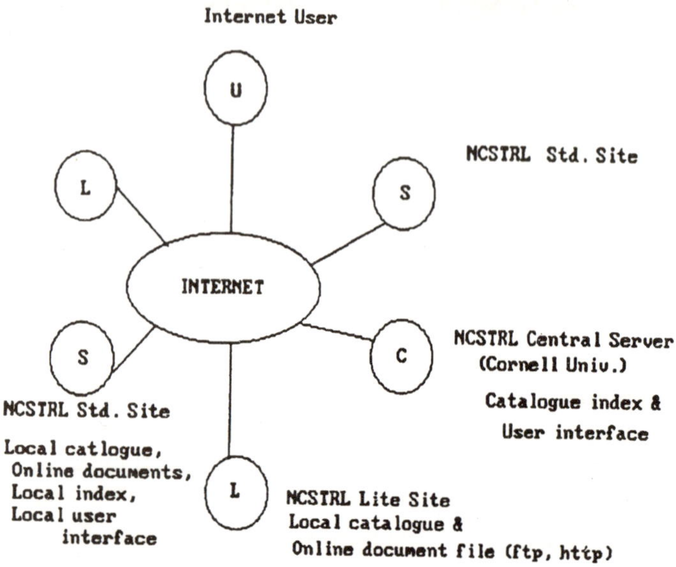

Fig.1 NCSTRL Architecture

Fig.2 NCSTRL — Portion of opening screen (http://www.ncstrl.org)

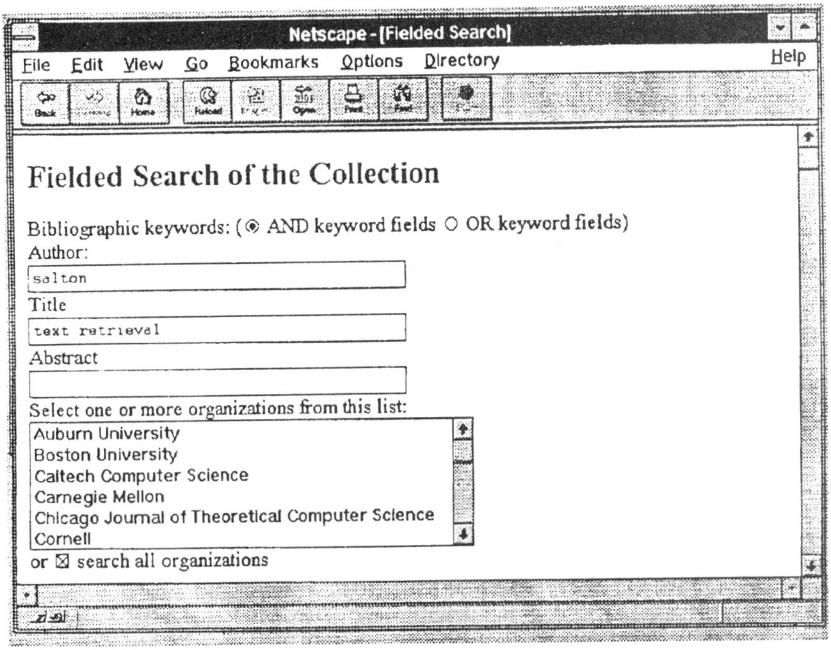

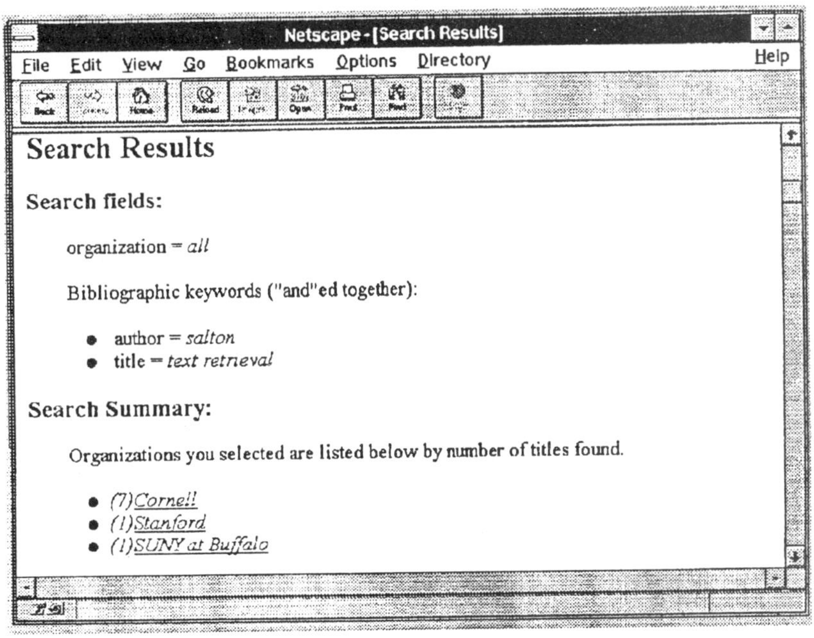

Fig.3 NCSTRL — Sample search for papers by 'Salton' on 'Text retrieval'

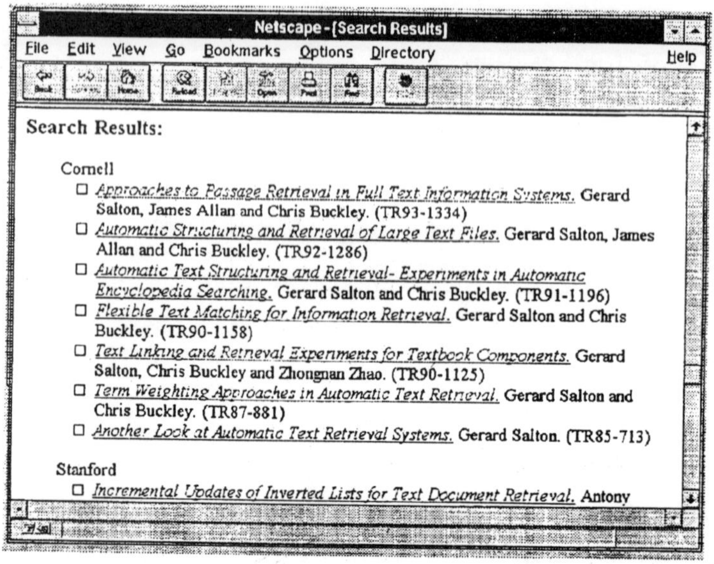

Fig.4 NCSTRL — Search result screens

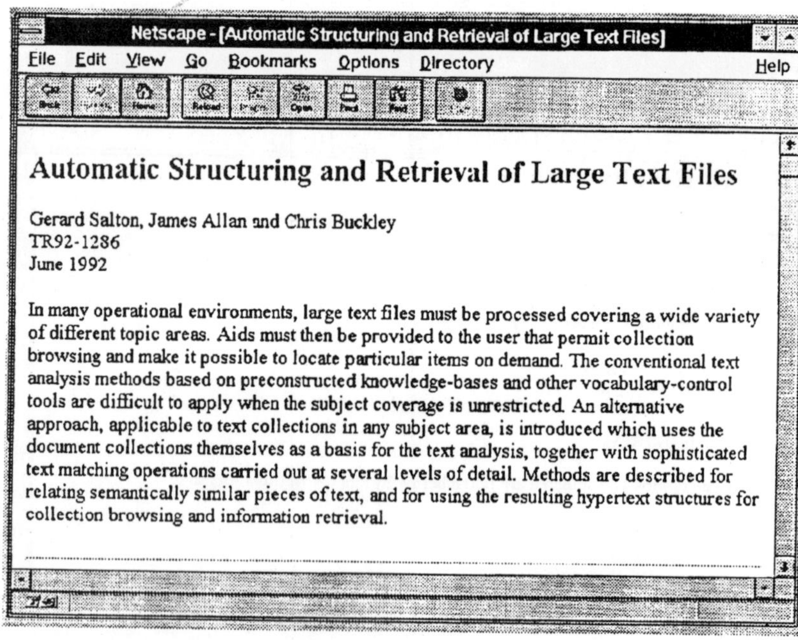

Fig.5 NCSTRL — Retrieving the abstract (Item No.2 in Fig.4)

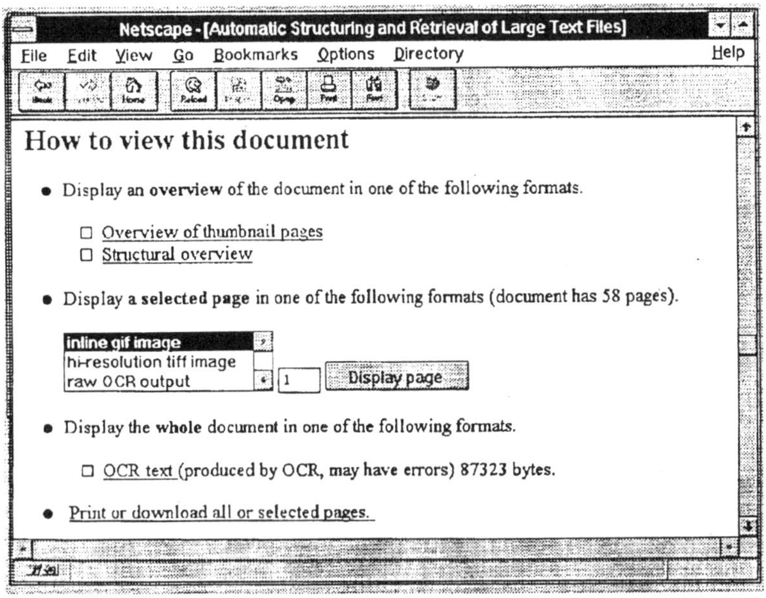

Fig.6 NCSTRL — Document view options

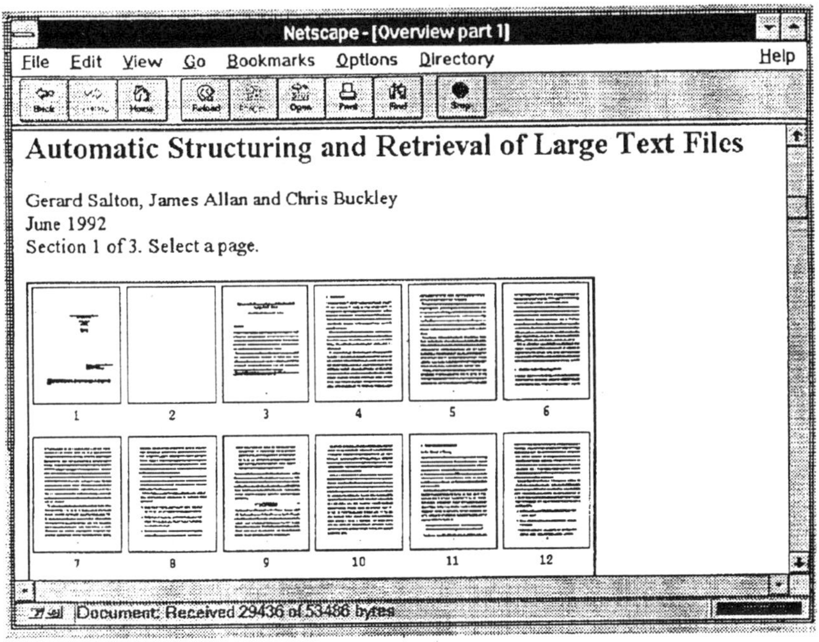

Fig.7 NCSTRL — Portion of the thumbnail pages display

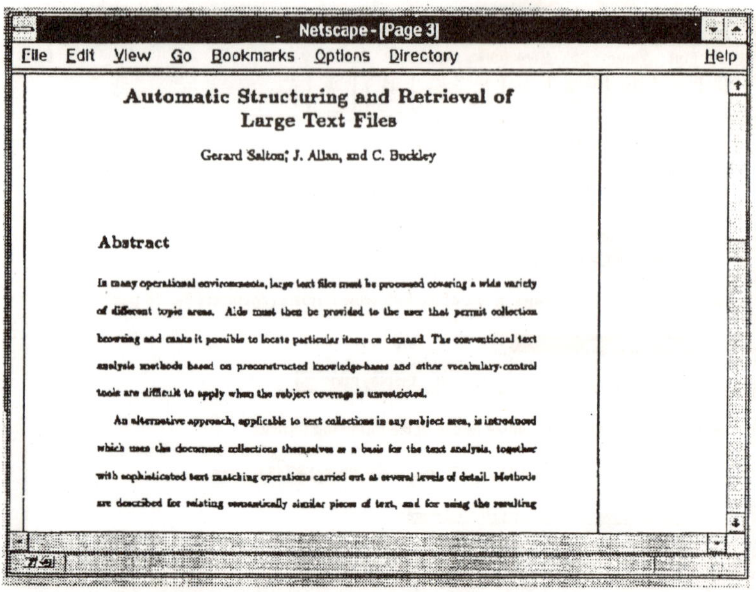
Netscape - [Page 3]

File Edit View Go Bookmarks Options Directory Help

Automatic Structuring and Retrieval of Large Text Files

Gerard Salton,* J. Allan, and C. Buckley

Abstract

In many operational environments, large text files must be processed covering a wide variety of different topic areas. Aids must then be provided to the user that permit collection browsing and make it possible to locate particular items on demand. The conventional text analysis methods based on preconstructed knowledge-bases and other vocabulary-control tools are difficult to apply when the subject coverage is unrestricted.

An alternative approach, applicable to text collections in any subject area, is introduced which uses the document collections themselves as a basis for the text analysis, together with sophisticated text matching operations carried out at several levels of detail. Methods are described for relating semantically similar pieces of text, and for using the resulting

Fig.8 NCSTRL — Portion of the full page display

Springer-Verlag, Blackwell Scientific, Chapman and Hall, American Chemical Society, Oxford University Press, etc.

The goal of the Red Sage project[7] is to explore the technical, educational, support and behavioural issues associated with the electronic delivery of primary journals to scientists and clinicians at their place of work, by building and deploying a working Digital Journal Library of the Health Sciences at UCSF. Participating publishers hope to gain understanding of how they need to modify their print production processes to produce electronic versions of journals. Eventually the Red Sage project hopes to develop a business model for electronic journals that will be satisfactory to universities and libraries, publishers and technology providers.

Content and access: 71 health science journal titles, beginning with the January 1993 issue. Initially, all content is stored in bit-mapped page images. The collection became available to UCSF faculty and students in January 1994. A demo version is available on the Web (http://www.ckm.ucsf.edu/Projects/RedSage/). Access to the journals is modeled on a traditional library metaphor, with journal titles arranged in alphabetical order, with most recent issue on top. Red Sage supports browsing the journals through table of contents, journal images and retrieve articles of choice. Users can also establish custom profiles for subscriptions and keywords, and receive alerting message by e-mail when new contents are loaded. An underlying text database also supports users to do limited full-text searching.

Architecture: Red Sage uses AT&T's RightPages software which is designed as a client/server system. Clients have been developed for different UNIX platforms, including SUN, DEC and Silicon Graphics, and Macintosh. WWW access through Windows clients is being developed. The file server is a 4 processor SPARCCentre 2000, with 640 MB RAM running SOLARIS operating system, connected through a high-speed FDDI connection to the campus backbone. A large disk cache allows new and recently used articles to be retrieved quickly. Also attached to the computer is a DISC Model 350 optical jukebox (expandable to 500 GB) providing 250 GB of permanent storage for the electronic journal collection. The database engine underlying Red Sage is EMASS AMASS.

The overall time required to display a page image ranges from less than one second to a maximum of 7 seconds when the system is being heavily used and images must be retrieved from the optical jukebox.

Some *current and future* plans of this project include :

- Extension of Red Sage from a campus facility to a regional Biomedical Digital Journal Library, is being evaluated, by linking (ATM line link) between UCSF library and Genentech, a major biotechnology firm, about 10 miles from UCSF. Scientists at Genentech have been able to access the Red Sage journals. Usage and network performance data is being collected.
- Direct input from publishers through SGML and other standards.
- Offer access to Red Sage through WWW.
- Linkages between the Red Sage journals and Medline.
- Evaluate eventual commercialisation of this experimental Digital Journal Library of the Health Science.

Attributes of digital libraries

What are the salient features of a digital library? Based on the digital library projects and architectures described earlier, we can arrive at an indicative list of important features of digital libraries. It is not intended to be an exhaustive list, nor does it suggest that a specific digital library should possess all the features.

Content : The unit of a digital library is a **'digital object'** (or information object)[1,2,3] which may be textual, audio, video, image, numeric, computer programs, or multi-media composites of such components. Some examples include books, magazines, videos, newspapers, satellite and spatial data (digital maps), scientific data sets (e.g. the human genome project), textual databases (e.g. of classic works), electronic journals, USENET news and listserv archives, digital encyclopedias and dictionaries, bibliographic indexes, directories and meta databases.

Key features: A digital library is expected to support the following features.

- Provide access to very large information collection(s)
- Focus on providing access to primary (or complete) information, not merely surrogates or indexes
- Support multi-media content
- Network accessible
- Provide user friendly interface
- Use declarative representation of documents (e.g. tagged SGML text), in addition or as against image, PostScript, etc. forms
- Unique referencing of digital objects[6]
- Enable 'link' representation to local/external objects (hypertext)
- Clearly separate the digital library and the user interface by employing client-server architecture
- Support advanced search and retrieval
- Available for a very long time (i.e., should not be dependent on specific hardware and software)
- Support traditional library missions of collection development, organisation, access and preservation
- Integrate personal, group, enterprise, public digital libraries
- Support publishing, annotation, and integration of new information.

Technical issues in the development of digital libraries

Some of the major technological challenges[2,4] and issues drawing the attention of workers in this area include:

— High band width computer networks supporting efficient multi-media document transfer
— Open communication protocols (client-server, e.g., Z39.50 for IR)
— Information access tools (browse, display and search tools)
— Meta databases (databases that describe and provide links to other databases/information sources)
— Electronic publishing tools (personal, institutional, publisher)
— Data compression
— Digital storage
— Scanning and conversion technologies
— Media integration technologies (multi-media)
— Advanced retrieval, indexing, natural language processing, routing and filtering
— Document description and representation standards (e.g. SGML)
— Inter-operability (how do multiple digital libraries interact?)
— Privacy, authentication and security
— Location independent naming of digital sources.

Conclusion

Digital libraries, as conceived by the digital library projects illustrated in this paper, are expected to provide several advantages, including, (i) accessibility from anywhere (home, school, libraries, during travel, hotel, etc.), (ii) provide access to more information than possible to physically acquire and maintain, (iii) support both formal and informal learning, (iv) media integration, (v) remote access to expensive and rare material, and (vi) greater opportunity for publishing.

The magnitude of the ongoing digital libraries projects, their funding and the complex technical issues involved may appear quite daunting and discouraging for library and information specialists in a country like India. This need not (and should not) be so. It is possible to initiate interesting and useful projects on institutional/campus local area networks, by innovative use of Internet and WWW technologies, to provide network access to in-house collections. These can then be expanded for external connectivity and usage. But what is important is to plan and design systems in a way that they can be integrated easily later into the emerging national and international digital library architectures. This of course means that we need to keep ourselves informed of developments in the digital library field.

References

1. Khan, Robert and Wilensky, Robert. A framework for distributed digital object services. 13 May 1995. (http://www.cnri.reston.va.us/home/cstr/arch/k-w.html)(wilensky@cs.berkeley.edu).

2. Lynch,Clifford and Garcia-Molina, Hector. (Eds.) Inter-operability, scaling and the digital libraries research agenda, 12 August 1995. A report on the May 18-19, 1995 IITA Digital Libraries Workshop. (http://www-diglib.stanford.edu/diglib/pub/reports/iita-dlw/main.html) (clifford.lynch@ucop.edu,hector@db.stanford.edu).

3. Larson, Ray R. Design and development of a network-based electronic library, March 2, 1994. (http://sherlock.berkeley.edu/diglib/asis.html) (ray@sherlock.berkeley.edu).

4. Association for Computing Machinery (ACM). *Communications of the ACM,* April 1995. (Issue devoted to digital libraries).

5. Davis, James R. Creating a Networked Computer Science Technical Reports Library. D-Lib Magazine, September 1995. (http://www.cnri.reston.va.us/home/dlib/september95/09contents.html), (davis@dri.cornell.edu).

6. Arms, William Y. Handles and the handle system. 27 July 1995. Corporation for National Research Initiatives, Reston, VA. (http://www.cnri.reston.va.us/home/cstr/handle-intro.html).

7. Lucier, Richard E. and Brantley, Peter. The Red Sage project: An experimental digital journal library for the health sciences. *D-Lib Magazine*, August 1995. (http://www.cnri.reston.va.us/home/dlib/august95/08contents.html), (rel@library.ucsf.edu, brantley@library.ucsf.edu).

Note : 'D-Lib Magazine' is an electronic journal, published monthly by the Corporation for National Research Initiatives (CNRI), Reston, VA, U.S.A., devoted to the reporting of R&D in digital libraries. In addition to full length articles, it contains news items, 'technology pen' reporting new software and technologies, review of progress made by various digital library projects, etc. First issue appeared in July, 1995. It may be accessed on the Web at http://www.cnri.reston.va.us/ home/dlib.

SIS–96, 18–20, Jan. '96, Bangalore

Digital libraries aboard ships and submarine — the US Department of Defence (DoD) CALS program payoff

B. RAMADEVI AND P. SUBBARAMAIAH
Naval Science and Technological Laboratory, Visakhapatnam-530 027

Abstract

The US DoD had launched CALS program in the mid 1980s to improve the process by which various weapon systems are built, maintained and supported. The program was initiated to digitize all active engineering data and information, store it at designated repositories and provide to Army, Navy, Airforce and Defence Logistic Support Agency etc., with what is termed as "Just in Time Information". CALS was a motivating technology both for the defence and industry as well. It enabled the contractors of the defence projects to interact with the defence authorities during the design process of a weapon or equipment so that the products that are being built really meet the defence customers end needs. Thus, it was an integrated, automated approach over the whole of technical information management from research, development, engineering, test, evaluation and procurement to the use of the data for production, operation, maintenance, training of the staff and finally, the disposal or de-militarisation of defence equipment, converting the whole product life cycle. The data is created one time with many subsequent uses.

The impact of Computer-Aided Acquisition Logistic Support (CALS) program on defence manufacturing is far reaching initially in defence, later with increasing "overflow" into commercial sector. Like the Internet, the CALS initiatives are also revolutionising the structure and performance of world economy.

This paper surveys the developmental background of CALS strategy to improve shipboard document publication and use thus paving the way for an information intensive ship. Considers the issues involved in changing from a paper based to digitized environment, standards adopted for presentation of technical manuals in digital mode. The dynamic features of technical manuals are discussed.

The ITs of the present

Present day technologies remind us of Allen Newell who described that there is a close resemblance between fairy tales and technology. Infact technology is a tool to build a land of fairies. It incorporates intelligence on all fronts. Some of the remarkable contributions for example are :

- Brakes that know how to stop on wet pavements;
- Bridges that watch out for safety of those that cross them;

- Automobiles that take over routing, scheduling, steering and control and relieving the driver to do what he likes including sleep!!

This is only a glimpse of the enchantment.

The information front, the life-blood of human society also has it's share of enchantment making it a land of fairies. It is equally fascinating and exciting to observe the breakthroughs made by the technologies in information presentation. Digital technologies have evolved for a dynamic presentation of information matched to the cognitive style of the user ranging from text, voice, image, animation, video, excitable simulations etc.

A mere click gets a photo or picture of a system in a window, another click provides a schematic of a system; yet another click enables to access selected text. The process continues. Users are offered a greater insight and detail into any subject concerned that is unattainable in conventional paper or microform media. For example, when a user asked about 'Traveling to Mars', Informedia Digital Video Library system has zeroed in on one of its "Books", a documentary, and brought up film clips of Arthur C Clarke and others discussing interplanetary exploration. The material thus provided to the user was more complete than a documentary shown on a TV. The same user queried about 'Parallel Processing'. The system tapped into a group of videotape lectures and also brought up a clip of "Thinking Machines" explaining the basis of parallelism.

The systems or mechanisms are being designed in such a way that they cater for what the user's query did not say, could not say but somehow made to manifest. Their developmental emphasis was:

1. How best to mimic the human thought process in grouping together related ideas, concepts and terminology even when these relationships are subtle and implicit;

2. How to give an optimum subject association similar to the way our own memory works by association and logic;

3. How to provide the magnets to attract pertinent information.

The developmental focus was entirely on the user. Systems have now evolved with the aim of helping the user to find pertinent information without his or her specifying and allowing them to develop a line of reasoning while searching with an adaptation for a person's changing viewpoint. They are not designed for a prototypical user but to suit users whose ideas change and evolve as they interact with the information presented at every step. They help even those users who may not know exactly what they are looking for, but somehow made to recognize it when they see it. Once the user performs this recognition function, then the newly evolved information store provides an intelligently guided browsing facility where by the user is exposed to sections that are likely to be relevant. The embedded mechanism allows the user to judge relevance quickly. If the retrieved sections are not felt relevant, then the inbuilt mechanism of the digital document suggests alternate search paths. Relationships in the text database are extracted automatically doing away with human indexing. The digital environment enables the individuals to interpret, amplify, reshape and reproduce the immense information resource at his disposal. The information is made more accessible as the users pick and choose what they want. Every one is a content creator.

The digitisation of information — the US DoD efforts

However, technology alone is not the solution. To reap the benefits of a particular technology it requires vision and foresight. The credit for incorporation of advanced technologies for generating, storing, reproducing and delivering technical information in digital form goes to defence and aerospace sectors. The goal of getting the right stuff to the right place at the right time, (termed as the "Logistics support infrastructure") has challenged the military organisations since time immemorial. Included in the mantle of "Logistics" are personnel, training, test equipment, technical manuals, plans, engineering drawings etc. Thus one the list of "Right Stuff" the most important ingredient is the Information ingredient. Weapon systems of today require a range and depth of information at the operating level which was not even dreamt of about a generation ago. Revolutionary changes in electronics have led to an interesting paradox. While electronics and computers make the defence services more capable, they also require more information for the job on hand. Thus defence is faced with an explosion in the amount of information needed to operate and maintain modern weapon systems of all three services — Navy, Airforce and Army.

CALS program

US Department of Defence (DoD) under it's CALS (Computer-aided Acquisition and Logistic Support) program had spent huge amounts for implementation of a digital, shared data environment in which all necessary information would be available to on-line users independent of location and time of the day. One of the reasons for triggering digitisation initiative in the form of CALs was an observation made in various services of Defence that instead of spending time devoted to their technical specialties, the highly trained engineers and crew members of a Defence Service were devoting too much time to being "Librarians" — maintaining technical information and technical manuals!!.

CALS Standards

The specifications and standard developed under the CALS initiative are important for the digital transfer and display of technical information and data. CALS documents released so far are:

MIT-STD-1840A-1987: Automated Interchange of Technical Information.

MIL-D-28000-1987: Digital Representation for Communication of Product Data.

MIL-M-28001-1988: Mark up Requirements and Generic Style Specification for Electronic Printed Output and Exchange of Text (SGML).

MIL-R-28002-1988: Requirements for Raster Graphics Representation in Binary Format.

MIL-D-28003-1988: Digital Representation for Communication of Illustration data.

MIL-HDBK-59-1988: CALS Implementation guide.

Navy's Approach

Since a detailed description of CALS project encompassing all the three services of Defence is out of the purview of this paper, we restrict our discussion to Navy's advanced technological approaches for generating, storing reproducing, and delivering technical information in digital form, the objective being to reduce the Navy's reliance on paper based information, and to automate the technical information process from initial acquisition through eventual delivery to the end user.

the storage problem of the material where space is an utmost constraint in war fighting platforms.

The task of going through these massive documents to identify and find the crucial nugget information to carry out the job on hand is overwhelming. Navy has found a solution by way of a combining document digitisation and logical linking approach. The end product of these effort is HYPERTEXT. The aim of CALS was to choose available and affordable technology with a growth capability. CALS had made use of the *"off-the shelf technologies"* hardware and software which already exist thus doing away with the overall system development, acquisition, and life-cycle costs. CALS had emerged to replace all contractor inputs and Government replies by a digital standard interface. It is a DoD and industry strategy to enable and accelerate the integration of digital technical information for weapon system acquisition, design, manufacture and support.

Recognition of the significant opportunities provided by the optical storage technologies in reducing the amount of paper on ships and in increasing the efficiency of operations have led to the choice of CD-ROM and WORM technologies which are capable of storing large quantities of test, databases, graphics or picture images and their retrieval. They can be duplicated locally and readily updated and backed up to prevent data loss and facilitate automatic indexing and cross referencing. The other added features of the chosen technology are: operating life of 50-100 years; compatibility of the medium with ship-board conditions and survivability requirements as the data stored on a CD-ROM are immune to environment hazards or electromagnetic interference or pulse damage.

The combination of optical disk storage technology with Hypertext in the realm of Naval documents offers access to large volumes of technical information while maintaining all of the advantages of traditional paper-based documents. The paper-less manuals so evolved are smart database of information in ASCII text that can be accessed with the touch of a finger.

The digital manual

In order to give a better feel of the salient features of a Naval technical manual delivered in digital mode, we present below the potentialities of digital documents aboard ships and submarines.

Paper-based manuals present a hierarchical structure, for e.g., 1st chapter deals with general information and safety procedures, and the 2nd operating procedures, the 3rd functional description and so on. Each chapter is further subdivided into sections, subsections and so on. In hypertext documents text and other information is segmented into topics. A topic can represent a chapter, section, subsection etc. Supposing a user is in search of information for a specific component-say, '*Lubricating Oil Cooler*', he can trace it instantaneously. This is retrieval of text part. Raster graphics facility embedded in the manual will facilitate the user with a flow chart diagram of the diesel engine lubricating oil system. similarly a link to vector node presents him with an engineering drawing of the lubricating oil cooler. Animation node presents him with a vision of the lubricating oil flow through lubricating oil cooler. Audio node depicts diesel engineer sounds under idling and full load conditions to contrast the engine noises under varying operating scenarios. Video node predicts safety procedures associated with operation of diesel engine. Computer programs make various functions available to the user. A simulation program can be run to decide on various operating parameters — temperature/pressure, fluid levels, etc. The Hypertext manual incorporates two additional features enhancing the usability of technical documentation. One is it allows the users to propagate their knowledge of system and equipment as they gain experience with them. Supposing documentation for a particular piece of information is found lacking in it's description, and during repairs the member gained an expertise in the repair that was not originally incorporated, he can append his knowledge base to the technical manual. This information comes handy during next repairs. The second is monitoring — it provides the developers of manuals with capabilities that allow them to improve the quality of documentation. Hypertext software monitors the frequency with which users access each topic. These usage statistics guide the designers for better presentation of later versions or other documents.

Important features of this media are replacement of individual Notebooks or diaries by allowing the user to make marginal notes to clarity or expand upon the text blocks and store them on the retrieval systems hard disk for later use. Clipboard allows the technician to isolate a section of text and clip it for transportation to another medium. The original text remains untouched, but the technician is free to manipulate the clipped text however desired and import it to other documents or databases. The graphics are explicitly faithful representations of the schematics, block diagrams etc., printed on paper manuals, but are color coded to highlight items of interest which is not done in paper format. The most innovative methods captured in the digital documents generate a splendid feeling amongst the users.

Evaluations carried out on the digital manuals aboard naval vessels revealed that the digital manuals are outstanding and greatly enhanced the operational readiness of the fleet. They enabled the junior personnel onboard to complex technical tasks with nearly the same effectiveness as senior technicians. They are said to be an information equalizer that significantly narrows down the margin of difference between experienced and inexperienced. The amount of information available for access is limited only by the user's capacity to assimilate and use it. They are considered as "One stop information center" providing the Just-in-Time-Information. In the area of training with digital manuals savings were reported to be $4000 per student and training time reduced by several days. US Navy could save about $3.12 million by fitting a ship with digital manual.

The eras of information age ERA4

We are in the Information Age. AD Little in his "Into The Information Age" (1987) observed that Era1 dealt with discipline/subject oriented questions, Era2 with Mission oriented, Era3 of problem oriented service and Era4 of individually oriented services customized for the individual providing him with access to Information of limitless variety. Era4 thus is marked with the innate objective of developments to mimic the human memory and thought process as realistically as possible so that the information is tailored to the individual. Digital Libraries are an end to personalized delivery of information. Digital libraries thus have marked the emergence of Era4. Era4 has become possible due to the pooling of researchers, developers, and users all with heterogeneous backgrounds but with a common commitment to harness the knowledge resource effectively.

ITs of the future

While in the paper-based world the information was doubling every 10 years or so, now in the technology-based world the doubling process is attained within 2 years. It is not the quantum alone that matters but the quality and means of presentation in a vivid form. Now the technology is being harnessed to make it possible for some personalisation like thing that recognizes each person and the information comes and presents itself! Efforts have yielded such technologies and systems that allow one to do much more in the same time and more effectively. It is exactly for this that the human civilization has been striving and the struggle goes on unending. The lead taken by the Department of Defence in USA, had provided a number of cost-effective and focused information systems for other industries as well. Storage technologies are evolving very fast and their is a likelihood of CD-ROM being taken over by yet another media called DVD (Digital Video Disk) which has an insatiable storage capacity, a single disk of which can hold database of 10 CD-ROMS. Under it's debut much more versatile applications can be expected.

Tools for accessing information sources are undergoing rapid improvements. With the launching of e-mail, Internet, WAIS, WWW, Hypertext links etc., the tasks are simplified to navigate amongst the myriad information sources around the world. Let us consider scientists of our laboratory working on a torpedo drag problem. They can look up for related information through the tools described above which are sure to provide them with an instant access to a number of references viz., all article on passive boundary layer control which is under peer review of a particular journal, but still accessible for public comment; another report on torpedo drag published by a Swiss company; another article deals with fish locomotion the principles of which can be applied to torpedo motion; another electronic group discussion on control and maneuver of underwater objects etc., Technology is the art of our time and expert communication is the alchemy of shared information, transforming the lead (data) into the gold (knowledge). No work, no endeavor, no effort can remain in isolation and everything is seen in a larger and wider context.

Salman Rushdie‘s vision of 21st century's communications is a perfect metaphor for what we perceive of the future information scenario...It (information) was made of thousands and thousands of currents, each one a different color, weaving in and out of one another like a liquid tapestry of breathing complexity... The ocean held all the stories (information) that had ever been told many that were still in the process of being invented...The ocean is infact the biggest library in the Universe. And because the stories (information) were held here in a fluid form, they retained the ability to change, to become new versions of themselves, to join up with other...unlike a library of books, the ocean of the stream was alive... This is a perfect metaphor of what is happening in the creation and use of information in the digital environment. The streams of information really do ebb and flow in various stages of creation and completion.

DIP YOUR CUP AND YOU CAN FILL IT...

References

1. Proceedings of the Annual Conference on "Optical Information Systems", 1990.
2. *Naval Engineers Journal*, 1991.
3. *Byte*, June 1992.
4. *Byte*, July 1995.

SIS–96, 18–20, Jan. '96, Bangalore

On librarianship in the emerging digital order

A. SREENIVASA RAVI
National Centre for Science Information, Indian Institute of Science, Bangalore-560 012
(E-mail: ravi@ncsi.iisc.ernet.in)

Abstract

Digital library can be broadly defined as a system of distributed full-text and multimedia databases accessible on computer networks. This article indicates that digital library is yet another product that resulted from the response of library and information professionals to the opportunities and challenges of the developments in information technology just as the products like OPAC and the CDROM database and so on. A number of digital library projects with large amounts of funding have been started in the developed countries, specially in the US, addressing a range of issues that include the design, implementation and maintenance. Access to digital library resources can significantly improve the library services and information provision and so digital library as a technological development cannot be ignored. With the available infrastructure in India a library can easily make a small beginning in utilising these information resources available on the Internet. The most important goal of any digital library effort should be publishing on the network as the librarian has to take on the additional responsibility of publisher in the new digital order. However, using the Internet and its resources for providing information services only requires a re-orientation of traditional skills of librarianship.

Introduction

Though the word *digital library* is approximately a year old now, a good deal of debate is going on and a number of definitions are being offered in the professional literature. However, a working definition which is generally accepted is that the digital library is a system of distributed databases, most often full-text and multimedia databases, accessible online on computer networks. Digital library surely is not a buzz-word or a concept that appeared overnight and gathered much ado about it. It is a definite, logical extension of the networked environment and the developments triggered thereof.

Library and information professionals have always responded to the opportunities and challenges of the developments in information technology with a high degree of enthusiasm and professionalism. The optical storage technology offered the CDROM and the library community was the first to find the best application which at once is economical and highly useful for its user community. The online database and the OPAC also are such examples of the yesteryear that utilised the high-performance computers.

Today, the Internet, available as a result of the R & D efforts in computers and communications, with hypertext-based navigating tools like the World Wide Web giving access to multimedia information, has opened out tremendous opportunities for providing and disseminating better information services. And the library profession responded to this, with the concept of the digital library. Innumerable databases of research papers, pre-prints and technical reports are made available on the Internet already via Web servers or for direct access and downloading. The word *digital library* is a generic term that is used to broadly describe these developments.

Two international conferences[1,2] were held on digital libraries in the US and the Association of the Computing Machinery (ACM) has brought out a special issue of the Communications of the ACM[3] on digital libraries. Several projects have been undertaken in the developed countries, specially in the US universities addressing a range of issues involved, like the design, implementation, maintenance of digital libraries. Other major players in the information field like publishers of primary journals such as Elsevier Science etc. have initiated developmental efforts to keep up with the new digital order.

Ongoing digital library projects

An overview of the ongoing digital library projects is out of the scope of this paper. The Cammunication of the ACM issue referred above gives a structured and detailed account of the digital library projects and a brief account appears in a review of this issue[4]. It would be sufficient to enumerate the R & D projects in digital libraries in order to give an idea of the trends and directions of these efforts.

The digital library research initiatives basically include:

- research in user interfaces
- search and retrieval of text, images and other multimedia objects
- representation of text and images in the databases or digital library resources
- creating and maintaining indexes or catalogues of the information resources
- advanced multimedia networking protocols.

A look at a few digital projects gives an indication of the future digital libraries.

UCSTRI (Unified Computer Science Technical Report Index) of Indiana University[5] is a system that builds a centralised master index by polling FTP sites and allows searching of the index and retrieval of the reports.

Harvest system of the IRTF-RD (Internet Research Task Force Group on Resource Discovery)[5] is designed as an integrated set of tools for managing information resources on the Internet by gathering and constructing indexes automatically through text analysis.

WATERS (Wide Area Technical Reports Service)[6] is another distributed database of computer science technical reports. WATERS is supported by a central server which provides indexing information and performs routing of queries. The reports can be distributed across systems and the end-users can use the system by accessing the central server through WWW.

DIENST[7] repository of the Cornell University is a protocol and implementation that provides Internet access to a distributed, decentralised, multi-format document collection. A distinguishing feature of DIENST is that the indexes are distributed and searches are processed in parallel across the index sites. Using WWW clients, users can search the document collection, browse and download the documents.

University of Illinois Digital Library Project[8] is building a large-scale digital test bed, planned to grow to thousands of documents and to thousands of users. The prototype implementation views the Internet as Interspace — a distributed space of inter linked information. The collection consists of full-text journals in SGML format supplied directly by major partners from the publishing industry. The software is based on NCSA's Mosaic, a multi platform WWW browser.

UMDL (University of Michigan Digital Library)[9] is a multi-disciplinary collaboration with the planned system consisting of three software agents — user interface, mediation agent and collection agent. Initial prototypes use the DIRECT system, a searching and browsing interface to about forty material science journals published by Elsevier Science, implemented under the TULIP project.

Numerous other projects are going on in various related areas such as OCLC's Cataloging of the Internet Resources, the British Library's Initiatives for Access Project. Publishers of primary journals are formulating and developing electronic publishing plans and products.

With such large-scale multi-disciplinary R & D efforts, one can expect the future digital libraries to be high-performance systems with a sophisticated user-interface, an intelligent retrieval engine, automated collection management tools or resource manager software and distributed document collections. Most of the test bed collections of these projects, in addition to several hundred other collections on the Internet, are available for accessing and downloading through Web browsers.

Librarians have to adapt to the new digital order as they did with the developments in the past, in order to improve the library services and to introduce newer ones. The general scenario in the country and infrastructure have to be looked at before considering the advantages or utilisation of the latest developments.

Digital libraries and the Indian scene

As we can see, all the projects mentioned above are multi-million dollar projects going on in the US and other developed countries. For us in India, the questions or doubts arise: 'is it not too early or premature to talk of digital libraries?' or 'perhaps we should wait to take advantage of the digital libraries!' The answer is a clear and definite no and the reasons are two fold. Firstly, the digital library is too important a development to sit down and wait to take advantage of the opportunity. And secondly, the infrastructure in the country is becoming available.

Use of computer networks in our country has come of age now. With the advent of ERNET (its sub-network SIRNET), and the NICNET, e-mail has gained acceptance and popularity and the networks have become an indispensable mode of information seeking and distribution in a number of campuses and laboratories. Certainly, the infrastructure is yet to catch up with the demand and to provide Internet access to all the institutions that require it. But it can be seen that things are steadily moving towards this ideal with ERNET improving its communication facilities and VSNL starting its Internet access services.

It is imperative that the library professionals have to upgrade their professional skills in order to exploit the opportunity and be able to use the digital libraries for the benefit of the local user community. Librarians have to find a cost-effective way of getting the Internet connectivity (preferably to the library rather than to their computer centre or other such place). There are easy and inexpensive ways of starting one's own World Wide Web server. The software is available free on the Internet and one can download the

MS-Windows version and start a server on a personal computer. In addition to providing information about the library services on the Web pages, one has to provide pointers to the Internet resources that are useful to the users. This list or collection of pointers to foreign sites has to be carefully maintained and by visiting the sites regularly to make sure that the site continues to provide the information by adding pointers to new resources to the list.

The librarians' tasks are no different in the new digital environment from the ones they have been performing in the past. 'Traditionally, librarians have performed a number of functions in the maintenance and the intellectual access to information'.[10] The development and maintenance of lists of Internet resources only requires a blend of skills in reference service, collection development and classification.

The most important function will be electronic publishing or making available local databases on the network. This again is not totally new in our profession since building and managing databases has been part of librarianship, the difference being the full-text nature of the digital library resources. In addition one has to present the local information sources like in-house newsletters, journals, technical reports, theses and dissertations etc. in the digital form for network access.

Lastly, funding agencies such as NISSAT, DBT and the like should promote the concept of digital library by funding projects with support for Internet connectivity and by identifying some libraries and information centres for specific functions based on criteria like subject areas etc. This type of support has met with considerable success in the past in certain aspects, as in the case of encouraging the use of online databases as well as the CDROM databases. Another example is wide-spread use of CDS/ISIS — today a number of libraries have developed in-house databases and applications on CDS/ISIS, thanks to the distribution and continued support of NISSAT.

From network-information services to digital libraries

It is not inappropriate to mention here the efforts at NCSI as a case in trying to use the computer networks as an effective means of information dissemination. After getting the e-mail connectivity we at NCSI considered the ways in which we can introduce new services and improve the existing services[11]. Besides e-mail delivery of SDI output to our users, we started an e-mail based bibliographic information server[12], which is now operational as CPSERVER. We also started using e-mail discussion lists like PACS-L and provided interactive access to a content page database on the campus-wide network.

Our next effort in this direction resulted in LIS-FORUM, an e-mail based discussion list for the library and information professionals in the country, run at NCSI as a project supported by NISSAT[13]. There are now more than a hundred subscribers to LIS-FORUM from within India and abroad who pose questions, seek solutions and share their professional experiences, and the number of participants is growing. We have archived the discussions going on, on the forum since its inception which is searchable through e-mail and interactive facility can be made available if necessary.

Now we have access to the Internet and have started and planned some subject-oriented services. One of the services is creation and maintenance of a classified or annotated list or catalogue of Internet resources in specific disciplines, so that a researcher looking for information will have a single gateway to the Internet resources in his/her subject. However, as mentioned earlier, a key service would be providing local or in-house information on the Internet through a software like the Web server. This does not require developing information resources afresh, as much as pooling of resources that are already in place and re-formatting them for publishing on the network.

We thus have made a beginning with a few network information services. With the availability of the technology, we are taking a path that is natural and logical, which is leading to the digital library. However, this cannot be considered just as a spin-off of the technology that is available as it requires deliberate and sustained effort to utilise technology and re-orientation of skills of librarianship with better information services as the goal.

Conclusion

Digital library is but a logical extension of the developments in information technology and a result of active response from the library profession to the challenges and opportunities presented thereof. A number of high-end tools and technologies are being developed through several digital library initiatives world over. But the advent of the digital libraries is too important to wait for the opportune time to take advantage of the resources. Using the Internet and its resources for providing information services only requires re-orientation of traditional skills of librarianship. With the available infrastructure in the country we can make a beginning in exploiting the digital library resources on the Internet for better and newer services.

References

1. Hassan, Scott W. and Metcalfe, Ted (Ed. — Electronic Version) Digital Libraries '94. First Annual Conference on Theory and Practice of Digital Libraries. June 19-21, 1994, Texas A & M University, College Station, USA. (URL: http://www.csdl.tamu.edu/DL94).

2. Shipman, Frank (Ed. — Electronic Version) Digital Libraries '95. The Second International Conference on Theory and Practice of Digital Libraries. June 19-21, 1994, Austin, USA. (URL: http://www.csdl.tamu.edu.DL95).

3. Fox, Edward et. al. (Ed.) *Communications of the ACM* (Special Issue on Digital Libraries). 38(4), April, 1995.

4. Rajashekar, T.B. Digital Libraries. *Information Studies.* 1(4), October 1995, pp. 223-238.

5. Fox, Edward. World Wide Web and Computer Science Reports. *Communications of the ACM.* 38(4), April 1995, pp. 43-44.

6. French, James C. et. al. Wide Area Technical Report Service: Technical Reports Online. *Communications of the ACM.* 38(4), April 1995, pp. 45.

7. Lagoze, Carl and Davis, James R. DIENST: An Architecture for Distributed Document Libraries. *Communications of the ACM.* 38(4), April 1995, pp. 47.

8. Schatz, Bruce. Building the Interspace: The Illinois Digital Library Project. *Communications of the ACM.* 38(4), April 1995, pp. 62-63.

9. Crum, Laurie. University of Michigan Digital Library Project. *Communications of the ACM.* 38(4), April 1995, pp. 63-64.

10. Furuta, Kenneth. Librarianship in the Digital Library. First Annual Conference on Theory and Practice of Digital Libraries. June 19-21, 1994, Texas A & M University, College Station, USA. (URL: http://www.csdl.tamu.edu/DL94/position/kfuruta.html).

11. Rajashekar, T.B. and Ravi, A. Sreenivasa. Information resources on worldwide networks — Possibilities of network information services in India. Seminar on Library Networks in India, 12-13 August, 1993. Documentation Research & Training Centre, Indian Statistical Institute, Bangalore.

12. Ravi, A. Sreenivasa and B.C. Indira. An e-mail based bibliographic information server. *Journal of Information Science.,* 20(4), 1994, pp. 295-299.

13. Gulla, Meenaxi, Rajashekar, T.B. and Ravi, A. Sreenivasa. LIS-FORUM: Electronic mail discussion forum for library and information services. *Information Today and Tomorrow,* 14(1), January-March 1995, pp. 25-26.

Seven

Social, Economical and Psychological Implications

SIS–96, 18–20, Jan. '96, Bangalore

Digital library not to surrogate but to supplement default library

S.VENUGOPAL
Bharathidasan University Library, Tiruchirapalli-620 024

Abstract

Internet wave has swept almost all countries that it could boast of fast-increasing larger communities in the world. Library has perforce to add digital-storey in quick succession over automated-storey built upon its long traditional ground edifice. Nothing to worry about its foundation, but its superstructure only adds feathers to its cap. The management of three-tier pyramidal-patterned library call for specialized skills. Traditional collection alone cannot be taken as the baseline for assessing the vitality or potentiality of the library. The trade-offs between long-range prospects and transitional problems have been brought forth in creating and maintaining a research-oriented digital library. The paper addresses several future trends that academic libraries could ill afford to ignore. The turbulent technological cascade has thrown the academic library out of its gears. It is a great challenge for the librarian to provide infostructure to accommodate online services and interactive multimedia CD-Net with the already existing automated systems. In sum, a maiden attempt has been made to explore the mystique of digital library.

Digital era

The advent of digital technology, which converts all communicating signals to 0s and 1s called bits, greatly expands capacity for transmission of text, audio, graphics and videos. Ever since the coinage of "cyberspace" by William Gibson in his novel Neuromancer (1984), cyberspace stands for the increasingly interconnected computer systems to the Internet. "Cyberspace is the land of knowledge.... And the exploration of that land can be a civilization's truest, highest calling," observes U.S. House Speaker, Newt Ginggrich. Hardly could there be an IT magazine in the world that has not featured a full-length article about Internet. For instance, Time has brought about a special issue starting with "Welcome to Cyberspace. What is it? Where is it? And how do we get there?" The combination of plummeting costs and soaring sophistication in communications technology is changing the nature of business competition. New found access to vast libraries of digitized data, combined with the means to communicate cheaply and rapidly, has given small firms tools that until recently were available only to big corporations. The futurist, Jim Willis, predicts that cybersociety will become exposed more to multimedia and turbonews. 'Turbonews' (a term coined by him) refers to the vast masses of news and information that can now reach us at the speed of light. The power of CD-ROMs to store massive amounts of information and the hyperspeed ability of fiber-optic technology to deliver all this to the user is astounding. We could become a much more learned and informed society if we took advantage of all this information. Multimedia communication technologies will profoundly alter the way we work in the decades ahead.

Digital library, the scholars' sanctuary

The ultimate purpose of research libraries must be to facilitate access to scholarly information — in other words, to be a means toward effective scholarly communication. The traditional library, based on storing physical books and journals, has become a large store of information. The quality of the more traditional libraries is measured by the ease with which the materials in the library can be retrieved by scholars. The desire to make information retrieval more efficient has prompted most major libraries to install computer-based, automated systems for handling bibliographic searches, circulation, cataloguing, acquisitions, and other library functions. But even after the introduction of these systems, libraries have continued to be ever-increasing stores of materials. Much material continues to be purchased on the principle of "just in case". Libraries have tried the mechanisms like resource sharing and inter-library loan not only to surmount the escalating costs of books and periodicals, but also to avoid duplication of rarely used items, but experience testifies to the ultimate analysis that they are neither economical nor efficient. The last decade has witnessed in quick succession many breathtaking technological innovations. The two principal ways by which process has occurred are the introduction of compact discs (CDs) and the general availability of electronic networks.

Ongoing digital library projects

In 1989, University Microfilms, Inc. (UMI), launched the first "full image" periodical database that offered researchers and students bitmapped access to hundreds of magazines with graphs, charts, text, photos, and illustrations. In 1993, UMI launched an electronic publishing system, proQuest PowerPages. It offers access to more than 18,000 periodicals and over 7,000 newspapers in various formats, including microfilm, microfiche, online, CD-ROM, and magnetic tape. Recovering royalties and other fees for each use of material is an added complication. But Case Western Reserve University has developed a promising software program that automatically tracks the uses of online materials through its campuswide network and eventually will bill directly for royalty charges.

Multimedia is the area that places greatest demands on the performance of computer networks. The networks at leading universities are designed to grow with essentially no limitations, but not all scholars have access to such networks. Carnegie Mellon University, which has a relatively small library for a research university, but an excellent campus network, has pioneered the notion of "distributed" computing resources and applied it to its Mercury Electronic Library. Two advantages of the distributed approach are that a variety of equipment can be accommodated through open standards, and no central facility big enough to store the totality of the collection will be needed.

One of the most ambitious digital library projects that spans the integration of many types of media is Cornell's "Making of America" project to be conducted in collaboration with a number of other institutions. This digital collection will grow in size over the next few years to be equivalent to about 100,000 volumes and will encompass a variety of disciplines bearing on the history of America. Books, articles, manuscripts, drawings, architectural blueprints, business records, maps, and other materials will be included. Cornell hypothesizes that providing worldwide network access to such an electronically integrated collection will open new opportunities for interdisciplinary research. The University also believes that the project will provide a challenging framework for digitizing a wide range of media into a coherent and readily accessible digital library for a large and diverse set of users. Cornell University has collaboratively pioneered the development of making high-quality facsimiles of deteriorating library books by using high-resolution production scanning and printing. Access across the Internet to the captured electronic images is also made available, and parts of the book or the entire book may be "printed on demand" from the scholar's workstation. In an effective incremental transition strategy to provide a bridge between old and new technologies, these facsimiles can also be reshelved to replace the embrittled original for use by scholars who prefer traditional formats. This approach to preservation and access is competitive in cost with microfilming and cheaper than photocopying, resulting in a growing library of several thousand digitized books and hundreds of thousands of scanned pages. The process is now so cost-effective that Cornell is applying the technology to other kinds of material, including doctoral dissertations, journals, and textbooks.

It is important to note in passing that another type of book, reference works, has been an obvious candidate for treatment in electronic form for a number of years. Dictionaries and encyclopedias, for example, typically enjoy very large sales, but over long periods of time. Publishers of reference works are therefore very much interested in exploring electronic formats. OCLC is now conferring with a number of professional societies about automating the editing and production processes of their proceedings. In electronic form, the proceedings would be available for archival record purposes, while the costs of producing, acquiring, and storing the proceedings would be significantly diminished. Photographs, paintings, maps and materials of artifactual value that require multibit scanning.

Digital library access (DLA) tools

Hypertext and Hypermedia: A hypertext system allows authors or groups of authors to link information together, create paths through a body of related material, annotate existing texts, and create notes that direct readers to either bibliographic data or the body of the referenced text. Using a computer-based hypertext system, students and researchers can quickly follow trails of footnotes and related materials without losing their original context; thus, they are not obliged to search through library stacks to look up referenced books and articles. Explicit connections — links — allow readers to travel from one document to another, effectively automating the process of following reference in an encyclopedia. In addition, hypertext systems that support multiple users allow researchers, professors, and students to communicate and collaborate with one another within the context of a body of scholarly material. Hypermedia is simply an extension of hypertext that incorporates other media in addition to text. With a hypermedia system, authors can create a linked body of material that includes text, static graphics, animated graphics, video, and sound. Harnad coined the phrase "scholarly skywriting" to describe the speed and breadth of dissemination that would result if academics eschewed the paper medium to publish over the network. If you want to get your message out on the World Wide Web, you have to use the Web's native language, Hypertext Markup Language, or HTML. Virtually every Web page that you see when you explore Internet with a Web browser is an HTML document that consists of text and HTML codes that define the way the text will look. If you want to publish your own pages on the Web, you will either need to learn HTML or find an editor program that generates HTML files for you. There are several HTML browers/editors (freeware/shareware) for the scholars.

Net-dwelling software agents

An "agent" to take the broadest possible definition is a program that can operate autonomously, carrying out tasks without direct human supervision. Think of a communications program that automatically dials a remote bulletin board late at night and downloads a large file when long-distance charges are lowest. Mobile agent paradigm is the network of the future. To create a mobile agent with Telescript, you just type out commands in much the same way as you might type out a program in BASIC. When you're done, you electronically feed the agent text into the Telescript "engine", a program that reads the written commands and carries them out step by step.

NCSA Mosaic and WWW: Hypermedia protocols

The WWW is a set of protocols that (i) allow for the location of any document on the Net through a naming system based on Universal Resource Locators (URLs); (ii) describe a way of placing links using URLs within text documents, called Hypertext Markup Language (HTML); and (iii) specify a way to request and send a document over the network, the Hypertext Transfer Protocol (HTTP). The introduction of functional search to the Internet coupled with standard classification of materials (using URNs and URCs) will likely change the character of the navigation of the Net by making digital libraries a widespread reality for the first time.

Information auditing

Digital libraries cannot be created and maintained like hanging roof-gardens where only aristocratic scholars could spend their past time. There is every possibility that in a research library the same materials could be available in printed form, electronic media and online. If the scholar's information requirements could be satisfied with the printed version, what's the fun of embarking upon a cruise on the Internet? Here information auditing is very essential. Resources available within the organization, and with the neighbourhood organizations should be taken stock of before resorting to expedition on the Internet.

Archiving the digital documents

The digital medium is replacing paper in a dramatic record-keeping revolution. But such documents may be lost unless we act now. If digital documents and their programs are to be saved, their migration must not modify their bit streams, because programs and their files can be corrupted by the slightest change. Ideally, bit streams should be sealed in virtual envelopes;

the contents would be preserved verbatim and contextual information associated with each envelope would describe those contents and their transformation history. This information must itself be stored digitally. We must adopt bootstrap standards for encoding contextual information, a simple, text-only standard should suffice. How will the archiving function be institutionalized? Who will do it and at what cost? How will savings in physical storage space affect the economics of archiving?

Manpower development

Digital library deliberately calls for dedicated development of manpower. How to make the digital library system excellent? To invoke Aristotle's conceptual framework, excellence means exercise of unique capacity. In the case of library, there are four components/factors that contribute to excellence: (a) sufficient resources, (b) leadership, (c) competent staff and (d) team work. Evidently human factors has a major share. TQM assumes that the major problems faced by most organizations are the lack of a quality focus caused by the work system and production process. Quality is achieved when workers ... cooperate with each other, not compete, and rely on customer feedback as the best measurement of whether the system is working effectively. Individuals, therefore, should not be evaluated; instead, if management wishes to enchance productivity, the system should be improved through more resources, training, or learning from the performance of superstars.

Not to surrogate but to supplement

With a role and a click of the mouse, we will summon Titian's masterpiece of *Assumption of the Virgin.* Thus the printed book, as a cultural delivery system, will become as obsolete in a cyberspatial society as the illuminated manuscript did after Caxton and Gutenberg. People have been saying this, in books of course, for several decades. But will it? The vast majority of books have not been converted to bits and almost certainly never will be, because they have no readership big enough to "justify" the huge task of digitalizing them all. One can well imagine digitalized versions of fundamental classics like *Antony and Cleopatra* or *Moby Dick*, or popular lit-kitsch like Maya Angelou's poetry, making it onto the small screen at some point, to satisfy mass demands from English Lit courses. In sum, what about the tens of millions of titles for which there is absolutely no popular demand and which can only be consulted as print on paper?

Nothing in the persuasively foreseeable future can or will replace the printed book, and the relation of cyberspace to literature hangs on a Rube Goldberg-like joke: the idea of needing an expensive electronic machine, available only to the relatively well-off and dependent on an external power source, to perform the act of reading. Besides there is not now and probably never will be a computer that you can get sand in and spill coffee on without impairing it, as you can with a book, a magazine or a newspaper. And the more you make information flow dependent on costly hardware, the more you separate the info rich and the info poor, thus adding new layers to a country's already vicious class inequalities. Any one and every can spend Rs.2 on a newspaper. It is by no means certain that the digital newspaper of the projected future, the silicon sheet you can plug into a wall jack for the day's info fix, will be widely accessible in the slums and ghettos of third world countries. Bill Gates has succeeded in spending $30.8 million on the only Leonardo manuscript that doesn't have a single drawing of real aesthetic significance in it. How many Gates could come forward to foot the bill for digitizing innumerable documents in the World?

The knowing gap

The gap between the knowledge available and the knowledge assimilated might actually increase rather than decrease. Knowledge hungry is not generally and largely felt by man as actue as biological hungry. Hardly could we expect even majority of educated people to take extra effort and time for surfing on the Internet. Another widening knowledge gap — that between the haves and have-nots — is the result of the rising cost of accessing information. Not everything free in the Internet. We have to subscribe to online services like America Online, Prodigy, CompuServe, Nexis and Lexis. In search for creative ways to lessen the technology gap, advocates of wider access are focussing on plans to put computers and Net connections into libraries, post offices and other public places around the contry to serve those who do not have home computers. Internet should be instrumental in narrowing the gap between the haves and have-nots in the knowledge society.

Conclusion

The results of technological innovation always take longer to reach fruition than early champions of change predict. But when change finally comes, its effect is likely to be more profound and widespread and unanticipated than anyone imagined. Digital library is a capital- and technology-intensive project. It is a great challenge for the academic library to build the digital library against the backdrop of shrinking budget.

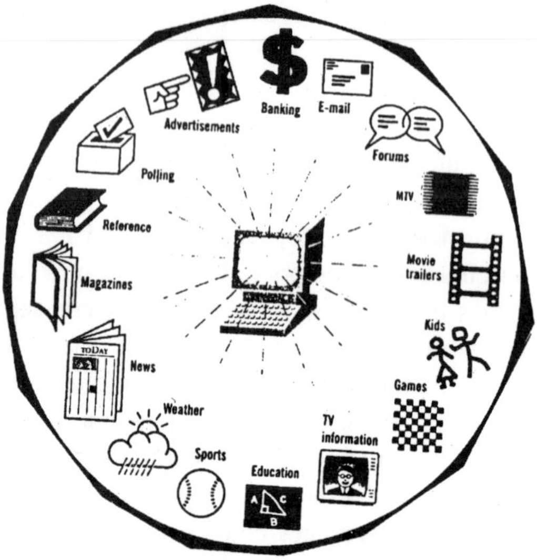

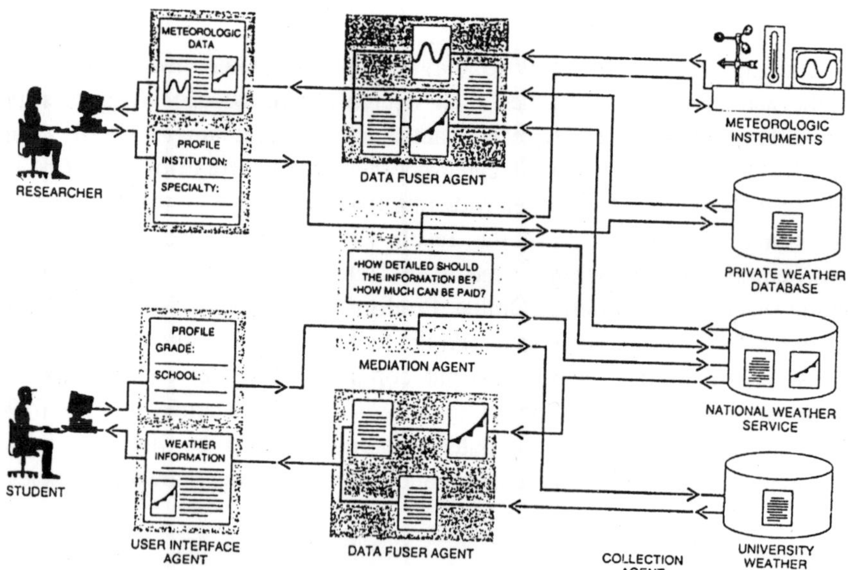

DOING THE BIDDING of research scholar or student, a network of software "agents" under development at the University of Michigan is intended to operate like an experienced reference librarian. After receiving a question—"What is the weather in Travers City?"—the user interface agent extracts a profile of the user from information in its database. The request is channeled to the mediation agent, which evaluates the profile to determine how detailed the information retrieved should be and how much the user can pay. The mediation agent decides what information resources should be allocated to what type of user. The researcher may get access to real-time meteorologic data and both public and private weather databases, whereas the student is relegated to less expensive public information sources. A collection agent then executes an actual search of the relevant databases. A data fuser agent assembles the collected information—text, maps, graphs, raw data—before relaying it to the user agent for display as a document on the student's or the researcher's screen.

References

1. Bowman, James S. At Last, an Alternative to Performance Appraisal: Total Quality Management. *Public Administration Review,* March/April 1994, p.129.

2. Clark, Charles S. Regulating the Internet. *CQ Researchers*, 30 June 1995, p.563.

3. Ekman, Richard H. and Quandt, Richard E. Scholarly Communication, Academic Libraries, and Technology. *Change,* January/February 1995, p.34.

4. Hughes, Robert, Take this Revolution... *Time*, Special Issue, May 1995, p.62.

5. Lyall, Sarah. Are These Books, or What? CD-ROM and the Literary Industry. *The New York Times Book Review*, 14 August 1994, p.3.

6. Max, D.T. The End of the Book? *The Atlantic Monthly*, September 1994, p.61.

7. Rothernberg, Jeff. Ensuring the Longevity of Digital Documents. *Scientific American*, January 1995, p.42.

8. Schatz, Bruce R. and Hardin, Joseph B. NCSA Mosaic and the World Wide Web: Global Hypermedia Protocols for the Internet. *Science*, 12 August 1994, p.895.

9. Stix, Gary, The Speed of Write. *Scientific American*, December 1994, p.106.

10. Waldrop, M. Mitchell, Software Agents Prepare to Sift Riches off Cyberspace. *Science*, 12 August 1994, p.882.

11. Willis, Jim. The Age of Multimedia and Turbonews, *The Futurist*, Sept-Oct. 1995 p.19

SIS–96, 18–20, Jan. '96, Bangalore

Beware of electronic libraries/media

M.S. SRIDHAR
Library & Documentation, ISRO Satellite Centre, Bangalore-560 017

Abstract

Print materials appeal to only one of the five senses, namely, the sight of man. Electronic medium provides for the effective use of the 'sight' and 'hearing' senses. With enormous dissemination capacity, easy acceptance by customers and monopolistic/profound effect on users a medium like TV acts as a 'Third parent' to children, a powerful and hypnotic gadget to adults and a 'cultural melting pot' for the society. The advantages and limitations of both print and electronic media for information acceptance, perception and use by man are discussed. Information industry is considered as belonging to leisure industries. Impact of electronic media on education, entertainiment, information supply and social, cultural and behavioural aspects are mentioned.

Introduction

Libraries having only print materials are restricted and useful only to functional literates. They appeal to only one of the five senses, namely the sight of man. 'Sight' is a very powerful sense of man and reading books makes highly inefficient by under-utilisation of this sense by requiring it to scan linearly printed black alphabets of a language against white background of paper. Imparting knowledge has necessarily to make use of all the five senses of man and break the monotony of alphabets.

Reading is believed to make man to close his mind to wider possibilities of imaginative expression. Print has formed a circle of aloofness around the reader and typing has reduced expression from art to craft and from personal to impersonal.

Electronic medium is a powerful tool having vast and wide applications in society. How much of it can be taken to their folds by libraries is left to one's imagination. Electronic medium emphasises effective use of the 'sight' and 'hearing' senses and naturally, rare use of the other senses.

Electronic media

Electronic media has pivotal role in information transfer, education, culture, environment, health, politics, commerce, etc. The entertainment value of the media has overshadowed the informational, educational and cultural values. As a double edged tool of 'third wave', electronic media is encroaching and eroding the readership of already under-used print medium. In the struggle for coexistence, books have been relegated to the position of 'inferior goods' (as per the economic analysis of income elasticity of demand). At the same time, electronic media is helping libraries to increase their efficiency and effectiveness by providing information in all its dimensions and colours. Unlike print medium, electronic media do not always require knowledge of script, comprehension and cerebral coordination on the part of users. Just understanding of the spoken language, access to the media and very little training are enough to use many services in electronic media. Electronic media coupled with advances in telecommunication make it economical to cover vast geographical area and almost complete population under information services. There is no limit on physical proximity of electronic libraries and their users. Above all, people perceive the utility of electronic libraries as quite high and there is no need for strong motivation to use them.

With enormous dissemination capacity, easy acceptance by customers and monopolistic/profound effect on users a medium like TV acts as a 'third parent' to children, a powerful and hypnotic gadget to adults and a 'cultural melting pot' for the society.

Information technology and computer based systems are now dominating and revolutionising libraries with versatility of their compact multimedia storage, electronic viewing and manipulation, instantaneous transfer and movement of information and inexpensive duplication. Print on paper is only one of the media for carrying information. Electronic libraries expand the horizon of information gathering, increase perception, processing, comprehension and understanding of information by users through the compactly, concisely, less ambiguously and directly stored information and provide for interaction with media as well as manipulation of information. At the same time limitations of electronic libraries/media like costs, compatibility, copyright, lack of standardisation and adverse/ill effects are to be noted.

Information and leisure industries

Libraries belong to two competing and complimentary industries, namely information industry and leisure industry. They are competing because both try to claim the leisure time and leisure expenses of people. They are complimentary because information technology is tending to increase the leisure time available without reducing the income from the work.

Three major inputs into the process of leisure production are time, money and technology. In other words, the available leisure time coupled with the level of consumers' disposable income and the state of technical knowledge determine the production of leisure. Leisure, though not solely a service industry, has been a part of the service sector of the economy relative to the manufacturing sector.

Many leisure activities are quite demanding in terms of the skills required to enjoy them full. Leisure time becomes boring without sufficient consumption skills. In such situations people resort to low skill activities like watching TV. Teenagers are often bored (and even resort to crime and vandalism for excitement) due to lack of adequate/better leisure facilities and lack of consumption skill if facilities are available. Activities like using a library or a database, reading a book, appreciating an art, etc., require adequate consumption skill on the part of customer. Even low skill activities like watching TV and movies require 'appreciation' training and skill to make maximum benefit out of the activities. This appears to be one of the reasons for decrease in reading habit and increase in watching TV.

Impact of electronic libraries/media

As mentioned earlier, some of the positive and negative effects of electronic media on education, entertainment, information supply and social, cultural and behavioural aspects are worth noting. Interestingly, information superhighway can virtually allow talking, learning (education), shopping, playing (entertainment), investing (finance), etc. on a global basis.

Education: By and large, electronic media/libraries aid all types of education — formal, nonformal, adult, vocational, distance and higher. But, if education is to give first place to the culture of the heart or the building of character as desired by Gandhiji, the 'violent and hot' electronic media may fail in some respects. Further, as found by U.S National Commission on Education, commercial electronic media (i) lead children to synthetic as opposed to analytic modes of learning, (ii) make the boundary between reality and fantasy unclear and (iii) cause rejection of the message when clashed with the expectation.

Entertainment: Electronic media has brought total democratisation and transformation of the concept of entertainment. Yet they fall short of 'family' expectations. The 'cocktail' of amusement and social education has not been effective as messages through amusement and entertainment are not perceived transparently sincere. Entertainment reflects something of the psychic drives that lie deeper than immediately apparent demands of the market. It is not possible for an 'entertainment-led' revolution to occur. But people want and are willing to pay for entertainment industry. Hence entertainment has dominated televideo and leisure time of the people.

Social, behavioral and cultural effects: Communication plays important role in bringing social change. Social change and economic development are closely related. Electronic media have changed the living habits, styles and values of people. They have shaken the traditional unwritten family norms, culture and behaviour. Aggregate flow of reiterated formulae, formats and ritualisation in electronic media cultivates the social environment. Minds are fertilised and nurtured, within shared cultural environment of the world. A 'cultural melting pot' like televedio provides common denominator and helps homogenisation of a heterogeneous society. Yet, it is not totally free from divisive and ill effects. As a powerful and hypnotic gadget, it affects behaviour of viewers particularly, children. The trends like, an average American child spends 10% of his or her time watching TV, gets exposed to over 1 lakh acts of violence by the time he or she becomes 13 year old and TV has moved from 8th to 3rd place out of top ten factors influencing the youth are quite disturbing. Even in India, the average time spent in watching TV is $14\frac{1}{2}$ hours a week (The Hindu, 26 Nov. 1995, Magazine Section PI). The result is that the margin between childhood and adulthood is cut and children are given an impression that they are more matured than what they are. Televedio causes diminishing respect fcr adults, exposes adolescents to unreal and provocative life and shakes the confidence and trust of children in traditional proven values.

Ill effects of electronic media on values and habits: Adverse or ill effects of electronic media on human values and habits cannot be easily ignored. It is difficult to say whether or not electronic media and modernisation of libraries through new technologies should conform to values. Of course, creativity of library users may not depend on whether a library is electronic or otherwise. Unlike nature, technology does not possess the virtues of being self-balancing, self-adjusting and self-cleansing. Further, modern technology has deprived man of the kind of work that he enjoys most, creative, useful work with hands and brains but has given him plenty of work of a fragmented kind, most of which he does not enjoy at all (Schumacher, 1973).

Social isolation: Social isolation is the major problem of today's world. One-fourth of the American households consist of a single person. The technology has eroded the bonds of neighbourly interdependence and has become 'solating technologies'. The 'cool' print medium isolates individual but sponsors rational and dispassionate analysis of the message unlike the 'violent and hot' electronic media which encourages group and even mob thinking (The Economist, 21-27 August 1993, p34). The Internet is knitting congenial sails together without visual contact and hence does not fully gratify the social machinery in our minds. Further, " ... the net adds to the information overload, whose psychological effects are still unknown but certainly aren't wholly benign" (Wright, 28 Aug 95, p.45).

"The pursuit of more communication keep us from better knowing our neighbour, better knowing our kin — in general, from cultivating the warm, affectionate side of human nature whose roots science is just now starting to fathom" (Wright, 28 Aug 95, p46). The electronically recorded messages are just taking over the place of a village headman, a school master or mistress, a doctor, a priest or a party functionary.

Developments like video on demand (VOD), virtual reality (VR) coupled with data super highways (DHS) are revolutionising entertainment, education and information supply. Spending time may become the central problem or opportunity of life. "The individuals of tomorrow would be subjected to greater isolation, though of a self pleasuring kind, and the lonely Disneylands of the future are atleast a stimulating substitute for lonely idleness" (Smith, September 1993). At the same time the modern technological societies need literate elites who depend substantially on print world.

Conclusion

It is still believed that print medium with its ease of use allows you to have more purposeful and fruitful time spending (by ordering what you want, when you want and where you want) and supports the basic human drive to self improvement than electronic media. Only print medium can break greater loneliness and isolation (like Disneylands) created by technology.

Electronic media do not respect freedom, autonomy, diversity and individuality. They have scant respect for intelligent viewers. Print as a 'cool' medium also appears to provide more real and rational messages than 'violent and hot' electronic media. Print is almost perception independent, overcomes perceptual constancy and misperception whereas electronic media depend on viewers' perception.

Print provides lasting experience rather than instant entertainment, education and information. Print upholds cultural values and electronic media has all the potential to set cultural degradation. Electronic media sometimes has inbuilt information hierarchies which, at times, affect ease of use. In addition, print has much less health hazards than televideo.

As on today, large chunk of information continues to be in paper medium. It is pertinent to note a finding of a recent study by M/s.Coopers and Hybrand (Hendley, 1988, p17) that "...of the information that enters an organisation in paper form, only 1% is coded and entered into computer systems, under 5% is converted to microfilm at some stage of its life and 94% remains in paper form throughout its life time. In addition, as the volume of transactions grows the volume of paper handled is rising at the rate of 25% per year". Thus, inspite of many mass-storage devices like microform, optical and electronic media, paper continues to have a major share. It is unrealistic to think of disposing paper system. In an automated environment also, it is desirable that manual system coexists to some extent to take care of SOS calls.

Digital representation of information in electronic media makes it amenable to cost-effective processing, communication and storage. But many attributes like ubiquity, quality of display, ease and speed of browsing and aesthetics like feel, texture, quality of binding, etc. of a printed book still score over electronic media. There are many tangible and intangible benefits of books which are not available in electronic form. For example, browsing, which is an important requirement of users, is slowed down by 40% if done on CRT (Gimson, 1995, p.141). Similarly, electronic media skips proof reading, makes editing (on VDU) more difficult and time consuming and creates tendency to skip an important process called refereeing required for quality control.

Regarding the cost of superhighway, it may be noted that "No matter who builds it, the global data network will be staggeringly expensive: estimates range from $400 billion over 20 years in North America alone upto more than a trillion dollars worldwide, and the truth is that no one knows how high the cost will be" (McGrath, 6 June 1994, p.19).

Lastly, there is a dire need for according equal importance to electronics in libraries. There is also a need for re-thinking and re-defining the role of libraries to accommodate dynamic multimedia information in electronics/ digital form and to provide mechanisms that will cater for 'living' information that can be modified and adopted by users. Further, it is equally important to impart necessary consumption skills for effective and efficient use of electronic libraries.

References

1. Deodhar, P.S. The Third Parent: Growth and development of Indian electronic media. New Delhi, Vikas, 1991.
2. Religion and communications: Feeling fundamentalism. *The Economist*, 328 (7825), 21-27 August 1993, 33.

3 Forthergill, Richard and Butchart, Ian. Non-book materials in libraries: A practical guide. 3rd ed. London, Clive Bingley, 1990.

4 Gilder, George. The death of telephony (why the telephone and TV will not be the stars of the communication revolution). *The Economist*, 11-17 September 1993, 328(7828), 69-72.

5 Gimson, Roger. Electronic paper — Can it be real? *Aslib Proceedings*, June 1995, 47(6), 139-149.

6 Hendley, A.M. Document image processing systems: Part II — Applications. *Information Media and Technology,* January 1988, 21(1), 17-18.

7 McGrath, Peter. Your electronic future, *News week,* 6 June 1994, 16-19.

8 Schumacher, F.F. Small is beautiful: A study of economics of people mattered. London. *Abacus*, 1973.

9 Sharada, P.V. Impact of television on political awareness of rural masses. New Delhi. Gyan Publishing House, 1992.

10 Smith, Anthony. The electronic circus. *The Economist*, 11-17 September 1993, 328 (7828), 72, 75-76.

11 Sridhar, M.S. Library applications of CD-ROM database with a case study of CD-ROM system at ISRO Satellite Centre Library. *CLIS Observer*, July-December 1994, 11 (3 & 4), 49-65.

12 Sridhar, M.S. Information technology and library services: A struggle for happy and healthy partnership. An invited guest lecture delivered at National Workshop on Impact of Information Technology on Libraries, August 6-11, 1995, Karnataka Regional Engineering College, Surathkal.

13. Sridhar, M.S. Modernising library services using IT: Potentials and problems. An invited paper for the Seminar on Services in Automated Libraries: Challenges and Opportunities, December 4-5, 1995, American Studies Research Centre, Hyderabad.

14. Sweetland, James H. Information poverty - Let me count the ways (The linear file - Guest editorial). *Database*, August 1993, 16(4), 8-10.

15. Teague, S. John. Microform, video and electronic media librarianship. London. Butterworths, 1985.

16. Wright, Robert. The evolution of despair. *Time,* 28 August 1995,146 (9), 40-46.

SIS–96, 18–20, Jan. '96, Bangalore

Towards digital libraries: Fear, aspirations and challenging opportunities

M. DEB AND BHAGWAN DAS
KDMIPE, ONGC, Dehradun

Abstract

The changing world of librarianship has paved to information highway from the traditionally embarked concept of printed world. The adoption of information technology (IT) for data readiness, accessibility and decision support excellence, has got into the virtual environment of electronic and electro-optical devices as visualised in ONGC. The paper pinpoints the gradual shift-overs towards digital info high-tech from traditional rudimentary adherence thus giving rise to the fears into the librarians to greater extent. The fears are like, phobia to computer exposures, stationary skills, regressive attitude, cognitive factors, perceived cost, etc. These are the pressing challenges before the professionals of coming generation to enthuse with high-tech information highway.

Unlike these intricacies, other side of Digial Libraries (DL) is quite fascinating. It draws the attention of befitting challenges of cutting edge technology, globalised socio-economic stresses, system friendliness, cost effectiveness of information use, R&D proliferation, effective strategic and managerial processes etc. The suggestions are also given as to how to overcome the fears and develop knowledge based confidence for high tech absorption of digitisation breaking the barriers of distance.

Introduction

The information revolution is rapidly widening the horizon of applications of upcoming technology promising the accessibility of relevant information to the users on one hand and enhancing the productivity of information work and services on the other. The revolution of digitisation is not instantaneous, it is likely to start with slow pace and accelerate over the time. But it is clear that the emergence of digital libraries will severely affect the traditional functions of libraries, readers, library professionals, authors, editors, publishers, book sellers etc. How soon these changes would occur, is hard to predict in Indian librarianship, but the technological foundations for digital library structures are in the gamut and the pressures of social and organisational changes will follow.

A digital library is popularly viewed as an electronic throughput replacing conventional archival and print media by electronic version with the inclusive sense of greater information exchange and value added professional elevations. This receives three major areas of differences: viz, (1) Storage in digital form, (2) Direct communication to obtain material and accessibility, and (3) Copying from a master version.

The perceived fears, uncertainties and frowning attitudes of resisting phenomena to the ensuing changes are worth mentioning. Generally speaking, the adoption of information technology in Indian environment is not applauded due to many distorting reasons at various levels.

Apart from all meanderings, the opportunities offered by digital libraries are a challenge before the professionals, experts, information workers, technocrats, corporate strategists, academicians, users etc.

The trends

The extrapolation of something today and its transformation into the reality of something tomorrow has been the tendency. To adapt the new ways and means or to resist the change in information handling and services is visualised through the cross sections of the technological insight. There has been massive changes in the nature or recorded knowledge akin to the revolution associated with printing. After all printing is barely 500 years old and the paper media is still dominant for authors, editors, publishers, book sellers and readers.

The librarians need to have parallel touch with the cutting edge developments even as the book as a source of knowledge becomes extinct. It ought to be augmented by some other media. While discussing the scope of the paper, the basic speculations are struck on electronic technology for preserving literature. The subtle thoughts contained in the existing sources need to be galvanised to correlate the imaginations — the images to the mind.

The end users in the industrial organisation are individuals who use information to make high level decisions, e.g., in ONGC, how more oil is explored, how economically oil is produced, how joint ventures are formalised etc. Decision makers always get their information from middle management, consultants, experts who come across the normal and informal organisational activities. The intangibility of information integration, simplification and presentation, arrests the fidelity of digital wares.

Characteristics of digital libraries

The gradual facelift of overall libraries from the past, there appears some tangible impacts recognising the predictions of Lancaster's paperless society to reality. The transformational effects that digital technology brings in to information system are as follows:

Collections: Digital library collections contain fixed, permanent documents. Not only that current libraries have more dynamic collections, but digital environment will enable of quick handling and/or ephemeral information.

Technology: Digital libraries are based on digital technologies. The underlying assumption is that the digital libraries will contain only digital materials, may be wrong. It is likely that both digital and non-digital information material will have to coexist.

Work: Digital libraries are to be used by individuals working alone. There is work oriented perspective focussing on group of information analysts, work being done and the documents and technologies that support it.

Transbordering of information: Breaking the physical boundaries of data transfers within and outside the countries. It is viewed that the support for communications and collaboration is as important as information seeking activities.

Compaction of data storage is enabling storage of conventional works in digital form. Electronic publishing is swiftly converting the bulk space onto the table top. The telecommunication is facilitating the use of electronic methods to get back, browse, and connect to teleconferencing, videotext, paging, messaging etc. With the capacity to copy from master version, the mechanical aspect of publishing and printing of books and magazines will gradually disappear as soon as the replicating facility of digital library takes in.

Fear and aspirations

The adoption and acceptance of new technology (digital libraries) will never be straightforward and monolithic, inspite of its expected dominance. Since this paper reveals the fears of most of librarians and end users for handling the digital libraries, the introspections of authors' observations and experiences are of paramount as discussed in the following sections.

Fears

The fears creeping in the minds are normally due to psychological aberrations and ambient environment. Some of the realistic fears as visualised and perceived are as under.

Technophobia

In general, some people do, however, fear or loathe any upcoming technology. Individuals may have several reasons for not using the new technology.

The underlying reluctance against the common users of electronic media, is generally the fear of getting the system scrapped and seem to be in pivotal state of mind. In Indian scenario, librarians in some organisations are happy with usual library routine services. Even during the hands-on training of on-line and library automation, most of the trainees are not susceptible to training opportunity of handling electronic devices.

Lack of knowledge

During the last decade, there has been parallel growth in technology, awareness, and services. The awareness of library professionals and end users, has been orthodoxical. The skill development modalities are evolved with new dimensions to familiarise the professionals and end users to accept the myths and reality of digitisation of the library environment. However, the lack of knowledge about any new system pinpoints the characteristics of individual librarians and their enthusiasm of learning.

There appears to be a need for an integrated approach to the problems relating to information storage and dissemination. It may be possible for information professionals to apply their knowledge to the facets of information handling for minimum distortion.

Technostress

Some experts are of opinion that there may be physical strains due to flare and glare of electronic operations. Sometimes atmospheric factors are also reactive and found unpleasant to health. RSI (Repetitive Stress Injury) which causes physical pain and apparent computer related stress[1].

To work overload and glutting of heterogeneous jobs invited stress to the minds of information handling personnel. The supercession and overlapping of cutting edge technology trends for arresting high value of economy, has also been the vital factors for inherent reluctance.

Fear of failure

The jargonisation of information products and services falling within the sense of digital libraries, has given rise to another kind of fear. As discussed above, the shallow insight about the understanding of the system always clicks to be the failure. The office bureaucracies, fiscal inputs, and maintenance implications are the major factors causing fear of fallsdrop. Sometimes audit's consequences in the organisational processes are also provoking the services with fearful blinkering to be minimum, optimum, or maximum.

On-line interactive services, facsimile services, e-Mail, WWW, WAIS, BBS are primarily cost intensive services. The end users should invariably have to be well versed about the system functions, execution and outputs to avert the loss mania from the minds.

Fear of fragility

The early days' librarians had been worried about the expense, safety and fragility of digital goods prone to scrapping, blasting, and flammability. The backroom computing for databases, e.g., geological interpretation, was predominant and the monolithic expertise had to prevail due to the singular situation.

Now the multidisciplinary approach in the digital age has been apparently advanced. The fear of fragility, safety and high cost against digital information services, has gradually vanished at the stage of global competitiveness, precision technology and economy.

Resistance to change

The problems of resistance put forth by individuals, potential users, publishers, distributors, editors etc. are of much interest within the scope of this paper. The rigid sense of some of the professionals/library work forces to change to the nascency and decency of the information system, remains always with the trends due to known reasons. The natural resistance of potential users to use electronic services as visualised by Newcomb[2], is of importance.

- Psychological preparation to change their reading habits forced to go on screens.
- Expense of electronic products as compared to print products.
- Prefer to selecting needed information faster by reading the printed products than is retrieved by watching the scrolled screens.

- Affordability to electronic products in totality.

Reverse attitude

The conceptualisation and social impact of digital libraries are two basic reasons for its proactive or reverse effects. The librarians and end users would definitely frown if the concept or background knowledgebase to digital devices is not skilled into them well in advance. The other side is the social recognition of merits of the digital system, which will push them to learn and accept. Even the most advanced information technology is of little use because of such reverse attitudes.

Fear of downsizing

With the advent of computer profiling data updating trends, the glare of status quo has occupied the corporatised organisational activities. Notwithstanding, the digital library surrogates would have been seen ideal on their table top. These decision makers/policy designers are either in tyranny of time resulting over occupation or due to the fear of downsizing the status as digital library accessibility, operations and back up as they think, relates to the operators themselves.

Ethical problems

The problems of ehical kind in terms of digital library operations, herein after concerned to end users, are prevalent almost in every working environment. The on-line searches, printing and organisation of digital libraries are ethically scrolled up and thus the acceptance of its predominant features gets delayed. The geoscientific community, oil explorationists, drillers, rigmen were not supposed to interpret the seismic data and other related information for their jobs. The backroom computing, i.e., the computing process was to be done only by the computer personnel, as prevailing just few years ago. Though the situation is improving yet it is imposing latent fear to digital library's success.

Aspirations

Apart from the intricacies of fears as discussed above, the scope of aspirations is increasingly wider. A schematic illustration is shown in Fig.1 In digital libraries environment, some novelties like CD-ROM database, micros with better peripherals, fax machines, smaller photocopiers, high speed modems, DTP, more on-line services, internetworking, highway communication, e-mail, multi-media have come up to information diligence.

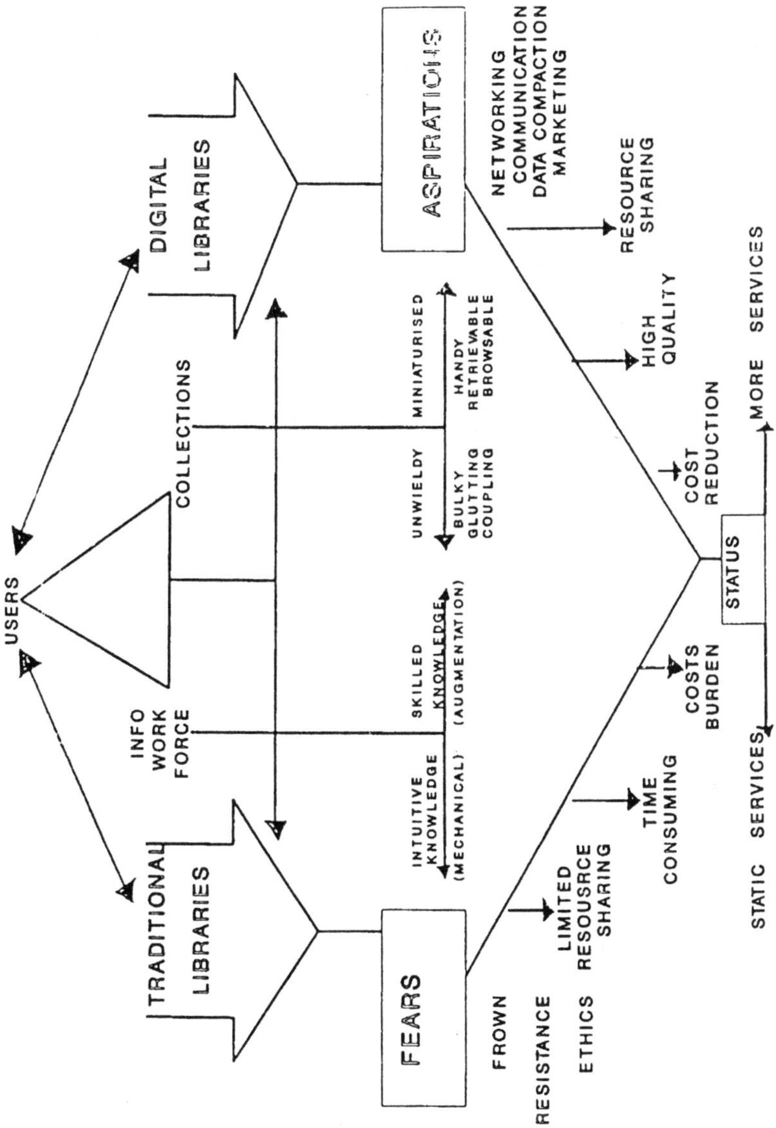

Fig. 1: EVALUATION OF FEARS & ASPIRATIONS

CD-ROM media, for example, have become popular in libraries because of lower storage costs and added features (Table 1).

Table 1. Storage costs per megabyte of DATA

Storage media	Costs in $
Hard disk	10.00
Paper	4.00
Floopy disk	1.70
Microfiche	0.76
Magnetic tape	0.25
CD-ROM	0.024

(Courtesy: SPE Comp. Applications, 1992 August)

Generally speaking the technical and communication environment is expected to be very rich, with proliferation of new devices, for creating, processing, storing, reorganising, replicating the digitised text, graphics, statistics etc. Bulletin Board, World Wide Web (WWW), Wide Area Information Server (WAIS), Internet, ORBIT, Dialog, Teleconferencing, paging, videophone, videotext are emerging as new vistas to information highway buzz. Driven to the valued features of digital libraries, following merits are visualised.

- Quick retrieval and time saving
- Reliability and quality of data seeking
- Shrinking of bulk space
- High speed communication and internetworking
- Greater output
- Increasing scope for information marketing
- Economy to the industry/organisation
- Scope for knowledge augmentation
- Decision support mechanism
- Thrusting global competitiveness
- Increasing resource sharing opportunities.

Internet and computer bulletin board are making it easy for oil industry workers to quickly access information for geologic, geophysical, drilling and other allied operations. The recent growth in the Internet has been "home pages" on the WWW offering hypertext links. According to Crow[3], oil and gas and geology home pages on the Internet's WWW have doubled in the last six months, while usage.has increased tenfold. SPE and AAPG are two professional groups active on Internet.

The other implicitness of digital libraries is miniaturisation of devices. As a result, the capacities are rising and the costs are dropping exponentially.

Challenges and opportunities

The changing world of today becomes even more challenging tomorrow. Despite carrying the lingering excellence of its own, digital libraries are the challenges on a variety of fronts in terms of their role and functions. While technology is advancing at an incredible pace, our ability to absorb and use the technology in an essentially human endeavours, is still limited. Even in cases where significant commitment has been made and resources invested, the human aspect of information processing and delivery have continued to limit the full utilization of available information wealth.

For librarians a hard nosed analysis of the value of the digital libraries services must be done. Librarians have to frame the strategies that demonstrate their ability and innovativeness to expand library services with the realisation of available digital technology. The users have to be alert of the off-the-shelf technology and the librarians must be educated in the ways of change. Lancaster[4] observes that the survival of the library profession depends on its ability and willingness to change its emphasis and image.

When cutback in budgets strikes, information services and libraries are often among the earliest victims. The downsizing of digital devices under such circumstances is depressing and technology switch overs seem to be bleak. The organisational view points need some inclusive resetting towards the digital libraries concept. The realisation of electronic mode will depend on the adaptability by their people, methodology and applications, attention and assistance offered by the organization, as well as the generic issues of the development approached from a global view point.

Traditional library schools' curriculum have tended to be too narrow, both in the conception of broadening the knowledge and application of information technology. Theoretically speaking, the modalities of curriculum specially in India, is in dilly dally position except in few exceptional appreciable cases. A new caveat is of much importance as the technology oriented hands on exercises during the studies would be highly warranted. The emphasis should now be to take an inevitable view to look to the digital technology for analysis, synthesis, and transmittal of data. The library academy must broaden beyond the home front to become international in scope, emphasising the global implications of knowledge.

Training and development opportunities for librarians and end users for optimal utilization of digital innovations, is to be encouraged and revitalised. NISSAT, NICNET, C-DOT, leading computer companies should regularly organise the training programmes for digital library users and novices.

Importing of technology has been a great barrier until recently but it has been simplified thanks to liberalisation programmes of government. A similar approach is to be launched by the Department of Telecommunication and other government agency to soothe the digital libraries intakes.

Security shocks are the most pressing challenges of digital affairs. Piracy of database, copyright infringement, viral invasions, parallel satellite networking stress are some of the issues for digital libraries to be confronted as a way of routine.

Suggestion/Recommendations

The shrinking world of information hardware necessitates the heightened sense of social responsibility. The thinking outlook must be global and action should be socially responsible. In the changing world, the librarians and information specialists must be upto the mark to stand with the future.

The user of the library of the future may be another knowledge system, i.e., any intelligent system. According to Martyn[5] the library of the future will be a network of knowledge systems. The professionals would take the advantages of the opportunities offered by the new technology and social changes as well as how best could they meet some problems of the future. The tendency to see the advances in digital libraries and communication technology need be formalised.

In the digital world of information highway, there should be stress on three things[6]: awareness of information, awareness of technology, and awareness of needs. The awareness of information gives the breadth of vision; awareness of technology gives the power to make the visions manifest; and awareness of needs gives the insight to use professional skills and talents to the greater effect.

The recommendations in view of the scope of the paper to aspire the library work force and users community with the digital libraries are as follows:

High cost of technology and inadequate skills of operations have to be taken on prirority. It can be sorted by facilitating users meet, specialised training, in-service training and motivating digital device users (librarians, scientists, system designers).

Consortia of digital libraries need be formed to look into the matter related to the implicit problems of individual libraries right from its procurement to applications. Recently the problem of networking being faced by ONGC in the present context, the selection of suitable hardware/software for networking at WAN is still unsorted.

The educative part of library curriculum should be of pragmatic sense. Internship project for library science students should be launched by UGC academic programme as being done in some of the professions. The syllabi of liberary science course need be reasonably restructured in the changed scenario.

The organisation, industries, institutes etc. should be given the exposure of digital libraries so as to make the authority affirm and applaud the decency of the new system. The digital library vendors, distributors, publishers should hold exhibitions, displays and trade fairs intermittently to familiarise with these innovations.

The policy of funding the libraries should be liberalised to encourage the information highway. As a matter of fact, libraries are funded in India not only on healthy economy but also on current policy of the organizations.

The monopolistic attitude and pricing policy of the database hosts should be taken seriously for discussion. Dual subscription burden to the user organisation need some relief due to stringent policies of the hosts. Petroleum Abstracts, USA has made the pricing policy for printed, digital and dual information product subscribers, based on the assets of the oil industries.

Conclusion

It is not the technology itself which is good or bad, it is what we do with it. The existence of the libraries of the future depends largely on the decision of present generation, if not thought well before, it will be vulnerable because other professionals start doing our job. Librarians have to see their primary role of maximising the effective use of their collection rather than acting as custodians. If well taken, the librarians of today can become the knowledge counsellors of tomorrow. The knowledge counsellor will be then much more intellectual, requiring much knowledge at selecting, analysing, and synthesising information. The digital libraries as visualised is, no doubt the benchmark in the information technology and practicing knowledge dissemination.

The action words for digital libraries are "do something, start getting involved, and must participate."

Acknowledgement

Authors are thankful to Director (E) of ONGC and Regional Director, KDMIPE, ONGC for granting permission to present/publish this paper to this conference.

References

1. Osakamp, S. and Spacepan, S. Ed: People's reactions to technology, 1990, Sage Pub, p.15.

2. Newcomb, J. Electronic information distribution, *Special Lib.*, 1983, 74(2), p.152.

3. Crow, P. Information access quick, easy with Internet, Bulletin Board. *Oil & Gas J*, 1995, 93(37), p.33.

4. Lancaster, F. W. Libraries and librarians in the age of electronics. Info Resource Press, 1982, p.150.

5. Martyn, J. Factors affecting the future of libraries. *Aslib Proc.*, 1991, 43(9), p.284.

6. Spaulding, F. H. Special librarian to knowledge counsellor in the year 2006. *Special Lib.*, 1988, 79(2), p.90.

SIS–96, 18-20, Jan. '96, Bangalore

Digital libraries and users: An analysis of interactions

K.S. CHUDAMANI AND B.C. SANDHYA
J.R.D. Tata Memorial Library, Indian Institute of Science, Bangalore 560 012

Abstract

Digital libraries are libraries wherein all information is available in digital form. They act as switching centres for local networks belonging to the user community. In order to understand the impact of digital libraries on users, in this paper the help of an anecdote from a traditional library reference query is solicited.

Further, it attempts to enlist the issues in information access, searching, retrieving, cost, etc. for a user of a digital library in contrast with the conventional library setup. Thereby interaction of users with the library system and the new role of library staff are analysed.

Introduction

With the advent of new technology, a great change is taking place in the information world. Information is made available in digital form. Hence people think that one day the conventional libraries will vanish and only digitised libraries will be in existence.

Keeping this in view, we thought of analysing a real life anecdote of a conventional library, in a digital context, to understand the various ramifications of interactions and role of libraries, library staff and the user, the three components around which the dynamics of a library revolves.

Digital libraries

According to the Berkeley Digital Library Project, Univ. of California[1], "the digital library will be a collection of distributed information sources; producers of information will make it available, and consumers will find it perhaps through the help of automated agents".

The Stanford Digital Library Project[1] states that the "Integrated digital library will create a shared environment linking everything — personal information collection to collection of conventional libraries to large data collection shared by scientists. Integrated virtual libraries provide an array of new services, uniform access to networked information collection".

As per the scenario presently conceived by digital library proponents, the basic assumptions underlying such a system are:

- Digital library collection contains fixed, permanent documents
- Digital libraries are based on digital technology
- Digital libraries are used by individuals working at their terminal.

The critical technology required for such a setup are :

- Fully automated indexing and intelligent retrieval
- Developing database to digital library application
- Developing a more effective protocol for client/server information retrieval.

However, current efforts in going digital, according to Levy[2] are "limited by a largely unexamined and unintended allegience to an idealised view of what libraries have been rather than what they actually are or could be". Now, before analysing the nature of their interactions with users, let us briefly understand the users and their needs.

Users and their information needs

Users are those for whom information systems are created; the ultimate beneficiaries. In the context of their direct use of an information system, they are often referred to as end-users to distinguish them in the sense of intermediaries who use and supply service on behalf of and for users. Their wants are always vague.

Very frequently it is impossible to know what it is needed, the need itself or the ability to express it or perhaps the ability to recognize what satisfies it all or any one of these may change with time. It is followed by cognitive processes, working hypothesis, the description of the want and its verbalization. Finally, it is the satisfaction or relevancy of the retrieved information, with minimum efforts and cost that is most important.

This need will be illustrated with the help of an anecdote.

The anecdote

A user approaches a reference staff with the following request — "I searched all the racks for a book, for two days and could not trace it. Can you help me to find the book?".

Then the library staff wants to know the details of the publication. The user says that he knows only the author's name and says that he searched all the racks with that information only. Then the reference staff points out that the user has wasted his time by not checking the catalogue first, to confirm the availability. Further, with the call number, the time required for searching could have been not more than 15-20 minutes.

Next, in order to assist the user, the staff consults the alphabetical part of the catalog and finds a number of titles, editions of titles by the same author. From the set, the user picks a specific title needed by him and wants it for borrowing. One of the edition readily available on the shelf is given to the user.

In this anecdote, the various characteristics of the users can be observed which relate to — vague/specific searching, requirement of personal assistance, losing time due to adhoc searching, satisfaction of the need, etc. Now, let us analyse the anecdote in the context of a digital library.

The anecdote in the digital context

If the query posed in the anecdote is analysed in the digital setup, the following sequence of actions may occur at the user terminal.

The user logs into a computer terminal of the digital library at his end. Therefore he needs at least minimum computer literacy. Here, he is not free to use it as he likes becuase he is already in a computer environment. He is guided by the program resident in the computer.

Therefore, when he keys in the author's name the program would allow him to navitage through the indexes automatically generating some output. The resident indexes, navigation tools play a vital role, whether visible or not. This can be explained by the fact that several indexes or tools such as thesaurus, hypertext links are searched without the knowledge of the user, when, only key is keyed in. In such a scenario, the loss of time in searching in conventional system is mostly avoided. Once an item is located, it is easily accessed without encountering the problems of misplacement or already borrowed or lost items, as is the case with the present day libraries.

Then, once a set of references or texts are retrieved by the system, user has to browse through them on the computer screen itself. This is a time consuming and physically strenuous job. So, the actual time gained in searching is lost in browsing. To avoid browsing for a long time, downloading the text/data from the database is the option. Downloading definitely involves cost of providing printing facility, royalty payment, etc. This inturn requires knowledge of copyright laws.

The following table presents all the issues discussed above in comparison with traditional libraries.

Comparison of issues in a conventional library with digital library

Issues	Conventional library	Digital library
enquiries	vague/specific	vague/specific
searching	through catalogue/ browsingon the shelf	only through indexes resident in the system
selection of titles	possible	possible
physical availability/ accessibility	not ensured	always ensured
loss of time	inconsulting the catalogue, physically locating items	in browsing on the screen and using inefficient search tools
assistance by library staff	more frequently needed	less frequently needed
cost of accessibility	very low or free	may not be free
computer literacy	can manage without it	essential
communication	mostly person to person, or telephone rarely by e-mail	mostly by e-mail rarely person to person or telephone

The nature of interactions between the user and library that can be visualised from this comparison are discussed in the next session.

Nature of interactions between users and digital library

From the table, it is evident that though the issues involved in both the systems are similar, their handling varies. In a traditional library searching of books/documents is physically on the racks. Libraries in general provide access to documents by a classified arrangement of books on the shelves, enabling the user to browse through a set of documents on a subject and its close allies. The knowledge of classified arrangment which was critical in libraries may not be essential in digital setup. This can be attributed to the capability of the computer in searching and linking various approaches automatically.

In libraries, for faster checking of availability, the catalogue is consulted. Many a times even without consulting the catalogue people go to the racks directly and browse because they know where to locate. Therefore, the minimum literacy requirement is the art of locating the books on the racks; may be without consulting the catalogue, even if a computerised catalogue is available. But, in the digital context the access is only through the computer. Hence, minimum computer literacy is essential. The loss of time due to adhoc searching is more common in libraries; and it can be expected that more time may be lost in browsing on the screen in the digital library.

Though, the nature of queries may be same in both systems, the way in which assistance is sought from the staff changes. That is, users seek the help of the staff both in locating the materials physically as well as for checking their availability in libraries. In a digital system they may still delegate the task of checking the availability to the library staff; but may not need any assistance in locating them. The delegation of the responsibility of checking may be communicated by e-mail instead of the usual means of telephone or fax or personal contact.

Cost of such accessiblity cannot be easily defined in both the systems. Though, at present, consultants charge fee for all information services, the institutions such as, public libraries, companies etc. who usually establish the facility for the sake of their obligation to their clientele provide almost free access to them. But, xeroxing is not free. Therefore, depending on the establishment cost of digital libraries, they may have to review their decisions regarding charging. However, the printing facility in the digital library which will be equivalent to the xeroxing facility of the present day may not be free.

All these differences visualised in the user-system interactions and many more issues not considered here, indicate that the role of the library and library staff in a digitial library setup will undergo a change. The new role of library and library staff is discussed in the next section.

Role of library and library staff in a digital setup

In the digital setup, everything is electronic. Hence, if we assume that some type of fee is charged by an electronic publisher for the right to access a particular database, it is conceivable that the libraries will and still play a role in making materials accessible free or at low cost.

Digital libraries will have to atleast collect, catalog and index materials of purely local interest. Libraries will have to subscribe to books and periodicals in electronic form.

For one thing, it seems reasonable to assume that some type of library will be needed to provide on-line access to individuals, who for one reason or the other do not have their own terminals. The library will be a centre in which access to worldwide databases and databanks will be possible.

They may become remote access points for some and turn out to be printout centres for some others. Digital library spacing requirements will be reduced drastically. In order to provide services, they may need a few highly trained personnel who can procure materials in digital form, create specialised indexes, searching tools etc., and assist users in:

- Searching indexes effectively and efficiently
- Searching network databases as intermediaries
- Education and training of new users
- Adhereing to copywright rules and regulations
- Procure required documents for the local database and process them to suit local requirements.

Conclusions

In a digital library system, the library and inturn the library personnel will have to be more specialised, highly technical and better equipped to provide high-tech services. Also, the user should become computer literate and develop the skills of exploiting computerised information services to the maximum. It can be foreseen that the dynamics of interactions in terms of creation and use of services increases.

Bibliography

1. *Communications of the ACM*, 38(4), 1995, p.59-60.
2. Levy, David M. and Marshall, Catherine C. Going digital: A look at assumptions underlying digital libraries. *Communications of the ACM*. 38(4), 1995, pp.77-84.
3. Lancaster, F.W. Towards paperless information society, New York, Academic Press, 1978.
4. Fleming, Hugh. Ed, User education in academic libraries, London, Library Association, 1990.
5. Wilson, Tom. In the beginning was the word...; Social and economic factors in scholarly electronic communication. *Aslib Proceedings,* 47(9), 1995, pp.195-202.

Eight

Indian Scenario, Problems and Prospects

SIS–96, 18–20, Jan. '96, Bangalore

Evolving digital library of petroleum: Efforts and achievements of Indian petroleum industry with special reference of ONGC

A.K. SRIVASTAVA
KDMIPE Library, Oil and Natural Gas Corporation, Dehradun

Abstract

The paper presents an overview of use of digital technology and communication system in petroleum information management, access and seeking pattern. Discusses the structure and architecture of digital library in Indian petroleum industry with special reference to Oil and Natural Gas Corporation (ONGC). Digitisation efforts of ONGC in developing digital library of indigenous geoscientific and petroleum information has turned out to be a system of specialised index text and bibliographic databases accessible through telecommunication system. Existing and planned facilities at different specialised digital libraries are elaborated. It critically examines the efforts and achievements of Indian petroleum libraries in developing various aspects of digital library system of petroleum information resources (out of copy-right). The leading role of the Oil and Natural Gas Corporation in evolving digital libraries through its overall setting and preparing for internetworksing with digital libraries of the world is highlighted.

Historical overview

Petroleum libraries around the globe witness increasing trends towards digitization of primary information sources, company profiling and use of electronic communication like Internet, Bulletin Boards, WWW (home pages) and Wide Area Information Service (WAIS) etc. Guthery's list indicates petroleum industry's use of Internet and Bulletin Boards, specifically for company profiles and news items is doubling every six months[1]. Giant petroleum database generating agencies like the University of Tulsa at USA, Society of Explorations Geophysics, Society of Petroleum Exploration and National Technical Information Service, USA etc. have already launched digitised petroleum information products accessible on-line or off-line. The coverage tantamounts and leaves scope for only indigenous information sources remaining uncovered and inaccessible to these agencies.

Although of recent origin, the digitisation efforts of Indian petroleum industry, and use of electronic communication for geoscientific data and information sources, as maintained by Singh[2] dates back to seventies. Library and Information units of Indian petroleum industry, especially the Oil and Natural Gas Corporation, have evolved various specialised text/bibliographic databases, on-line public access catalogs of holdings and retrieval services while efforts are currently on to cover full text of articles andother in house publications (out of copyright), images, maps, graphics and animation etc. Singh mentions that the nature, scope and information needs of both upstream and downstream Indian petroleum industry differ significantly because of their scope and style of functioning[3]. This demands a distributed but internetworked digital library system that provides a comprehensive range of library services for collection of spatially indexed data, maps and graphical information. Such collections includes besides literature sources, in company communiques, siesmic maps, animated images of exploration equipments and subsurface structures. Information resources structure of ONGC includes 7,00,000 lakhs of magnetic tapes, with annual addition of 70,000 tapes per year, 5,000 maps, VSP, 3,000 files and thousands of R&D reports besides regular bulletins and other inhouse publications.

Conceptual framework

Digital library represents digitised version of basic components of library i.e., documents, retrieval system, archival, information processing, dissemination and stand —alone/shared access mostly aided by or unaided by information worker. Thus the digital library evokes an impression of change perspectives of carrying out the library functions using electronic technology. This influences the form of information resources, acquisition policy (especially with more shared and subscription services), methods of storage and presentation, approaches to technical processing like classification and cataloguing, modes of interaction with information resources by the users, communication system and networks, and dramatic shifts in intellectual, organisational and economic practices. ONGC's system is a mix of both digital and non-digital library.

Model of a digital library system

ONGC proposes to develop distributed petroleum database system that serves as an on-line library of ONGC's inhouse information not available through digitised packages like GEOROM, AAPG Bulletin, Proceedings of the Society of Petroleum Information to its entire workforce and offer a range of useful information service to entire petroleum industry.

Digital library system being evolved is not restricted only to distributed specific knowledge bases developed at different work locations of ONGC but also covers commercially available full text and bibliogrphic databases. The configuration of hardware, software and structure of datasets reveals stand alone heterogeneous unit that presently do not correspond to each other. Coverage of subject domains are highly specific to objectives of patron institute/work centres such as exploration and exploitation, drilling, reservoir engineering, production technology, ocean engineering and environment pollution etc. Access points to datasets include bibliographic details of monographs, serials, society publications, journals holding and availability information, article index accessible through author, title, thesaurus based keywords subject index, accession number, contents of books, journals article series etc. approachable individually or in combination with author and subject.

Full text of documents both macro and micro are yet to be converted to digital form. Only retrieval aspects and secondary sources have been tried out in different magnitudes and dimensions at different locations of ONGC.

Development process is being carried out in phases. The process involved a team for designing, developing and implementing the software, information processing, database development internet worked dissemination and access. Basic assumptions are:

- Acquire the suitable software/hardware and communication channel for library operations.
- Develop specific databases for bibliographic/text archival and retrieval.
- Develop database for full text in combination to bibliographic details for indigenous publications (out of copyright) and provide multimedia integration for images, graphics, maps, animation etc.
- Provide internetworking through servers for interactive login, file transfer and e-mail.
- Provide connectivity of indigenous database with international databases.

System architecture

The architecture is heterogeneous. Some knowledge bases are developed on flat file basis and some on relational database system partitioned into modules and sub-modules. These databases provide a simple access to each of the library services by combination of textual and visual languages; a query manager component providing appropriate response to queries, particularly those involving a content based search, a database manager component providing storage for and high speed access to specialised collection of isolated and spatially indexed items and ingest component allowing information workers and programmers to add/modify items to the library collections.

Table 1 Configuration of library system

Institution	Location	Comments
KDM Institute of Petroleum Exploration	0135-625265	Information on petroleum exploration and exploitation. Good links with other petroleumlibraries DIALOG on-line connectivity.
Institute of Drilling Technology	0135-628965	Specific to drilling information
Institute of Reservoir Engineering	079-7487662	Reservoir and production information. R & D Unit.
IOGPT	022-7451690	Specific to production technology. Good links with other petroleum libraries. EASYNET connectivity.
IEOT	022-7451690	Ocean technology and corrosion management
IPSEM	0834-737609	Safety and environment specific information

Interface component is to support both text and visually based query lanauges that return information about the availability of datasets that satisfy various constraints. It supports procedures that allow the users to browse and visualise pertinent datasets and have selected datasets communicated to different work locations. Interface at each site is highly user friendly and menu driven for populating, browsing, listing, editing and selective retrieval of information. CICS/VS, IMS and VMS combination is used for inhouse developed system while various application packages like Clipper, dBASEIII+ and CDSISIS have been used either on IBM mainframe or on PCs. Data input is possible at acquisition as well as cataloguing stage.

New services

Access to literature sources on various subjects domains related to petroleum is being provided to users. Digitised databases and collections on optical discs, on-line system available through international networks developed by outisde agencies and Oil and Natural Gas Corporation forms the data store which the users of this industry can search, extract, and retrieve. Full text and image database of industry's own publications will also be made available. On-line public access catalog is kept open for access and various personalised services like selective dissemination of information, current awareness service, new arrivals information, retrospective search services and audio/video viewing is currently available. Some databases provided browsing contents pages of books and other documents on-line.

Table 2 A view of facilities available in selected specialised knowledge bases of ONGC

Knowledge bases	Indexes	Text	On-line	Image	Graphics	Maps	File transfer	E-mail	Remote login
Petroleum E&P	Y	Y	Y	N	Y	Y	Y	Y	N
Rservoir Engg.	Y	Y	Y	N	N	Y	Y	Y	N
Drilling Engg.	Y	Y	N	N	N	N	Y	Y	N
Petroleum Production/ Simulation	Y	Y	Y	Y	Y	Y	Y	Y	N
Corrosion/ Ocean Engineering	Y	Y	N	N	N	N	Y	N	N
Safety and Environment Management	Y	N	N	N	N	N	Y	Y	N

Discussion

Efforts of ONGC is evolving digital library has been restrictive to immediate needs. The achievements indicate partially digitised library concentrating on secondary sources for indicating existence and availability of published literature sources of Indian and foreign origin. Provision for full text database, downloading from CD-ROM based databases and multimedia integration for images, graphics, animation etc. was not planned. Structure of datafiles needs standardisation or retrospective conversion into similar fields and dataset structures enabling real time parsimonious updating and compatibility. Retrieval features especially Boolean approach need to be incorporated. Structure of subjects and its relation to fields needs logic intensive reconfiguration and relook. Digitised archival, access and retrieval of technical data, maps, graphics, seismic profiles etc had started in seventies but it is not in the library's purview. The very nature of the exploration data is such that its access is restrictive, but published information needs to be converted digital. Password based controlled access system and time-use accounting is essential for opening access to outside agencies. The efforts of Library and Information unit of ONGC should now be directed to capture indigenous publications, internetwork all the spatially developed isolated specific knowledge bases and hook these data nodes with international networks. Efforts in this direction are on and are likely to complete in near future.

References

1. Patric Crow. Information access, quick, easy with Internet, Bulletin Boards. *Oil and Gas J.*, Sept.11, 1995, p.33.

2. Singh Kharak. Computerisation in ONGC during VIII plan. *Energy Review.* Vol.3(I), May 1994, p.113.

3. Singh Sodan, Naresh Chandra and Dhar, P.C. Management of exploration data resources in Oil and Natural Gas Corporation, India. *Indian J. Petroleum Geology*, 2(I), 1993, pp.43-54.

SIS–96, 18–20, Jan. '96, Bangalore

Digital libraries — Dream or reality?

NAINA PANDITA AND MD SIBLI SIRAJEE
National Informatics Centre, New Delhi

Abstract

Libraries serve at least three roles in learning. They serve a practical role in sharing expensive sources — a cultural role in preserving and organizing artifacts and ideas, a social role by bringing together people and ideas. Digital libraries extend roles of traditional libraries by making diverse information resources available beyond the physical space. These roles are discussed high lighting the efforts of NIC.

Introduction

The explosive growth in networked connectivity and rapid advances in computing power are replacing the older notion of stand alone information utilities with newer notions on interconnected digital libraries. Libraries exist in many forms and are of many types. With multimedia technology we have image libraries, audio libraries, and even digital video libraries. We might also think of libraries when we refer to collections that now reside in databases, text bases, gopherspace, or the World Wide Web (WWW).

Traditional libraries' budgets devote an ever increasing share of their funds to electronic services, whether in the form of CD-ROMs, on-line public access catalogs, or on-line databases. As digital storage costs go down relative to cost of library shelf space, and as electronic services become more useful, affordable, available and usable, there is a move towards the grand challenge of a World Digital Library System.

In the digital library, users will need to work simultaneously with multiple distributed information sources that differ in content, form and sources types. They will need to understand displays of larger sets of objects from these sources, organized in ways that allow them to make rapid decisions about what is relevant and what overall patterns exists among the objects. They will need to manipulate the access results and incorporate the information into larger tasks. In short, the digital library will require effective means for amplification of information intensive work (Samuelson).

Libraries serve at least three roles in learning. They serve practical role in sharing expensive sources — both physical and human resources. Libraries serve a cultural role in preserving and organizing artifacts and ideas. Third, libraries serve social and intellectual roles by bringing together people and ideas. Libraries serve as centres of interdisciplinary places shared by learners from all disciplines. Digital libraries extend such interdisciplinarity by making diverse information resources available beyond the physical space shared by a group of learners.

The information resources — both physical and human are customized for specific missions that have traditionally separated, although common technologies such as printing, photography, and computing are found across all settings. Digital access breaking down all physical barriers between resources. Digital libraries have obvious roles to play in formal learning by providing teachers and learners with knowledge bases in a variety of media. One clear difference between traditional libraries and digital libraries is that digital libraries offer greater opportunity for users to deposit as well as to use information (Becker).

A digital library is viewed as an electronic version of a public library. By replacing paper with electronic storage will lead to three major differences: storage in digital form, direct communication to obtain material and copying from a master version. These differences will lead to a plethora of further differences so that eventually the digital library will no longer mimic a traditional library (Weiderhold).

Transformation of digital libraries

The change in a society calls for a change in attitude of the management, technologist, institutions and users. Again, the innovations are not readily accepted by the community at once due to lack of awareness, expertise, cost benefit analysis and suitable end-user cost. In case of libraries, after print media the revolution was taken up by microform and audio-visual materials. In case of computer-communication facilities, the revolution is both in media of information and speed of communication. Changes in case of libraries are:

a) The initial innovation is that the material (books, journals, magazines, newspapers, videos, etc) are to be stored in digital form.

b) The second innovation is in communication.

c) Material will be always copied from the master version of the work in electronic library.

All these changes will have wide ranging effects (Weiderhold).

The information will be available in digitized format and be accessible on World Wide Wed. There will be a change in the management of copyrights in the electronic world. The introduction of digital libraries will affect the traditional functions of authorship, editing, publication, critical review, book selling, libraries, readers and customers.

The challenge of handling electronic publication will require radical changes in the way libraries are organized and managed (Demas).

The management strategies required are:

- Promote flexibility in the organization
- Facilitate coordination and collaboration across organizational divisions
- Promote the ability of the staff to adopt to constant change, and
- Eliminate territoriality in the organization and develop a set of shared goals and values that will promote cooperation among administrative units in collection development for the digital libraries.

Electronic publishing has profound implications for collection development, which is defined as the intentional and systematic building of the set of information resources to which the library provides access. The selection of electronic publications profoundly affects every functional unit in the library. The idiosyncrasies of the new media and the far reaching organizational implications of deciding to acquire or to provide access to publications in new formats require the development of a new organizational model for selection and a conceptual framework for making the transition to the electronic library (Demas).

In the process of development of the digital library there is need for a model for collection development. On the basis of the characteristics of the information resources and how these resources are used, Demas has identified five genre which he called as "information genres". These are: (i) Application Software, (ii) Bibliographic Files, (iii) Full Text, (iv) Numeric Files, and (v) Multimedia.

Characteristics of digital libraries

The three important features which characterize digital libraries are (Levy and Marshall): (i) Documents: Digital library collections contain fixed, permanent documents; (ii) Technology: Digital libraries are based on technology; and (iii) Work: Digital libraries are to be used by individuals working alone.

As an example one can say that the future of biomedical enterprises and biomedical libraries is tied closely to digital information. The changing of print information to digitized information will create new pressures on libraries, particularly, in health care organization. Libraries must learn to deal with these pressures (Erhardt-Domino, et al).

The Indian scenario

India has to be in the Information Highway as a sea of information is knocking at its doors. India has the expertise to meet the challenge and to set up digital libraries in the country. We are at the threshold of breaking into Cyberspace and navigate through Internet and World Wide Web. Through Internet it has now become possible to a part of "Global Village" and exchange information instantly. World Wide Web (WWW) is the most advanced browsing and searching system deployed on Internet based on hypertext paradigm. WWW allows one to explore a seemingly unlimited world wide digital "WEB" of human knowledge. With all these facilities it is possible to access hundreds of databases and make the information available to the user community in the country. Availability of CD-ROM databases accessible through LAN and WAN is an added advantage.

The tools are there and the technology is there, so there is no excuse for us, in India, not to start planning for digital libraries. A number of biomedical institutions in the country have already made a start and notable among these are National Informatics Centre, All India Institute of Medical Sciences in New Delhi; National Institute of Mental Health and Neurosciences in Bangalore and MGR University in Madras.

National Informatics Centre (NIC): NIC through NICNET (NIC satellite based communication network) has 500 odd VSAT at state and district offices. NIC has digital capabilities to support any kind of computer-communication facilities.

- On-line access to MEDLINE and AIDS databases
- Full text of selected journal articles
- Information from databases accessible via internet
- Information from other NLM databases
- Interactive access to CD-ROM databases
- On-line search of catalogue of biomedical databases
- Union catalogue of journals available in various biomedical journals
- Assistance in setting up MEDLARS search facilities
- User awareness programmes
- End-users training

- Assistance to many specialist institutions for developing databases in various speciality organization.

The NIC has been providing biomedical information services to the medical community in the country since 1987/88 staring from the MEDLARS (Medical Literature Analysis and Retrieval Systems) of National Library of Medicine, USA it has now reached a point where a number of databases are being accessed through Internet and WWW. Information from over 40 databases of MEDLARS is being provided to hundreds of doctors/clinicians, postgraduate students and the paramedical staff. Medical institutions and libraries in India can access MEDLINE data from almost any part of the country.

Special information packages on specific drugs and diseases are prepared for medical and health professionals during epidemics for patient care needs. This information can be transferred instantly over NICNET to the remotest parts of the country. Other major institutions like AIIMS and NIMHANS have procured a number of databases on CD-ROMs and are providing information services to their faculty. The DBT Centres are subscribing to gene, DNA and other protein sequence databases on CDs and are also accessing these databases through Internet.

NIC also understands to train the end users, largely including medical and health professionals in the information retrieval techniques. This enables them to shed all inhibitions and feel comfortable in accessing information in digitized format. With the existing scenario in India, it will not be a difficult task to start a network of digital libraries. This would enable a faster and reliable information access and satisfy the information seeker.

Conclusion

One cannot dispense with the print media. The digitized media is a supportive tool for searching, locating the information faster to the targeted users. In achieving that end a national network, expertise and demonstration of results is essential, which NIC is trying to establish with the libraries in India. It is upto the participating libraries to exploit the facilities, expertise of NIC and NICNET.

SIS–96, 18–20, Jan. '96, Bangalore

Coverage of Indian literature in social science bibliographic databases on CD-ROM — Sociofile, EconLIT, LISA and PsycLit

N. PARVATHAMMA
Department of Library & Information Science, Gulbarga University, Gulbarga 585 106

Abstract

Availability of indexing and abstracting services, in printed form, online and on CD-ROM have eased the task of literature searching for scientists and social scientists to a greater extent. Further, having data on CD-ROM has many advantages over print media or online access. The results of the study of some bibliographic databases in social science on CD-ROM, namely, Sociofile, EconLIT, LISA and PsycLit shows that the coverage of Indian publications and Indian periodicals, on an average, amounts to 0.5 percent and 1.16 percent respectively. Among 626 Indian periodicals published in Sociology, Economics, Library and Information Science, and Psychology, 489 (78.1%) periodicals are published in English language. Among these 489 English periodicals, only 45 (9.2%) are covered in the four bibliographic databases under study. Therefore, there is need to publish bibliographic databases covering Indian literature in the above areas on CD-ROM and other machine-readable forms, preferably by private enterprises to ensure promptness in publication and market-oriented approach.

Introduction

Accelerated rate of accumulation of knowledge as a result of increased R & D activities has led to information society of high productivity. In addition to the continued use of traditional channels such as books, periodicals, theses and dissertations and technical reports for communicating research information, there is a gradual increase in the use of digital technology for publishing activities. Availability of the indexing and abstracting services, in printed form, online and on CD-ROM have eased the task of literature searching for scientists and social scientists to a greater extent. Further, having data on CD-ROM has many advantages such as fast retrieval of information, ease of use, fixed price and no telecommunication cost. This aspect has already been discussed.[1,2,3] Directory of CD-ROM Products published by TFPL has listed about 8000 titles in 995[4], which is an indicator of its popularity. The possibility of accessing CD-ROM databases on digital networks similar to Internet is being debated and it is speculated that networked digital information environment is going to be part of our day-to-day professional activities in the next couple of years[5].

In the light of the above developments, a glance at the Indian scenario shows that, at present, India is not much behind the advanced countries in the computer software development, library management methods and techniques and in telecommunication field. But, the use of Information Technology in libraries and in publishing activities is quite low. However, it is expected to go up in the coming years with the price of hardware coming down and increase in awareness among library professionals and scientists regarding the advantages of using IT tools[6]. At the same time, it is observed that, even though Indian scientists and social scientists are contributing significantly to the world knowledge through traditional channels of communication, most of these information are not covered in the international indexing and abstracting services. In this context, an attempt is made in the present study to find out the coverage of Indian published literature in some bibliographic databases in social science on CD-ROM, namely, Sociofile, EconLIT, LISA and PsycLit.

Methodology

A systematic search of the bibliographic databases on CD-ROM, namely, Sociofile, EconLIT, LISA and PsycLit, produced by SilverPlatter Inc., USA, were conducted using the following combination of keywords: "India OR India* in Title". Later, the title and source of publication of the entries retrieved work examined individually to eliminate the entries with the words "American Indian, Navajo Indian" etc. The periodical titles of Indian origin were noted down. Facts about the bibliographic databases under study are given in Table 1. While collecting the data regarding the languagewise distribution of periodicals, since many periodicals are being published in more than one language, they are counted as an individual periodical under each language.

Discussion

Coverage of Indian literature in terms of the number of publications and periodicals covered, on an average, amounts to 0.5% and 1.16% respectively (Tables 2 and 3). Languagewise distribution of 626 Indian periodicals published in the areas of Sociology, Economics, Library and Information Science, and Psychology shows that 489 periodicals (78.1%) are in English language[7] (Table 4). Among these 489 periodicals in English language, 45 (9.2%) are covered in the four databases under study (Table 3; Annexure 1). Hence, it is clear that the literature published in the remaining 444 (90.8%) Indian periodicals in English language are not being brought to the cognizance of the international community due to their non-coverage in the international databases. Even though a few indexing and abstracting serials are being published in India, they do not have much impact on the Indian and

Table 1 Facts about the bibliographic databases on CD-ROM under study

Sl. No.	Name of data base	Source	Coverage	No. of CDs	Print equivalent	Online equivalent	Abstracts added	Update frequency	No. of records covered	No. of Periodical covered
1.	Sociofile	Sociological abstracts Inc.	1975 to April 1995	01	Socioloical abstracts and social planning, policy and development abstracts	Sociological abstracts	Yes	3 times a years	2,06,313	1600
2.	EconLit	Journal of economic literature	1969 to March 1995	01	J. of Econ. literature; Index of Econ. articles in journals	Economic literature index	Yes	Quarterly	3,11,866	423
3.	LISA	Library Asso. Publ. Ltd.	1969 to March 1991	01	Current res. in library and Inf. science	LISA	Yes	Semi-annual	1,05,483	550
4.	PsycLit	American Psycholoical Association	1974 to March 1995	02	Phychological abstracts	PsycInfo	Yes	Quarterly	6,16,087	1300

Table 2 Indian publications covered in social science databases under study

Sl. No.	Name of the database	Period covered	Number of publications indexed	No. of Indian publications indexed	Percentage of Indian periodical cover
1.	Sociofile	1974-Apr.95	2,06,313	1990	0.965
2.	EconLIT	1969-Mar.95	3,11,866	2358	0.756
3.	LISA	1969-Mar.91	1,05,483	584	0.554
4.	PsycLit	1974-Mar.95	6,16,087	1302	0.211
	Total		12,39,749	6234	
	Average		3,09,937	1559	
	Percentage			0.5	

Table 3 Indian periodicals covered in social science databases under study

Sl. No.	Name of the Database	Total Number of periodicals covered	Number of Indian periodicals covered	Percentage of Indian periodical covered
1.	Sociofile	1600	11	0.688
2.	EconLIT	423	10	2.364
3.	LISA	550	14	2.545
4.	PsycLit	1300	10	0.769
	Total	3873	45	
	Percentage		1.16	

international social science fraternity due to various reasons such as time lag in the coverage of primary literature and delay in publication (Table 5). On the other hand, there are ample number of communication networks emerging in the country and Indian scientists and social scientists have easy access to computer and CD-ROM facilities at their work place. Also, the concept of in-house CD-ROM publishing is gaining popularity. In this context, there is an urgent need to publish bibliographic databases covering Indian literature in the above areas on CD-ROM and other machine-readable media, preferably by private enterprises to ensure the promptness in publication and market-oriented approach. It would be desirable to include publications of other Indian languages and dissertation and theses also. Further, the technical skills available with professional librarians regarding the preparation of the

Table 4 Languagewise distribution of Indian periodicals in Sociology, Economics, Library & Information Science and Psychology *

Sl. No.	Language	Sociology, Social-work, Social. Welfare	Economics and Commerce	Library and Inform. Science	Psychology	Total	Percent
1.	English	46	361	39	43	489	78.1
2.	Hindi	21	50	3	2	76	12.1
3.	Marathi	6	8	1	0	15	2.4
4.	Bengali	3	5	2	1	11	1.8
5.	Gujarathi	1	7	1	0	9	1.4
6.	Malayalam	1	4	1	1	7	1.1
7.	Tamil	3	1	0	0	4	0.6
8.	Telegu	1	1	1	0	3	0.5
9	Kannada	0	2	1	0	3	0.5
10.	Assamese	2	1	0	0	3	0.5
11.	Urdu	1	1	0	0	2	0.3
12	Oriya	0	2	0	0	2	0.3
13.	Punjabi	0	1	0	0	1	0.2
14	Sanskrit	1	0	0	0	1	0.2
	Total	86	444	49	47	626	100

* Source: Kaur & Sapra, 1994[7]

bibliographic entries, and the expertise available with academicians in the areas of database creation, maintenance, etc. can be utilised. This would also help in the much sought interaction among the library professionals, academicians and the information industry.

Conclusion

Coverage of Indian literature in some bibliographic databases on CD-ROM, namely, Sociofile, EconLIT, LISA and PsycLit is found to be very low (0.5% for publications and 1.16% for periodicals). While 626 periodicals are published in Sociology, Economics, Library and Information Science, and Psychology in India, 489 (78.1%) of them are in English language. Among these 489 Indian English periodicals, only 45 (9.2%) are covered in the databases under study. Hence, the remaining 90.8% of Indian periodical literature published in English language, in the areas under study are not brought to the cognizance of the international social science fraternity. The

Table 5 Indian indexing and abstracting periodicals in English in the areas under study

Sl No.	Name of the indexing and abstracting service	Publisher	Address	Current Issue (as on 1994)*
1.	ICSSR Journal of abstracts & reviews: sociology & social anthropology (1972-)	Indian council for social — science Res.	35, Ferozeshah Road, New Delhi-110 001	V.20, 1991 delayed publication
2.	Social science research index (1986-)	Indian council for social — science Res.	35, Ferozeshah Road, New Delhi-110 001	Irregular
3.	Index to Indian economic journals (1966-)	Information research academy	Flat No.9, 37, Amir Ali avenue Calcutta-700 019	Regular
4.	Indian economic abstracts (1992-)	Information research academy	Flat No.9, 37, Amir Ali avenue Calcutta-700 019	Regular
5.	Indian library science abstracts	Indian association of special libraries & information centres	P291, CIT Scheme, No.6M, Kankurgachi, Calcutta-700 054	V.22, 1988 delayed publication
6.	Indian psychological abstracts	Indian council for social science research	35, Ferozeshah Road, New Delhi-110 001	v.28, 1990 delayed publication

* Source : Kaur and Sapra, 1994[7]

situation demands for the publication of indexing and abstracting services in these areas covering Indian literature on CD-ROM and other machine-readable forms, preferably by private enterprises to ensure the promptness in publication and market-oriented approach.

References

1. Oppenheim, C. CD-ROM. Fundamentals to applications. Aditya, New Delhi, 1992, 307p.

2. Parvathamma, N. Emerging trend in CD-ROM technology and its use: A case study of Gulbarga University. In: C.P. Vashishth (Editor), Library Movement in India. 39th All India Library Conference, Bangalore, January 7-10, 1994, pp.385-393.

3. Satyanarayana, B. Multimedia CD-ROMs: Library Networking. In: M.A. Gopinath and Rama Reddy (Editors), Information Access Through Networks. CALIBER-95, University of Hyderabad, Hyderabad, February 10-12, 1995, pp.55-67.

4. Tedd, Lucy A. The changing face of CD-ROM. *Journal of Documentation*, V.51, No.2, 1995, pp. 85-98.

5. Rajashekar, T.B. *Communications of the ACM*, Special Issue on Digital Libraries (April 1995): Review. Preprint, 1995.

6. Murthy, S.S. Information technologies in libraries: A futuristic perspective. ILA Bulletin, V.31, No. 1-2, 1995, pp. 27-33.

7. Kaur, S. and Sapra, P. (Compilers). Directory of Periodicals in India, 1994. 3rd Ed., Sapra and Sapra, New Delhi, 1994.

ANNEXURE 1

Indian periodicals covered in the databases under study

I. Sociofile

1. Indian Journal of Social Work
2. Indian Journal of Social Science
3. Indian Journal of Social Research
4. Indian Journal of Criminology and Criminalistics
5. Indian Journal of Youth Affairs
6. Indian Journal of Clinical Psychology
7. Indian Linguistics
8. Indian Journal of Politics
9. Indian Economic and Social History Review
10. Indian Journal of Psychology
11. Indian Journal of Sociology

II. EconLIT

1. Economics of Planning
2. Indian Economic Journal
3. Indian Economic and Social History
4. Indian Journal of Quantitative Economics
5. Journal of Developing Areas
6. Journal of Development Economics
7. Journal of Development
8. Journal of Policy Modeling
9. Margin
10. Indian Economic Review

III. LISA

1. Journal of Library and Information Science (India)
2. Indian Library Association Bulletin
3. Indian Energy Abstracts
4. Indian Journal of Library Science
5. Indian Archives
6. Indian Librarian
7. Indian Library Movement
8. IASLIC Bulletin
9. Library Herald
10. Herald of Library Science
11. Annals of Library Science and Documentation
12. Timeless Fellowship
13. Library Science with a Slant to Documentation and Information Studies
14. Lucknow Librarian

IV PsycLit

1. Indian Journal of Behaviour
2. Indian Journal of Psychometry and Education
3. Indian Journal of Disability and Rehabilitation
4. Indian Psychologist
5. Indian Journal of Clinical Psychology
6. Indian Journal of Current Psycholqgical Research
7. Indian Journal of Psychiatry
8. Indian Journal of Applied Psychology
9. Indian Journal of Psychological Medicine
10. Indian Psychological Review

SIS–96, 18-20, Jan. '96, Bangalore

Digital libraries: assumptions and adaptability

H.S. SIDDAMALLAIAH
NIMHANS, Bangalore

Abstract

The paper concentrates on assumptions and adaptability of digital library, considering the existing facilities, expertise and technological needs in India. It examines the problems, perspectives and the role of librarians.

Introduction

Man is a communicator of information not simply a user of tool. The history of civilization is the history of improved means of communication of information. The man always desires to improve the means of communicating. Documents are the artifacts of recorded knowledge that is information. Documents are meant for communication knowledge to larger audience. Libraries have stored and served the documents to the users. Thus libraries have performed as one of the links between generators of information and its users. The developments of libraries from print-paper-based libraries to digital libraries seems an illustration of man's never ending desire to improve his means of communication.

In the context of digital library, four assumptions can be identified. These are:

(i) Digital library is totally a paperless system with computer networks and communication facilities.

(ii) Digital library is a supplementary facility to traditional library for better retrieval and faster communication.

(iii) Any individual can have a direct link to electronic publishers, their agents/through computer-communication facilities, with or without knowledge of librarianship.

(iv) Any commercially interested organization or an individual, with or without knowledge of librarianship, having a direct access to electronic publishers/can become local promotional trade agent in information service, like one of the IST/STD centres, electronic typing centre, reprography centres at ice cream parlors.

These assumptions are made on the basis of our experiences at National Neurosciences Information Centre (NNIC), Bangalore.

National Neurosciences Information Centre (NNIC)

The NNIC, as a national information centre for mental health and neurosciences is equipped with adequate document backup and computer-communication facilities, attracted good number of users. It has provided a VSAT connected to NICNET; a pentium system (both unixware and DOS) with 6 terminals; interactive access to MEDLINE, AIDSLINE, AIDSTRIAL and AIDSDRUG; and Internet access for e-mail, FTP and WEB browser.

In addition, NNIC has CD-NET (seven drive), provides access on LAN (10 users), subscribed to many databases on CD-ROM viz. EMBASE-Psychiatry, Neurosciences, OCLC, Extra MED and many other complimentary CD databases. NNIC has created a national bibliographic database of Indian literature in the field of mental health and neurosciences. It has a proposal to publish the database including full-text of journal articles on CD-ROM and put it on WEB server (Internet).

In the process of establishment, services and interaction with the users, many misconceptions and problems were experienced, such as, ownership of digital media, digitized information, administrative problems, customs payment/clearance, user education, user appreciation and providing terminal to each user for simultaneous access to all the databases on CDs and on-line (minimum 15 users at a time), throughout working hours. It was felt that, for digitized information system, there is a need for full time staff for demonstration, on-site guidance and user education, particularly, in choosing suitable databases, search logic and locating the physical/digitized full document. It was experienced that, in case of digital systems, one time establishment of hardware is not possible. Updating hardware or change of hardware to accommodate changing requirement from time to time is essential. Here the problem is, "how long can we go on spending money, for every change/augmentation and new requirement of the hardware?" After all information may remain the same but the technology used for storage, searching and faster communication is ever changing. Further, the choice of media is of users.

User needs information, a conducive place to study and expert guidance to search/locate information. In case of information needs, it may be bibliographies, facts, full text of an article or a book. In case of usage, it may be to get a solution to his routine problem, updating his knowledge or just entertainment.

At same time, community views are broadening to a global view by popular gimmicks of information providers for publicity. In this process libraries, database hosts, search service agents, database mediators, and network and information providers bring out overlapping information that is confusing users.

Users in R&D centres are trying to establish links among scientists/ institutions, through Internet, WEB servers (WWW), with the support of interpreter and navigators. It is observed that majority of users are not aware of sources and services available in digital form. Hence, it is essential to create user awareness in this regard by preparing guides to the available digital information sources.

Dissemination need

The dissemination/circulation of information should address the user's choice and information seeking behaviour, irrespective of whether it is a traditional or digital library. The usage of information depends on awareness of users and facilities available to them. To fulfill and popularize the service from digital library, it is essential that:

- Librarians (in service) should have expertise and libraries should have adequate facilities.
- Teachers of library and information science should have the expertise and the facilities to teach/expose students to the latest technological development.
- Updating the syllabus, to cope with the frequent changes in technology.
- The access to information from digitized media be made user-friendly and helpful to review/recollect or memorize.

Cost depends on infrastructure requirements and expertise needs. Affordability depends on priority/fund of individuals/institutions.

Technology needs

The requirements of a digital library vary with the purpose, targeted users, affordability of funding agents, level of users and its participation with various national/international networks. The digital library requires convergence between computers, and synthesis of digital text, video and audio. Output required by user are still or motion video, animation computer generated images, sound synthesis, audio, text and interactive. The facilities required are, like powerful time-sharing computers; fast-access disc storage devices; telecommunication networks; video-telecommunications; video-teleconferencing; multimedia PCs, MPCs, CD-I, CD-ROM and CDTV; machine readable databases; television and fast, low cost computer terminal etc.

Expertise needs

Considering the existing curriculum at the school of library and information sciences in india, it is very essential to reconsider the curriculum in line with the digitized facilities.

- Training about the computer skills to make them familiar with DOS, windows, Macintosh and Unix and latest development in information technology.
- Building tools for accessing information; design and implementation of information systems; networking of CD-ROM and other facilities on campus network to the users terminals; human-computer interface issues; database construction/design and electronic publishing.
- Actual development of end user systems; translating request for information search; mediated literature search services; on-line public access catalogue and accessibility to variety of sources via international networks.
- Training for remote login, FTP, e-mail and public access Internet Web servers; Internet navigators and interpreters for cultivating working relationship with their counter part; telecommunication software, serial line Internet protocol (SLIP), transmission protocols etc.

Marketing of information

Administrative needs

Further, the execution of work and acquiring new equipment depend on the administrative perception. Hence it is essential to look at the administrative needs. The administrative analysis depends on advantages, disadvantages and technical limitation of traditional or digital facilities.

The disadvantages foreseen in adaptation of digitized facilities are: misuse of password; time lag for to change password; awareness and tutored education to users (usage and locating relevant one); lack of consistency of digital approach; obsolescence of technology; publisher (electronic) control or grip through term of contract; security of data; maintenance of equipment and upgradation of the system for changing needs. The limitations include; Overhead cost of digitized system, such as: training costs; cost of connecting time; use of software; installation charges in case new equipment; recurring fee for telecommunication services; charges of misuse of the password; renewal fees of the password; reproduction/downloading costs and stationary cost.

In case of many databases on CD-ROM, in the absence of copyright law, they are in fact using binding contracts by terms of agreement. They explicitly prohibit rental or lending. In fact it indicates the fear of electronic publishers about damage to the productivity, economics and credibility, returns due to the provision of network access to users by libraries, etc.

Silver Platter company USA, has introduced Electronic Reference Library (ERL), a multi-users software for databases on CD-ROM, a client server technology, to provide network access in campus, charging proportionate to the number of simultaneous accesses. The libraries, as information providers, do not have guarantee of returns (social or economic) for value added services.

Adaptability Needs

Considering the existing expertise, the adaptability calls for redefining the role of librarians and schools of library and information science, with respect to changing technology. The adaptation needs are:

- Not a wise decision to think of a total transformation to digital library.
- Acquisition of digital media be planned with respect to the type of library.
- End-user cost and payment attitude of users should be ascertained before establishment.
- Charging should be planned carefully as users are not used to pay for usage of printed media.
- Digitized product should not duplicate the printed products in case of primary sources of information.
- Staff development should be carefully planned considering the existing development and future needs of the library and information service.
- Regular user-education programme should be developed.
- Integrate digital library concept in the curriculum of all disciplines of studies, at least at graduation and post-graduation level.
- Regular demonstration centres have to be established to facilitate continuing education.

- Seminars/workshops should be conducted, at least once a year, for discussing the latest development in the field.
- Professional journals/newsletters should cover the state-of-art report on digital libraries.

Conclusion

It is well established fact that no body can dispense the printed media. Now there is a demand for information, a facility for searching tailor-made information services and faster communication. Hence, digital library seems a suitable solution at the moment. Authors are paying to get their contributions (particularly in journals) published, users are paying to get their relevant information, libraries are suffering to cope with frequent changes in technology, then librarians are struggling to cope technological changes and electronic packages. If librarians are trained suitably, one can really become information practitioners in digital society.

Reference

Communications of ACM Spl. Issue in Digital Libraries. 38(4), 1995.

SIS–96, 18–20, Jan. '96, Bangalore

Storage and retrieval of information in digital libraries

D. GAYATRI AND N. KALIDAS
Library and Documentation, Indian Institute of Chemical Technology, Hyderabad

> "Knowledge is of two kinds : we know a subject ourselves, or we know where we can find information upon it"
> — SAMUEL JOHNSON

Abstract

Organisations are increasingly replacing conventional storage & retrieval systems with digital systems. This conversion happens due to discrete analysis of documents, with the current data as a basis. The user specific requirements for a digital storage and retrieval system can be defined to develop a target concept. The focal point of analysis is : Document analysis, Context analysis, Qualitative analysis, Legal analysis. The paper discusses these in the context of ISR systems in digital libraries.

Introduction

Digital medium is fast replacing paper in a dramatic revolution. As we prepare for the 21st Century, emergence of increasingly ambitious unprecedented relationships harness. The contemporary information environment is fraught with uncertainty. In this turmulitious environment like Jurassic Park, forces of change threaten exintinction for all, but the most nimble, intelligent, organizations and individuals!

How can we redesign our institutions which embrace the access rather than the ownership? How do you organize and manage a library in which users expect service 24 hours a day, in which most of technical services staff are not even in the library, in which many of your heaviest users may never enter the building or may be located in another town or state? The changes, libraries face will be profound, as many libraries fear them, sometimes with good reasons. And yet these changes offer many positive opportunities.

Storage of information

This paper is based on the premise that what happens in libraries is result of what happens in the society at large. We are in the early stage of a transition from a print based to a digital society.

The latest technologies offer cheap computer processing power, cheap mass storage, inexpensive and ubiquitous access to high speed networks, and retrieval devices give us the ability to create, to manipulate, to store and especially to transfer large quantities of information in digital form at low costs. The products of these technologies are today as primitive and imperfect as the book in 1494s, but the abilities they offer will have profound effects on the academic world.

Digital information can be stored on any medium that is able to represent binary digits 0 & 1.

Conversion from the conventional storage to digitized format requires discrete analysis as the primary function. Based on user electronic storage and retrieval systems could be defined and a target concept could be developed. The document analysis includes : Formal analysis, Analysis of content, Qualitative analysis, Legal analysis.

Some of the common digitized storage media that are presently used world over are : Hyperbooks, CD-ROM, Multi-media.

Hyper books

Books are par excellence the traditional storage media of information and represent a classical tool for information delivery. They have a deep historical value and a well defined structure; they are easy to read and are accessible. In the traditional library, computers are applied to back office services. The book collection is still available in paper form, this brings a number of disadvantages.

- once identified a book of interest may not be available.
- it is difficult to retrieve publications of interest, even if they are present in the library.
- large and costly physical space is necessary for storing.

Most of these problems are overcome in the electronic library. Hyperbooks are electronic books defined on the basis of the paperback metaphor. Metaphors have been widely used to facilitate learning of computer system. A model with which the user is familiar is provided in order to enable users to exploit their existing knowledge of other domains when learning to use a system. The metaphor which appears to be the most suitable for presenting electronic books is the paperback metaphor stated by several authors.

Advantages:

- It can be shared by users in different geographical locations.
- It is quick, accurate, easy to locate by using searching and browsing mechanisms.
- Binding, preservation and shelf maintenance do not exist.
- AI and language techniques are exploited in fields such as cataloging, indexing and abstracting.

Hyperbook contains text and graphical images. Graphical object is always visible and appears in the text as in a paper book. The feature of the text is that it contains embedded links i.e., active text that is connected to other parts of the book. Hyperbook links can be grouped into categories such as:

Hierarchial links : Defined in the table of contents, list of figures, list of the table and index.

Transverse links: which are defined in the text may be divided into two groups a) Window links consisting of links whose activation causes the display of additional information in an overlapped window without changing the current position b) Jump links consists of links whose activation allows access to cross-referenced information in another part of the same book or another book.

CD-ROM

The first product in evolutionary optical storage of information is CD-ROM. It is a permanent optical based storage device, that in conjunction with an associated drive becomes a powerful peripheral for the PC. The CD-ROM puts mulitmegabyte permanently stored data bases at user front end of a PC. Its only drawback is that the end user cannot put his own information on it.

The advantages of storing data on CD are:

- high Storage capacity (600 MB)
- no head crash
- low error rate, correctable data
- long life
- random access
- early transportable
- OS independent file system

- low cost
- reliable medium
- less shelf space.

The advantages that made CD-ROM practically attractive in today's competing information environment are;

- Multi-Media : The ability to deliver unlimited end users access to over 600 MB information delivered using ordinary post means. It can be used for text, graphics, data, audio and video in one simple purchase.
- Multiplatform : It is the first truly system independent media with appropriate SWI CD-ROM allows equal access to information regardless of the computer HW or SW platforms used by the end users.
- Multilingual : Sophisticated CD-ROM systems today allow the end users to select the operating language at choice and change it on-the-fly.

The technology which will most characterise the 90's is multi- media. Multi-media technology integrates text, images, graphics, video, animation, sound or music. It is interactive on the lines of hypertext and hypermedia. The multimedia has a number of technological barriers for example, extra disk space required to store multimedia formats and broad bandwidth to transmit the text.

Retrieval of information

"More than any other time in history, mankind faces at cross roads. One path leads to despair and utter hopelessness. The other, to total extinction. Let us pray that we have the wisdom to choose correctly" - WOODY ALLAN.

The analysis of document retrieval in a library helps in identifying

- How many search queries occur per weekday, per peakday and on an average?
- What is the time taken for each search query?
- How successful are the searches?
- How quickly the information as a rule has to be made available?
- What aids the user has at his disposal for retrieving a document?
- Are the search criteria of formal nature or more to do with content?
- How often several users access the same document simultaneously?
- How access is protected?

The following stages are important in retrieval

- The analysis of search question
- The translation of the question into the indexing language of the system
- The formulation of the search strategy.

In addition, a lot of service problems occur such as, how to provide copies of documents, how to display them, how to manage search and retrieval, how to protect, copyright and how to manage loans.

To avoid these problems, in electronic environment interface design is a very important issue. There are various ways for example :

- Plain text interface :Electronic documents are presented as plain (ASCII) text, without images or other multimedia elements.
- Image based interface : The material is presented in image form of only some relevant parts.
- Hypermedia based interface : Electronic documents are presented following the paper book metaphor and the electronic library design reproduces the main features of the physical library.

The catchwords in the retrieval systems are Online, Internet, Fidonet etc. What are these? How does one retrieve information? How do they work? A brief description is given.

Fidonet

Fidonet is just one form of electronic communication that provides a means to bridge time and distance, to facilitate interpersonal communications. The simplest is a bulletin board system. In its basic form, the idea of the system can post a message in a public area. Any other member of the system can bowse through the bulletin board reading items of interest.

Main services: Electronic Mails (one to one), Conference Mails (many to many) and file transfer (can handle both text and binary files) when these services are integrated with an interactive electronic bulletin board system such as remote access, they can be accessed by people using only a modem and ordinary phone lines.

Internet

The Internet is a co-operative computer network of networks that links libraries, schools, governments, corporations, individuals and others to each other and to vast information resources. The internet protocol links many independent networks together so that they appear as a single network to the user. The internet currently consists of about 28,000 registered networks about

2 million host computers and an estimated 15 million users. About 149 countries have connections to some sort of an international computer network; of these about 63 countries have direct connections to the Internet.

Internet can be used to send and receive electronic messages, to contact and search other computers — Telnet, to copy files.

The internet is an open network. Anyone or any group is welcome to use it as long as that person or group has a terminal or a computer with the correct software and the ability to pay the costs. Since most users of internet are affiliated with institutions, the computers they use are attached to LAN which are inturn connected by a router (a device that connects networks together and passes information among them) to a regional or wide area network.

You may also be limited in the applications you can use since the transmission control protocol/ Internet Protocol (TCP/IP) does not really come to your own computer, it stops at the host. For this type of connection, you will need a modem and access to a standard voice grade telephone line.

Gopher, Archie, Veronica, Jughead, WAIS and the WWW are the tools supported by Internet that help users to find and retrieve information.

Online

Online makes information available in different formats. It is a means of constant access to databases around the world from any location using an inexpensive telecom link and PC terminal.

Eliron

Eliron is one of the first electronic library developments in the UK. It has given the user aspects of the electronic library a high priority in the research programme. In fact, from the outset it included a user friendly interface as one of the important selection criteria, on which the electronic library system (ELS) could be based.

Basic objective of ELIRON is to setup a large image database of complete books, journals and course materials which can be directly accessed by students and teaching staff via Windows-based IBM and Macintosh PC's. ELIRON ELS employs current Graphical User Interface (GUI) technology, the basic feature which is WIMP i.e. Window, Icon, Mouse and Pull-down menu. It may be divided into broad aspects such as

Finding document

Browsing and searching the Electronic Library database are two possible routes to find a document, which may be either a known citation or any relevant document related to a topic. The browsing - related interface provides graphical presentation of the hierarchial structure of the data fileroom eg. books, computer, computer architecture, from logic to page. The searching and browsing routes may be combined to find a relevant document. e.g. : The user can first select certain drawers in the electronic library fileroom and then enter a free-text search clue to find relevant documents in the selected drawers.

Reading a document

The PIX/TEX/EFS system links OCR'ed text page of a document with its corresponding image page. The user can, therefore switch the display between the text and image pages. Within the text pages, the users can enter simple searches on terms, which is similar to the "Find" function commonly available in word processors. For image viewing, the user can easily drag the page up/down and right/left. He can also reduce or enlarge the size of the image by simply double clicking the mouse. It is also possible to zoom into a particular area of the image page. Images may be rotated to 90, 180, 270, 360 degrees for viewing. The user can flip through the pages by clicking the next or previous buttons, or the go to button to select any given page. It is also possible to lock up to four windows each displaying an image page of one or several books. The user can, therefore compare different parts of a book or read several books on the screen. Because the user station runs on Windows-based interfaces, the user can create notes with any Windows-based editor while viewing a page.

The above two procedures can to a certain extent be used interchangeably. The user can highlight a term or sentence in he text page being read and go on to request an additional search of other documents matching that new pattern.

Hyperbook Retrieval

The mechanism which the library provides in order to access the collection are :

Catalogues, Subject-browser.

The alphabetical catalogue is a particular book. The search catalogue consists of an input and output window, through which the reader can enter the search terms and see the search results respectively. A database of biliographical records, and a number of indexes to facilitate the search in the database. The subject browser allows a document to be accessed by subject. A hierarchial structure of subjects has been defined, starting from a global classification, going down to the lowest level, which includes the shelves of book.

According to BNF (Backus Naur Form) notation, the library components highlighted as follows :

<Library> : = <Co llection> < Librarian> < Access> < Resources>

<Collection> : = <Electronic Books>

<Librarian:> = <<Expert Systems>> <<Human Librarian>>

<Electronic Book> : = <<Cover >> <Double page> << Cover>>

<Double Page> := <Page> <Page>

<Page> : = <Page-Component>

<Page-Component:> : =<text> / <table> / <Figure>

<Text> : = <Active text> / <<Simple text>>

<< >> —-> Terminal Elements.

Conclusion

In conclusion we can only say that the full transition from print to electronics can only occur when :

- — the terminal infrastructure needed to support electronic distribution is in place
- — the cost of electronic publication drops below that of print on paper
- — the Online market is large enough to support the local cost of producing and distributing publication.

Developments in the application of computers in publishing, in e-mail and the paperless office, in computer conferencing and other manifestations of interactive television allow us, to conceive a paperless information system of the future.

From library and information service professional point of view, in this period of transition of paper/print to electronics can best be summed up in a single word "DEINSTITULISATION" although reinstitulisation, may perhaps be more accurate. As more and more information resources are available online, the librarianship must change in two important respects.

Firstly, it will make sense to view the collection of a library as not merely set of publications obtained within its four walls.

Secondly, major change concerns the librarians. When the libraries have become deinstitutilised, so must the librarians. Infact with the information resources already available online, the searching function of libraries could be performed outside the library. The librarians of Electronic Age do need to work within a library. They could perform their major professional function in support of research from an office or indeed, from the home. This means that *the value of the librarian has increased* but may greatly *decrease the value of the library*. Electronic age may also bring in a number of free-lance librarians, not individuals but working in small groups resembling the present group of the doctors and lawyers. It is noteworthy to note that in the electronic age, librarian could be valued as professional colleague of chemists, physicists, physicians, attorneys, educationists and other professionals.

Acknowledgement

We would like to thank Mr.Hari Hara Prasad & Mr. Divakar, (CCMB) Library, IICT for their encouragement and guidance to write this paper.

References

1. Networks and Resource sharing in the 21st Century, *Resource sharing and information networks*, 10(2).
2. Skinner, Robert Multimedia Resource Access, *Resource sharing and information networks* 10(2).
3. Keys, Marshall. Librarians and emerging digial revolution - *Resourch sharing and information networks*, 10(2).
4. *Communications of the ACM*, 38(4), April 1995.
5. Kind, Joachim. The need for office analysis in the introduction of electronic document management systems, *Information Media and Technology*, 24(6), 1991.
6. Zimim Wu, The user perspective of the Elinor Electronic Library. *Aslib Proceedings*, 47(1), Jan.1995.
7. *Electronic and Optical Publishing Review : an International journal*, 7(2), 1987.
8. Internet Primer - *Information Development* , 11(2), June 1995.
9. Fidonet - *Information Development*, 11(3), Sep.1995.

10. Gopinath, M.A. CD-ROM technology and its impact on library and information services. *Library Sciences*, 31(4), Dec 1994.

11. Rothenberg, Jeff. Ensuring the longevity of Digital Documents. *Scientific American*, Jan.1995.

12. Catenazzi, Nadia. Hyperbook: a formal model for electronic books, *Journal of Documentation*, 50(4), Dec.1994.

13. Catenazzi, Nadia. Hyper Library: a formal model for an electronic library based on Hyper books. *Journal of Documentation*, 51(3), Sep.1995.

14. Lancaster. F.W. Libraries in the year 2001. *Herald of Library Science*, 32(3-4), 1993.

A Select Bibliography

Digital Libraries: A select bibliography (1992-95)

compiled by

V.A. SUBHAN

J.R.D. Tata Memorial Library, IISc, Bangalore-560 012

(A project sponsored by the Society for Information Science, Bangalore Chapter for the SIS'96 – 15th Annual Convention and Conference on Digital Libraries)

The digital library concept has emerged very recently and getting deeply rooted in the field of Library and Information Science. The bibliography clearly indicates through the number of publications which were very few in 1992 and 1993 have increased to hundreds of references in the years 1994-95. Due to the shortage of time and rthe limited resources available at the JRDTML and NCSI at the Institute were consulted. Hence, it is very likely that the bibliography might have left out some important publications which might have appeared in the same period. The references are arranged according the classification followed by LISA and a personal author index is provided. It is hoped that the bibliography will be useful for many of the University, College Libraries and the library science departments where the identification of the references on the subject is limited.

For data entry Shri V.N.Nagendra helped and the computer programmes were developed by Shri V.A.Subhan.

DIGITAL LIBRARY: A SELECT BIBLIOGRAPHY

8 LIBRARY TECHNOLOGY

1. Adams, J.A. and Bonk, S.C. Electronic information technologies and resources: Use by university faculty and faculty preferences for related library. *College and Research Libraries* 56 (2) 1995 p119-3.

2. Anderson, Laura Challman. and Lotspiech, Jerry B. Rights management and security in the electronic library. *Bulletin of the American Society for Information Science* 22 (1), 1995 p21-23.

3. Barker, Philip. Electronic libraries — vision of the future. *Electronic library* 12 (4) 1994 p221-230.

4. Barnes, S.J. The electronic library and public services. *Hi Tech* 12 (3) 1994 p44-62.

5. Benedict, Philip J. Document revision process for the electronic library system. SAE Technical Paper Series. Publ by SAE, Warrendale, PA, USA, 1991 p1-9.

6. Benest, I.D. and Morgan, G. Humanised model for the electronic library. *IEE Colloquium (Digest)* 1985/80 1985 p1-9.

7. Biddiscome, R. Networking CD-ROM in an academic libraries environment. *British Journal of Academic Librarianship* 6 (3) 1991, p175-183.

8. Brennan, Patrick W. The impact of technology on libraries: a view to ongoing change. *Bibliotheca Medica Canadiana* 12 (3) 1991 p137-143.

9. Buckland, M. Redesigning library services, A manifesto. American Library Association, Chicago, 1992.

10. Burg, B. and Tallent, E. Silver-Platter's electronic reference library (ERL) technology. *Search* 3 (5) 1995 p66-8.

11. Callahan, Diane R. Librarian as change agent in the diffusion of technological innovation. *Electronic Library* 9 (1) 1991 p13-15.

12. Dahms, Moshie. Influence of library automation on the subject-divisional reference, service at the University of Quelph Library. *ABI-Technik (Archiv Bibliotheks und Informationswesen)* 6 (3), 1986 p189-193.

13. Drapeau, Ann L. Patterson, David A. and Katz, Randy H. Toward workload characterization of video server and digital. *Performance Evaluation Review* 22 (1) 1994 p274-275.

14. Dutcher, G.A. DOCLINE: A National Automated Interlibrary Loan Request Routing and Referral System. *Inf. Technol. Libraries* 8 1989 p359-370.

15. Fox, E.A. Sourcebook on digital libraries: Report for the National Science Foundation. Tech. Rep. TR-93-35, Computer Science Dept., VPI&SU, Blacksbur, 1993

16. Fox, E.A. and Lunin, L. Introduction and overview to perspectives on digital libraries. *Journal of the American Society for Information Science* 44 (8), 1993 p441-443.

17. Fox, E.A. Hix, D. and Nowell, L. Users, user interfaces, and objects: envision a digital library. *Journal of the American Society for Information Science* 44 (8), 1993 p480-491.

18. Gladney, H. Fox, E. and Ahmed, E.Z. Digital library: Gross structure and requirements: Report from a March 1994 Workshop (Texas A&M Univ., College Station,tex., June, 1994). Proceedings of the 1st Annual Conference on the Theory and Practice of Digital Libraries: Digital Libraries '94 1994, p101-107.

19. Graham, Peter S. Requirements for the digital research library. *College and Research Libraries* (July) 1995 p331-337.

20. Hix, D. Nowell, L. and Fox, E.A. Users, user interfaces, and objects: envision, a digital library. *Journal of the American Society for Information Science* 44 (8), 1993 p480-491.

21. Hurt, C. Building the foundation of Virginia's virtual library. *Information Technology and Libraries* 14 (1) 1995 p50-3.

22. Kawauchi, K. Multimedia and libraries: special feature [in Japanese]. *Toshokan Zasshi/Library Journal* 88 (10) 1994 p733-52.

23. Kels, J.J.F. Electronic delivery of scientific information and the role of libraries. *Information Management Report* (September) 1992 p1-5.

24. Lakshmana Moorthy, A. and Rajendran, V. Information technologies for libraries and information centres. *Aglis Journal* 8 (1-4) 1990 p6-16.

25. Lamont, B.L. School libraries and new technologies. *Illinois Libraries* 76 (2) 1994 p83-5.

26. Lancaster, F.W. Electronic publishing and their implications for libraries and Beyond, 1984 /ed. by Peter Gelatly.

27. Larsen, Gitte. Maggie's place III: an electronic library revisited. *Electronic Library* 6 (6) 1988 p404-406.

28. Levy, David M. and Marshall, Catherine C. Going digital: a look at assumptions underlying digital libraries. *Communications of the ACM* 38 (4) 1995.

29. Marchionini, Gary. and Maurer, Nermann. The roles of digital libraries in teaching and learning. *Communications of the ACM* 38 (4) 1995 p67-75.

30. Marchionini, Gary. and Maurer, Hermann. The roles of digital libraries in teaching and learning. *Communications of the ACM* 38 (4) 1995.

31. Marshall, C. Shipman, F. and McCall, R. Putting digital libraries to work: issues from experience with community memories. Proceedings of Digital Libraries '94(College Station, Tex., June, 19-21) /ed. by J.L. Schnase, J.J. Leggett, R.K. Furuta & (...), 1994 p126-133.

32. Martin, Susan K. Defining "It": NRENS opportunities for librarians. Paper Presented at the Clinic on Library Applications of Data, 1991.

33. McCue, J. Technical services and the electronic library: designing our. *Library Hi Tech* 12 (3) 1994 p63-70.

34. Miksa, F.L. and Doty, P. Intellectual realities and the digital library. Proceedings of Digital Libraries '94 (College Station, Tex., June, 19-21) /ed. by J.L. Schnase, J.J. Leggett, R.K. Furuta & (...), 1994 p1-5.

35. Oxman, Rivka. and Oxman, Robert. Remembrance of things past: design precedents in libraries. *Automation in Construction* 2 (1) 1993 p21-29.

36. Raitt, D., ed. The electronic library managers guide to the transfer and diffusion of new technology. *The Electronic Library* 10 (4) 1992, p191-193.

37. Raitt, D.I. Look — No Paper! The Library of Tomorrow. *Electronic Library* 3 (4) 1985 p276-289.

38. Ramana Rao. Pedersen, Jan O. and Hearst, Marti A. Rich interaction in the digital library. *Communications of the ACM* 38 (4) 1995.

39. Riggs, Donald E. Digital libraries: Assumptions and characteristics (editorial). *Library Hi Tech* 13 (4) 1995 p5,60.

40. Riley, John. Electronic library system (ELS). Safety through efficient data management. Flight Safety — An Endless Task Intl. Air Safety Seminar Proceedings. Publ by Flight Safety Foundation Inc. Arlington, USA, 1990 p94-10.

41. Samuelson, P. and Glushko, R.J. Intellectual property rights in digital library and hypertext publishing systems. *Harv. J. Law & Techn.* 6 (237) 1993.

42. Samuelson, Pamela. Copyright and digital libraries. *Communications of the ACM* 38 (4) 1995 p15-21,110.

43. Sasse, Margo Q. and Winkler, B Jean. Electronic journals: a formidable challenge to libraries /ed. by Irene P. Goddar. *Advances in Librarianship* 17 1993 p149-173.

44. Schnase, J.L. Leggett, J.J. and Furuta, R.K. Proceedings (Texas A&M Univ., College Station, Tex, June 1994). Proceedings of the 1st Annual Conference on the Theory and Practical, 1994.

45. Steele, Colin. Libraries and new information technologies. *Outlook on Research Libraries* 11 (11) 1989 p8-10.

46. Steele, Colin. The E-library it's time- but is it the best of times or the worst of time? *Australian Academic and Research Libraries* 22 (2) 1991 p83-87.

47. Still, J. and Campbell, F. Librarian in a box: the use of electronic mail for reference. *Reference Services Review* 21 (1) 1993 p15-18.

48. Tennant, R. The virtual library foundation: staff training and support. *Information Technology and Libraries* 14 (1) 1995 p46-9.

49. Williams, Bernard J.S. ELINOR: ushering in the electronic library? *International Journal of Micrographics & Optical Technology* 12 (3) 1994 p111-117.

50. Yerkey, A Neil. A course in digital libraries. *DESIDOC Bulletin of Information Technology* 16 (1) 1996.

51. Zhao, Dian,G. ELINOR electronic library system. *Electronic Library* 12 (5) 1994 p289-294.

52. Zhao, Dian G. Usage statistics collection and management in the ELINOR electronic library. *Journal of Information Science* 21 (1) 1995 p1-9.

53. Argentesi, F. and Rana, A. An electronic library for publishing and consulting information distributed across Internet. Proceedings of the 18th International Online Information Meeting, 1994.

54. Banchieri, A. Electronic library. *Biblioteche Oggi* 13 (2) 1995 p8-14.

55. Barker, James. Fiber-optic library. *Inform* 7 (8) 1993 p30-33.

56. Bartenbach, B. CD-ROM challenges and opportunities: Issues of concern to librarian. An introduction. *Inspel* 28 (3) 1994 p298-306.

57. Bassman, W. CD-ROM in the public library: signpost to the information highway. *Show-Me Libraries* 45 (2) 1994 p20-2.

58. Becker, Herbert S. Library of Congress digital library efforts. *Communications of the ACM* 38 (4) 1995 p66.

59. Bell, Timothy, C., etc. The MG Retrieval System: Compressing for space and speed. *Communications of the ACM* 38 (4) 1995.

60. Bevan, N. Transient technology? the future of CD-ROMs in libraries. *Program* 28 (1) 1994 p1-14.

61. Birmingham, W.P. Drabenstott, K.M. and Frost, C.O. The University of Michigan Digital Library: This is not your. Proceedings of the ACM Conference on Digital Libraries, 1994.

62. Blagden, J. and Ford, J. The electronic library: a view from academia and the computer industry. *Managing Information* 1 (6) 1994 p36-8.

63. Braid, A. The problem of digitising non-electronic media. *Libri* 44 (4) 1994 p311-16.

64. Brown, J.M. The Internet and visual architecture library. *Art Library Journal* 19 (4) 1994 p16-20.

65. Bryant, P. Library and information: progress on priorities for the UK 1992-1994. *Library and Information Briefings* (55/56) 1994 p1-41.

66. Burrows, T. Integrating electronic services into the academic library: the Scholar's Centre at the University of Western Austria. *Australian Academic and Research Libraries* 25 (4) 1994 p213-20.

67. Cargill, J. and Hay, R.D. Achieving a vision of a statewide academic library network. *Journal of Academic Librarianship* 19 (6) 1994 p386-7.

68. Catlett, Charles and Terstriep, Jeffrey A. The use and effect of multimedia digital libraries in a national network. Paper Presented at the Clinic on Library Applications of Data, 1991.

69. Dijkstra, J. A digital library in the mid-nineties, ahead or on schedule. *Information Services & Use* 14 (4) 1994 p267-77.

70. Eaton, J. Using the Internet in an academic library. *Online and CD Notes* (June) 1995 p3-4.

71. Emerson, P.R. The college librarian's guide to accessing the Internet. *College and Undergraduate Libraries* 1 (1) 1994 p135-63.

72. Entlich, Richard., etc. Making a digital library: the chemistry online retrieval experiment. *Communications of the ACM* 38 (4) 1995 p54.

73. Ewers, A. and others. Libraries, networks and Europe: a European networking study. *Library and Information Research,* Report 101 1994 p91.

74. Farrell, J.O. Working towards a library without walls. *Library Association Record* 97 (3) 1995.

75. Halmagyi, Z. Multimedia - megy, mint a karikacsepas [Multimedia-going on smoothly]. *Tudomanyos es Muszales Tagekoztates* 42 (5-6) 1995 p179-83.

76. King, G. Kung, H.T. and Grosz, B. The Harvard self-enriching library (SELF) project. *Proceedings of the ACM Conference on Digital Libraries*, 1994.

77. Konnur, M.B. and Rajendra, A.R. Automated libraries: some experiences. *Herald of Library Science* 33 (1-2) 1994 p24-8.

78. Kreitz, P.A. An annotated bibliography on networking: past, present, and future. *Resource Sharing & Information Networks* 8 (1) 1992 p159-96.

79. Krishnan, R. and Steier, D.H. Adaptive access to a digital library of corporate information. Digital Libraries Workshop. Rutgers Univ. Newark, NJ, May 1994.

80. LaGuardia, Cheryl. and Bentley, Stella. We teach the networks electric: the networked library classroom. Proceedings — National Online Meeting 1994 p319-327.

81. Lagoze, Carl. and Davis, R. Dienst: an architecture for distributed document libraries. *Communications of the ACM* 38 (4) 1995 p47.

82. Lancaster, F.W. The future of the library in the age of telecommunications. Telecommunications and Libraries: a primary for librarians and 1981,

83. Lang, B. The electronic library: implications for librarians, academics and publishers. *Libri* 44 (4) 1994 p265-71.

84. Larsen, Gitte. and Qvortrup, lars. Third library revolution: experiments with electronic community libraries in Denmark. *Electronic Library* 6 (5) 1988 p332-337.

85. Lee, H.-W. Networked, electronic and virtual library: libraries of the 1990's. *Journal of Educational Media and Library Sciences* 32 (2) 1995 p119-29.

86. Leggate, Peter. and Dyer, Hilary. Microcomputer in the library: II Hardware and Operating Systems. *Electronic Library* 3 (4) 1985 p260-274.

87. Lynch, Clifford A. Networked information: a revolution in progress. Paper Presented at the Clinic on Library Applications of Data 1991.

88. MacDonald, A.H. Electronic Alexandria: destination or final resting place? *Canadian Journal of Information and Library Science* 19 (4), 1994 p23-43.

89. Mantey, Patrick E. and Levy, David E. Electronic libraries and optical jukebox server scheduling. Proceedings of SPIE — The International Society for Optical Engineering 1662 1992 p146-153.

90. Maurer, H. Muelner, H. and Schneider, A. The PC library and applications in an educational settings. Symposium Didaktik der Mathematik, Klagenfurt 1994.

91. Mayo, John S. Global communications in the information age. *IEEE Circuits and Devices Magazine* 8 (3) 1992 p38-39.

92. McKnight, C. Meadows, J. and Pullinger, D. ELVYN-Publisher and library working towards the electronic distribution and use of journals. Proceedings of the ACM Conference on Digital Libraries, 1994.

93. Miah, A.J. Automated library networking in American Public Community College Learning Resource Center. *Journal of Interlibrary Loan, Document Delivery and Information Supply* 5(1) 1994 p67-95.

94. Nelson, T. Computer Lib-Dream Machines Distributors, South Bend, IN, 1974.

95. Norbie, D. The electronic library emerges at US West. *Special Libraries* 85 (4) 1994 p277-6.

96. Packard, P.W. Information technology: you can't beat it (you may as well) join it. *Journal of Youth Services in Libraries* 8(2) 1995 p197-203.

97. Pitman, R. Welcome to Jurassic Library. *American Libraries* 26 (4) 1995 p352-4.

98. Prietto, C. Automating the archives: a case study. *American Archivist* 57 (2) 1994 p364-73.

99. Raitt, David. Teleports: opportunities for electronic libraries. Proceedings - National Online Meeting 1986 1986 p359-368.

100. Relan, S. Adoption of CD-ROM in libraries. *Herald of Library Science* 33 (1-2) 1994 p35-40.

101. Rowland, L.M. Libraries and librarians on the Internet. *Communication Education* 43 (2) 1994 p143-50.

102. Saltzer, Jerome. Technology networks and the library of the year 2000. Future Tendencies in Computer Science, Control and Applied Mat, 1992.

103. Schatz, Bruce. Building the interspace: the Illinois digital library project. *Communications of the ACM* 38 (4) 1995 p162.

104. Senkevitch, J.J. and Wolfram, D. Equalizing access to electronic networked resources: a model. *Library Trends* 42 (4) 1994 p661-75.

105. Shiba, M. and Kita, K. The era of multiple library networks: current situation and prospects. *The Library World* 45 (3) 1993 p288-93.

106. Slonim, J. Networked information systems as digital libraries. Summary Report from IBM Academy Digital Library Workshop, Briarcliff Manor, New York (Sep. 12-13) 1994.

107. Somerville, I. and Curtis, G. CD-ROM networking at the state library Tasmania. *Australian Library Review* 11 (2) 1994 p157-64.

108. Spriggs, M. Providing access technology within the library setting. *Link-up* (June) 1995 p10-12.

109. Tedol, L.A. An introduction to sharing resources via the Internet in academic libraries and information centres in Europe. *Program* 29 (1) 1995 p43-6.

110. Troll, Denise A. and Richards, Barbara G. From vision to reality: implementing the distributed electronic library. Proceedings of the ASIS Annual Meeting 1992. Publ by Learned, Information Ltd. Medford, NJ, USA 29 1992 p144-149.

111. Valauskas, E.J. Alternatives to CD-ROM: issues and prospects. *Inspel* 28 (3) 1994 p382-9.

112. Wiggins, R. What to say when MIS won't connect your library to the Internet. *Searcher* 3 (1) 1995 p18-21.

113. Wilensky, Robert. UC Berkeley's digital library project. *Communications of the ACM* 38 (4) 1995 p61-62.

114. Williams, B.J.S. Elinor: ushering in the electronic library? In *International Journal of Micrographics and Optical Technology* 12 (3) 1994 p111-17.

115. Zhao, D.G. The ELINOR electronic library system. *Electronic Library* 12 (5) 1994 p289-94.

116. Zwu, A. Ramsden. and Zhao, D. The user perspective of ELINOR electronic library. *Aslib Proceedings* 47 (1) 1995 p13-32.

117. deGruyter, M.L. The Texas State electronic library. *Library Journal* 71 (1) 1995 p24-8.

13 COMPUTERISED INFORMATION STORAGE AND RETRIEVAL

118. Al Gore. The information superhighway: what it will mean. The World Almanac and Book of Facts [Maheiah, N.J.] World Almanac, 1994 p35-36.

119. Anon. Japanese Ministry of International Trade and Industry programme for advanced information infrastructure. *Electronic Library* 12 (5) 1994 p298-300.

120. Bambrick, J. BRS gone but not forgotten. *Online* 19 (4) 1995 p75-9.

121. Berleant, D. and Berghel, H. Customizing information. *IEEE Comput.* 279 (September) 1994 p96-98.

122. Carson, Ken. and Danielson, Jason. Integrated digital production suite. *SMPTE Journal* 100 (6) 1991 p423-426.

123. Cutting, D.R. Halvorsen, P.K. and Pedersen, J.O. Information theater versus information refinery. AAA/Spring Symposium on Text-based Intelligent Systems (March), 1990.

124. Denning, Peter J. Inside risks: information superhighway 2015. *Communications of the ACM* 38 (4) 1995 p138.

125. Diaz, M.L., and others. Hipertaxtos, una alternativa [Hypertext, an alternative]. *Ciencias dela Information* 25 (1) 1994 p22-6.

126. Ehrlich, K. and Cash, D. Turning information into knowledge: information finding as a. Proceedings of Digital Libraries '94 (College Station, Tex., June, 19-21), J.L. Schnase, J.J. Leggett, R.K. Furuta (Eds). 1994 p119-125.

127. Erickson, T. and Solomon, G. Designing a desk top information system: observation and issues. Proceedings of ACM Conference on Human Factors in Computing systems 1991 p49-54.

128. Farner-Hines, J. and Willett, P. The use of hypertext in libraries in the United Kingdom. *Vine* (97) 1994 p45-9.

129. Foster, W. Information retrieval: towards the multimedia network. *British Book News* (August) 1993 p488-93.

130. Frei, H.P. Bartfchi, M. and Jauslin, J.F. Caliban: it's user-interface and retrieval algorithm. Tech. Report,62, Institut fur Informatik, ETH Zurich (April) 1985.

131. Gimson, R. Electronic paper: can it be real? *Aslib Proceedings* 47 (6) 1995 p139-43.

132. Greenbaum, J., ed. and Kyng, M., ed. Design at Work: Cooperative Design Computer Systems. Erlbaum, Hillsdale, N.J., 1991.

133. Jenda, Claudine Arnold. Electronic journal publishing and the scientific scholarly communication system. Proceedings — National Online Meeting 1994 p223-232.

134. Lamping, J. Rao, R. and Pirolli, P. A focus+context technique based on hyperbolic geometry for visualizing large hierarchies. Proceeding of the ACM SIGCHI Conference on Human Factors in Computing Systems (May) 1995.

135. Mackinlay, J.D. Robertson, G.G. and Card, S.K. The perspective wall: detail and context smoothly integrated. Proceedings of the ACM SIGCHI conference on Human Factors in Computing Systems (April) 1991 p173-179.

136. Malone, T.W. How do people organize their desks ? Implications for the design office information systems. *ACM Transactions on Office Information Systems* 1 (1) 1983 p99-112.

137. Penniman, W David. Tommorrow's library, *Computer Methods and Programs in Biomedicine* 44 (3-4) 1994 p149-153.

138. Rao, R. Card, S.K. and Jellinek, H.D. The information grid: a frame work for building infomation retrieval and retrieval-centered application. Proceedings of the ACM Symposium on User Interface Software and Technology (November) 1992.

139. Rao, R. Russell, D.M. and Mackinlay, J.D. System components for embedded information retrieval from multiple disparate information sources. Proceedings of the ACM Symposium on User Interface Software and Technology (November) 1993.

140. Shaw, Debora. (Ed.) Proceedings of the 55th. Annual Meeting of the Society for Information Science. Proceedings of the ASIS Annual Meeting, 1992. Publ. by Learned Information Ltd. Medford, NJ, USA 29 1992 p357.

141. Taylor, P. The shape of things to come. *Assistant Librarian* 86 (7) 1993 p104-5.

142. Tenopir, C. Goodbye BRS, hello EDP online. *Library Journal* 120 (4) p26,28.

143. Wiederhold, G. Mediation in the architecture of future information systems. *IEEE Comput.* 1992 p38-49.

144. Wiederhold, G. The roles of artificial intelligence in information systems. *Journal of Intelligent Information Systems* 11 (1) 1992 p35-56.

13.1 COMPUTERIZED INFORMATION STORAGE AND RETRIEVAL - ECONOMIC ASPECTS

145. Ahlberg, C. Williamson, C. and Shneiderman, B. Dynamic queries for information exploration: an implementation and evaluation. The sparks of innovation in human-computer interaction, B. Shneiderman, Ed. Ablex, Norwood, New Jersey 1994 p281-294.

146. Alberti, B. Anklesaria, F. and Lindner, P. Internet Gopher Protocol: a distributed document search and retrieval protocol.

147. Anon. (Ed.) Proceedings of the 11th. Annual International Conference on SIGDOC '93. Proceedings of the 11th. Annual International Conference on SIGDOC '93, Proc. 11 1993 p382.

148. Bane, A.F. and Milheim, W.D. Internet insights: how academics are using the Internet. *Computers in Libraries* 15 (2) 1995.

149. Berners Lee, T. Cailliau, R. and Groff, J. World Wide Web: the information universe. *Electronic Networking: Resarch Application and Policy* 2 (1) 1992 p52-58.

150. Berners-Lee, T. Cailliau, R. and Groff, J. World-Wide Web: the information universe. *Electronic Networking: Research, Applications and Policy* 1(2) 1992 p52-58.

151. Blake, P. Where does networking leave the library? *Library Manager* (3) 1995 p12-13.

152. Bowman, C.M. Danzig, P.B. and Hardy, D.R. The HARVEST information discovery and access system. Proceedings of the Second International World-Wide Web Conference, (Chicago, Illinois, Oct. 1994) 1994 p763-771.

153. Bruce, H. Internet services and academic work: an Australian perspective. *Internet Research* 4 (2) 1994 p24-34.

154. Case, D.O. Conceptual organization and retrieval of text by historian:the role of memory and metaphor, *Journal of American Society for Information Science* 42 (9) 1991 p657-663.

155. Cleveland, G. Introduction to the World Wide Web. *UDT Newsletter* (27) 1995 p5-8.

156. Cox, B. Superdistribution. *Wired* (September) 1994.

157. Cronin, B. Networking: some root definitions and issues. *British Journal of Academic Librarianship* 6 (3) 1991 p163-194.

158. Cutting, D.R. Karger, D.R. and Pedersen, J.O. Constant interaction-time scatter/gather browsing of very large document collections. Proceedings of SIGIR' 93 (June) 1993.

159. Cutting, D.R. Karger, D.R. and Pedersen, J.O. Scatter/gather: a cluster-based approach to browsing large document collections. Proceedings of SIGIR'92 (June) 1992.

160. Davis, J. and Lagoze, C. Drop-in publishing with the World Wide Web. Proceedings of the 2nd. International WWW '94 1994 p749-759.

161. Deutsch, P. Resource discovery in an internet environment: the archie approach. *Electronic Networking: Research Application and Policy* 1 (2) 1992 p45-51.

162. Dillion, Martin. et al. Assessing information on the Internet Dublin: OCLC 1993.

163. Enser, P. Image database for multimedia projects. *Journal of the American Society for Information Science* 46 (1) 1995 p60-4.

164. Faloutsos, C. Barber, R. and Flickner, M. Efficient and effective querying by image content. *Journal of Intelligent Information Systems* 1994 p231-262.

165. Fenn, B. and Maurer H. Harmony on an expanding net. *ACM Interactions* 1 (3) 1994 p26-38.

166. Fishman, B.J. and D'Amico, L.M. Which way will the wind blow? Networked computer tools for studying the weather. Proceedings of ED-MEDIA '94 (Vancouver, B.C., June 25-30) 1994 p209-216.

167. Fonss-Jorrgensen, E. Future international patterns of AV archive use: reaching out to new users. *IASA Journal* (1) 1993 p26-32.

168. Garrett, John R. and Lyons, Patrice A. Legal marketplace and social considerations in online network environments. Proceedings - National Online Meeting, 1993. Publ by Learned Information Ltd. Medford, NJ, USA 1993 p153-157.

169. Gordon, M. Electronic readers/electronic reserves. *DLA Bulletin* 14 (2) 1994 p3-7.

170. Harman, D. Overview of the first text retrieval conference. Proceedings of the 16th Annual International ACM/SIGIR Conference, 1993 p36-48.

171. Hearst, M.A. Multi-paragraph segmentation of expository text. Proceedings of the 32nd Meeting of the Association for Computational Linguistics (June) 1994.

172. Hearst, M.A. Tilebar: visualization of term distribution information in full text information access. Proceedings of the ACM SIGCHI Conference on Human Factors in Computing systems, Denver Co. (May) 1995.

173. Hernon, P. Disinformation and misinformation through the Internet: findings of an exploratory study. *Government Information Quarterly* 12 (2) 1995 p133-9.

174. Hogarth, J. and Martin. Non-texual archive material and document image processing: results of a survey conducted in 1992. *Journal of the Society of Archivists* 15 (1) 1994 p27-38.

175. Jacob, M.E.L. Networking applications for research libraries. Paper Presented at the Clinic on Library Applications of Data, 1991.

176. Jones, R. and Seale, C. Three electronic networks: their potential international roles for library communications. *Collection Management* 15 (3/4) 1992 p425-437.

177. King, Shirley V. ELNET: the electronic library database system. *Electronic Library* 9 (2) 1991 p6.

178. Knox, J. Access to library catalogues through electronic networks: views from a university library's users. *LASIE* 22 (6) 1992 p128-139

179. Lago, K.N. The Internet and the public library: practical and political. *Computers in Libraries* 13 (9) 1993 p65-70.

180. Levy, D.M. Naming the nameable: names, versions, and document idntity in a networked environment. Scholarly Publishing of the Electronic Networks: filling the pipeline and paying the piper. Proc. of the Fourth ARL/AAUP Symp. 1995 p153-159.

181. Louis, Gros. The real costs and financial challenges of library networking: Part 1. Paper Presented at the Clinic on Library Applications of Data 1991.

182. Mackinlay, J. Robertson, G. and Deline, R. Developing calendar visualizer. Proceeding of the Symposium of User Interface Software and Technology (November) 1994.

183. Mackinlay, J.D. Rao, R. and Card, S.K. An organic user interface for searching citation links. Proceedings of the ACM SIGCHI Conference on Human Factors in Computing Systems (May) 1995.

184. Maly, K. French, J. and Selman, A. Wide area technical report service. Proceedings of the 2nd. International WWW '94 1994 p523-533.

185. Maurer, H. Advancing the ideas of World-Wide Web: Hyper-G. Proceedings of the Distributed Multimedia Systems and Applications. Honolulu 1994 p201-203.

186. McFarland, M. The Tex-Share Gopher and Web server. *Library Journal* 71 (1) 1995 p16-20.

187. McKee, M.B. A day in the life of a virtual librarian: helping you zip around the Internet. *School Library Journal* 41 (4) 1995 p30-3.

188. Moore, James W. Use of encryption to ensure the integrity of reusable software components. Software Reuse: Advances in Software Reusability - International, Conf. 1994, IEEE 1994 p118-123

189. Negroponte, N.P. Products and services for computer networks. *Scientific American* 265 (3) 1991.

190. Nowell, L. and Hix, D. Visualizing search results: User interface development for the Project Envision database of computer science literature.

191. Oard, D.W. The Information Filtering Laboratory. WWW 1994.

192. Obraczka, K. Danzig, P. and Li, S. Internet resource discovery services. IEEE Comput. 26 (September) 1993 p8-22.

193. Oswald, A. *Bibliotheksdienst* 27 (4) 1990 p496-501.

194. Pedersen, J.O. Cutting, D.R. and Tukey, J.W. Snippet search: a single phrase approach to text access. Proceedings of the 1991 Joint Statistical Meetings. American S. 1991.

195. Peters, Paul Evan. Networked information services: next steps on the road to the distributed digital libraries of the Twenty-first Century. Paper Presented at the Clinic on Library Applications of Data, 1991

196. Peterson, C. Getting on the Internet: eating in or dining out? *Texas Library Journal* 71 (1) 1995 p10-14.

197. Piller, C. Dreamnet. *Macworld* 1994 p96-105.

198. Rao. R. Card, S.K. and Johnson, W. Protofoil: storing and finding information worker's paper documents in electronic file cabinet. Proceedings of the ACM SIGCHI Conference on Human Factors in Computing Systems (April) 1994.

199. Rostek, L. Mohr, W. and Fischer, D. Weaving a web: The structure and creation of an object network representing an electronic reference work Electronic Publishing-Origination, Dissemination and Design. Special Issue. Wiley, New York 6 (4) p495-505.

200. Runkle, Martin. Changing economics of research libraries. Paper Presented at the Clinic on Library Applications of Data, 1991

201. Rush, James E. Keeping the window of opportunity open for the private sector. Paper Presented at the Clinic on Library Applications of Data, 1991.

202. Salton, G. Automatic text processing: the transformation analysis, and retrieval of information by computer, Reading(Mass): Addison-Wesley 1988.

203. Schmidt, D. The electronic library: a bibliographic instruction course for graduate students in the life sciences. *Science and Technology Libraries* 14 (2) 1993 p49-60.

204. Shaughnessy, Thomas W. The real costs and financial challenges of library networking: Part 2. Paper Presented at the Clinic on Library Applications of Data, 1991.

205. Studer, William J. The real costs and financial challenges of library networking: Part 3. Paper Presented at the Clinic on Library Applications of Data, 1991.

206. Sutton, Brett. Libraries and networked information systems: selected bibliography. Papers Presented at the Clinic on Library Applications of Data, 1991.

207. Tuss, J. Roadmaps to the Internet: finding the best guidebooks for your needs. *Online* 18 (1) 1994 p14-26.

208. Uhlmann, D. Digitizing of archival materials for displays. *Apple Library User's Group Newsletter* 12 (3) 1994 p20-1.

209. VanHeyningen, M. The unified computer science technical report index: lessons. Proceedings of 2nd. International WWW '94 1994 p535-543.

210. Wu, Z. Zhao, D. and Ramsden, A. From automated library to electronic library: challenges for. Proceedings of the 15th Research Colloquium of the British Computer Society Information Retrieval Specialists Group; 1993 — 1994 p24-38.

13.2 COMPUTERIZED INFORMATION STORAGE AND RETRIEVAL - IMAGES

211. Abid, A. and Pellissier, D. CD-ROM in developing countries: a Unesco perspective. *Inspel* 28 (3) 1994 p366-76.

212. Akscyn, Robert M. and McCracken, Donald L. PLEXUS: a hypermedia architecture for large-scale digital libraries. Proceedings of the 11th. Annual International Conference on SIGDOC '93 1993 p11-20.

213. Andrews, K. Kappe, F. and Maurer, H. On second generation hypermedia systems. IIG Report, Graz 1994.

214. Baker, N. DisCards. *The New Yorker Magazine* (April) 1994 p64-86.

215. Balas, J. Online help for CD-ROM. *Computer in Libraries* 15 (4) 1995 p46-8.

216. Beiser, K. CD-ROM middle-aged crazy after all these years. *Database* 16 (6) 1993 p91-95.

217. Beynon-Davies, P. A semantic database approach to knowledge-based hypermedia system. *Information and Software Technology* 36 (6) 1994 p323-9.

218. Bowman, C.M. Danzig, P.B. and Hardy, D.R. The harvest information discovery and access system. Proceedings of the International WWW 1994 p763-771.

219. Budd, J.M. and Williams, K.A. CD-ROMs in academic libraries: a survey. *College and Research Libraries* 54 (6) 1993 p529-35.

220. Chakravarti, A.K. Vasanta, B. and Shroff, N. ASA CD-ROM electronics. *Information and Planning* 22 (2) 1994 p106-112.

221. Chen, R.-S. Chen, D.-J. and Ting, K.C. Multi-user access to library CD-ROM databases via a campus network. *Asian Libraries* 4 (1) 1995 p39-46.

222. Christel, M., et al. Informedia digital video library. *Communications of the ACM* 38 (4) 1995 p57-58.

223. Conway, paul. Digitizing preservation. *Library Journal* (February) 1994 p42-45.

224. Cox, J. and Hanson, T. CD-ROM: still transient after all these years? *Library Association Record* 96 (4) 1994 p210-11.

225. Coyne, Robert A. Hulen, Harry. and Watson, Richard W. National Storage System Foundation (NSSF). Digest of Papers - IEEE Symposium on Mass Storage Systems 1994 p45-46

226. Crosnier, H.L. L'hypertexte en reseau: repenser la bibliotheque [The WorldWide Web: a new look over foundations of libraries]. *Bulletin des Bibliotheques de France* 40 (2) 1995 p23-31.

227. Devan, P. A survey of applications of CSCW including some in educational settings. Proceedings of ED-MEDIA '93 (Orlando, Fla., June 23-26). AACE, 1993 p147-152.

228. Everett, D. Localizing CD-ROM databases in the college library: eliminating the negative and accentuating the positive. *College and Undergraduate Libraries* 1 (1) 1994 p35-40.

229. Faier, J.A. The truth about multimedia: what is it, where it's at, where. *Multimedia Today* 3 (1) 1995 p25-8.

230. Faloustos, C. Barber, R. and Flickner, M. Efficient and effective querying by image content. *Journal of Intelligent Information Systems* (3) 1994 p231-262.

231. Faloutsos, C. Barber, R. and Flickner, M. Efficient and effective querying by image content. Special Issue on. Integrating Artificial Intelligence and Database Technology.

232. Gladley, H.M. Storage subsystem for image and records management. *IBM Systems Journal* 32 (3) 1993 p512-540.

233. Haan, B.J. Kahn, P. and Riley, V.A. IRIS hypermedia services. *Communications of the ACM* 35 (1) 1992 p36-51.

234. Haber, Stauart. and Stronelta, W Scott. How to time-stamp a digital document. *Journal of Cryptology* 3 1991 p99-111.

235. Herala, M. Krishnanda. Srinivasa Ravi, A. and Rajashekar, T.B. Automated SDI service using CD-ROM databases. *Online & CD-ROM Review* 19 (3) 1995.

236. Herther, N.K. CD-ROM in libraries: a ten year anniversary report. *Online* 19 (3) 1995 p109-14.

237. Horowitz, L.R. CETH workshop on documenting electronic texts. Tech. Rep. 2, Centre for Electronic Texts in the Humanities, N, 1994

238. Jacso, P. Role of your own CD-ROM disc.(Part 1). *Information Today* 12 (4) 1995 p32.

239. Jipson, Victor B. Directions in optical storage (Invited Paper). Proceedings of SPIE — The International Society for Optical Engineering 1499 1991 p2-4.

240. Kappe, F. Maurer, H. and Scherbakov, N. Hyper G: a universal hypermedia system. *Journal of Education, Multimedia and Hypermedia* 2 (1) 1993 p39-66.

241. Kermit, H. CD-platen og biblioteket. [The CD disc and libraries]. *Synopsis* 25 (1) 1994 p26-9.

242. Lange, Holley R. Voice as computer interface. A look at tomorrow's technologies. *Electronic Library* 9 (1) 1991 p7-11.

243. Levy, D.M. Fixed or fluid? Document stability and new media. Proceedings of ECHT '94 (Edinburgh, sept. 18-23). ACM, New York, 1994 1994 p24-31

244. Li, W.-S. and Clifton, C. Semantic integration in heterogeneous databases using neural. Proceedings of the Twentieth Conference on Very Large Data Bases (VLDB), Morgan-Kaufmann 1994 p1-12.

245. Lynch, Clifford A. The integrity of digital information mechanics and definitional issues. *Journal of the American Society for Information Science* 45 1994, p737-44.

246. MacKinnon. MICROLIAS: Online Personal Access Catalog. Proceedings — National Online Meeting 1986 1986 p53-58.

247. Marcella, R. and Middleton, I. Key factors in help desk success. *Managing Information* 2 (6) 1995 p37-39.

248. Marchionini, G. and Crane, G. Evaluating hypermedia and learning: Methods and results. *ACM Transactions on Information Systems* 12 (1) 1994 p5-34.

249. Markee, Katherine M. Searching for such and such ... the key is instruction. Proceedings — National Online Meeting, 1993. Publ by Learned Information Ltd. Medford, NJ. USA 1993 p301-305.

250. Marshall, C.C. A mult-tiered approach to hypertext integration: negotiating. Proceedings of the Hypertext Standardization Workshop

(Gaithersburg, Md, Jan.16-18) /ed. by J. Moline, D. Benigni and, (...) 1990 p167-177.

251. Mas, M.T. CD-ROM end users in the university library. What to do. *Inspel* 28 (3) 1994 p377-81.

252. McSean, T. CD-ROM: is the game over? *British News* (September) 1992 p606-607.

253. Melton, L.R.A. and Ismail, N. Distant knowledge of distance education: an online database. IFIP Transactions A: Computer Science and Technology (A-29), 1993 p591-600.

254. Murugappan, Palaniappan. Yankelovich, Niwle. and Sawtelle, Mark. Linking active anchors: a stage in the evolution of hypermedia. *Hypermedia* 2 (1) 1990 p47-66.

255. Nieuwenhuysen, Paul. Criteria for the evaluation of text storage and retrieval software. *Electronic Library* 6 (3) 1988 p160-166.

256. Nieuwenhuysen, paul. Bibliography of text information management software for IBM. *Electronic Library* 8 (4) 1990 p254-278

257. Nondal, L. Full text and bibliographical databases on CD-ROM in research libraries: costs, services and technology. *Inspel* 28 (3) 1994 p355-65.

258. Omaji, A. None-use of CD-ROM databases in academic environment. *Computers in Libraries* 14 (9) 1994 p45-6.

259 Osterbye, L. Structural and cognitive problems in providing version control for hypertext. Proceedings of the ACM Conference on Hypertext (Milan, Italy,Nov. 30-Dec.4) /ed. by D. Lucarella, J. Nanard, M. Nanard & (...) 1992 p33-42.

260. Pesch, O. Electronic information: options for access. *College and Undergraduate Libraries* 1 (2) 1994 p25-48.

261. Quint, B. The inevitable Internet onslaught. *Wilson Library Bulletin* 69 (9) 1995 p64-65.

262. Ramdhian, S. Multimedia 94: what is multimedia? and what has it got to do. *Audiovisual Librarian* 20 (3) 1994 p224-6.

263. Rao, R. and Card, S.K. The table lens: merging graphical and symbolic representation in an interactive focus+context visualization for tabular information. Proceedings of the ACM SIGCHI Conference on Human Factors in, Computing Systems. ACM (April) 1994.

264. Ritchie, I. Ofcourse multimedia is hot — so be careful or you will burn yourself. *Aslib Information* 20 (10) 1992 p375-376.

265. Robertson, G. and Mackinlay, G.D. The document lens. Proceedings of the ACM Symposium on User Interface Software and Technology (November) 1993.

266. Rowe, G.R. Multimedia technology as the catalyst for a new form of literacy. *The Information Society* 8 (2) p83-90.

267. Rowly, J. Multimedia kiosks: a new medium of information provision. *Audiovisual Libraries* 21 (1) 1995 p40-2.

268. Rus, Daniela. and Subramanian, Devika. Multi-media RISSC informatics: retrieving information with simple structural components. Proc. 2 Int. Conf. Inf. Knowl. Manage. - ACM 1993 p283-294.

269. Small, R.V. and Ferrira, S.M. Multimedia technology and the changing nature of research. *Reference Librarian* (44) 1994 p95-106.

270. Vasi, J. Creating a library electronic classroo. *Online* 18 (5) 1994 p75-84

271. Watson, M. From academic library to CD-ROM database publisher. *Assignation* 11 (3) 1994 p13-18.

272. Weiss, Joachim W. The challenge to the library and information professionals in the visual information age. C.cChen Festschrift in Honour of Dr. Ahmed H. Helal., Essen, 1992.)

273. Welsch, L.A. Multimedia and hypermedia: model and framework. *Information Services and Use* 13 (2) 1993 p89-91.

274. Yglesias, A.E. Mathematics at the Amparo Museu. *Information Services and Use* 14 (3) 1994 p161-8.

275. deZegher-Geets, I. Freeman, A.G. and Walker, M.G. Summarization and display of Online Medical Records. M.D. Comput. 5 (3) 1988 p38-46.

13.3 COMPUTERIZED INFORMATION STORAGE AND RETRIEVAL - VIDEOTEX

276. British Library. The effect of digitisation on library and information science. BLRD Report; 6098-1993 p156.

277. Hiltz, S.R. and Turoff, M. Virtual classroom plus video: technology for educational excellence. Proceedings of Ed-MEDIA '94 (Vancouver, B.C., June 25-30) 1994 p26-31.

278. Kamps, T. and Reichenberger, K. A dialogue approach to graphical information access, Designing User Interfaces for Hypermedia /ed. by W.Schuler; J.Hannemann; and N.Streitz 1995 p141-55.

279. Robertson, G.G. Card, S.K. and Mackinlay, G.D. Information visualization using 3-D interactive animation. *Communications of the ACM* 36 (4) 1993.

280. Robertson, G.G. Mackinlay, G.D. and Card, S.K, Cone trees: animated 3-D visualization of hierarchical information. Proceedings of the ACM SIGCHI Conference on Human Factors in, Computing Systems. ACM (April) 1991.

14 COMMUNICATIONS AND INFORMATION TECHNOLOGY

281. Beiser, K. High-density discs move closer to reality. *Online* 19 (3) 1995 p118-20.

282. Cochrane, Peter. IT- a glimpse of the future. *Aslib Proceedings* 47 (10) 1995 p221-228.

283. Norton, B. Human resource implications of adopting information technology (IT). *Aslib Proceedings* 49 (9) 1992 p289-303.

284. Tomer, C. Information technology standards for libraries. *Journal of the American Society for Information Science* 43 (8), 1992 p566-570.

14.1 COMMUNICATION AND INFORMATION TECHNOLOGY - COMPUTER INDUSTRY

285. Arnfield, R. Electronic mail a road to the information super highway. *Library Journal* 119 (13) 1994 p16-19.

286. Crowcroft, J. The Internet: evolution or revolution. Internet World and Document Delivery World International, (1998) 1994 p124-8.

287. Dornet, J.J. Rajkumar, T.M. and Yen, D. Multimedia networking: a leading edge communication technology. *Information Systems Management* 11 (4) 1994 p39-45.

288. Falk, H. CD-ROMs: at the heart of multimedia. *Electronic Library* 11 (6) 1993 p419-22.

289. Fox, B. CD's: the next generation. *New Scientist* 143 (1942) 1994 p33-5.

290. Gartner, R. The Internet. *Paper Conservation News* (72) 1994 p11.

291. Green, C. From paper to CD-ROM documentation. *Computer Communications* 18 (6) 1995 p423-428.

292. Kantor, A. and Neubarth, M. The greatest network story ever told. *Internet World* 5 (6) 1994 p74-5.

293. Learn, L.L. Deregulation and privatization; What's it mean for libraries. *Library Hi Tech News* (120) 1995 p1-4.

294. Lurie, B.N. Imaging today and tomorrow: where are we going and will we be happy when we get there? *International Journal of Micrographics and Optical Technology* 12 (4) 1994 p155-9.

295. Mostafa, J. Digital image representation and access. *Annual Review of Information Science and Technology* 1995 p91-135.

296. Poel, W. The Internet: how does it happen? *Managing Information* 1 (10) 1994 p35-6.

297. Priestly, J. Using the information superhighway. *Information Services and Use* 15 (1) 1995 p25-9.

298. Schlapfer, K. The Information content of images. *Professional Printer* 39 (1) 1995 p10-15.

299. Snaprud, M. and Kaindl, H. types and inheritance in hypertext. *Internal Journal of Human Computer Studies* 41 (1/2) 1994 p223-41.

300. Walker, T.D. Libraries and the Internet: education, practice, and policy. *Library Trends* 42 (4) 1994 p585-758.

AUTHOR INDEX

Steier, D.H. 79
Still, J. 47
Stronelta, W Scott. 234
Studer, William J. 205
Subramanian, Devika. 268